Linkage, Inc.'s Best Practices in Knowledge Management and Organizational Learning Handbook

CASE STUDIES   INSTRUMENTS   MODELS   RESEARCH

EDITORS:
PHIL HARKINS
LOUIS L. CARTER
AMY J. TIMMINS

FOREWORD BY HUBERT SAINT ONGE

Copyright© 2000 Linkage, Inc. Published by Linkage Press

ISBN 0-9677965-1-2

Library of Congress Cataloging-in-Publication Data
Linkage, Inc.'s best practices in knowledge management and organizational learning
hanndbook: case studies, instruments, models, research/editors, Louis Carter, Phil
Harkins, Amy Timmins; foreword by Hubert Saint Onge
Library of Congress Card Number : 99-091848
ISBN:0-9677965-1-2

Printed in the United States of America

Published by

LINKAGE
INCORPORATED

One Forbes Road

Lexington, Massahchusetts 02421

(781) 862-3157; Fax (781) 862-2355

Visit Our Website at:

www.linkageinc.com

Table of Contents

Part One

Introduction

Acknowledgements

Linkage Team

Phil Harkins, President & Founder

LINKAGE EDUCATIONAL RESOURCES

Taavo Godtfredsen, Director

Louis Carter, Publisher/Consultant

Melissa McLaughlin, Manager

Amy Timmins, Acquisitions & Copy Editor/Product Development Specialist

LINKAGE RESEARCH GROUP

Marc Pramuk, Director
Derek Smith, Research Consultant
Crystal Thorpe, Research Associate

GRAPHIC DESIGN

Lynda Jemson

SPECIAL THANKS TO:

Byron Woodman
Tobin Kelly
Lok-Sze Wong
Kristin Flynn

Contributors

Dave Pollard, Ernst & Young

Peggy Parskey , Hewlett Packard

Marilyn Martiny, Hewlett Packard

Adam Flar, AT& T

Christine Costello, AT&T

Sheldon Ellis, Buckman Labs

Michael Pommier, World Bank

Michael Crandal, Microsoft

Richard McDermott, Shell Oil

John Kendrich, Shell Oil

Carol Zuluaff, Massachusetts General Hospital (MGH)

John Couris, MGH

Cliff Kennedy, MGH

Jeannie Rice, Norske Skog Flooring

Claes Wennerth, Norske Skog Flooring

Lasse Kjaer Hansen, Norse Skog Flooring

Rebecca Wilmot-Lynch, InFocus

We are drowning in information and starving for knowledge.

ABOUT THIS BOOK

The principal goal of this book is to provide you with the key ingredients taken from the best-practice companies to help you create and maintain your knowledge management and organizational learning initiative. Through a case study approach, this book provides practical, easy-to-apply tools, instruments, training, concepts and competency models that can be used as benchmarks for the successful implementation of your specific program.

Within each case study, you will learn how to:

- Analyze the need for KMOL

- Build a convincing business case for KMOL

- Identify the proper audience for the initiative

- Design the KMOL program

- Implement the design of the initiative

- Evaluate the effectiveness of the initiative

HOW TO USE THIS BOOK

Direct Application

Because this book contains actual forms, guides, training, competency models and methodologies for implementing a Knowledge Management and Organizational Learning program, you can immediately apply many of its parts directly to your job and company initiatives. Many of the evaluation and assessment forms, models, reference guides, and training exercises can be easily implemented and customized to your specific organizational needs.

Master's Degree or Executive Workshops

This book is ideal for a master's degree or executive workshops and/or seminars on designing, implementing, and evaluating a KM/OL system or initiative. The case studies are instructive in nature and can be used as actual examples of KM/OL programs or systems. For more information on Linkage's organization development and corporate education products and services, contact Linkage Customer Service at (781-862-3157) or visit Linkage on the Web at: www.linkageinc.com

Online or Virtual Learning

This book is perfect for virtual teams that are separated by long distances but still must work together. Many of the chapters include a blueprint for this exact situation.

Getting the Most from this Book

1. Read over the Introduction to get a feel for the book's landscape.

2. Skim over the table of contents for each chapter, mining for information on the types of interventions, key features in each program, competency models, strategic objectives of the program, critical success factors, and evaluation methods.

3. Examine all of the exhibits.

4. Go back and choose specific case studies to read over carefully. Work with a team to develop a list of the components in a few case studies that fit your organization. Analyze why these components are most applicable to your organization and its culture. What interventions and key features best fit your organization's goals and objectives? How might you implement such a program at your organization? Why do some programs seem to be more tailored to your organization than others?

FOREWORD BY HUBERT SAINT ONGE

Every month, the World-Wide Web triples in size. Thousands upon thousands of terabytes of information are continuously uploaded and downloaded at whim. The U.S. Department of Labor predicts a shortage of the technically savvy workforce by the year 2002. The constant barrage of information, combined with a shrinking workforce, provides a strong basis for training employees to learn and assimilate knowledge for increased productivity and enhanced performance.

In 1999, Linkage, Inc. surveyed senior executives, most of whom would most likely be leaders of change within their organization. (See Table One) The main topic of the survey was to assess the areas of interest and concern in knowledge management and organizational learning (KM/OL).

Table One: KMOL Hottest Topics, ranked in order of concern

KMOL Topic of Concern	Ranking of Topic (Scale: 1 - 5, 1 Being Highest Ranked Topic of Concern)
Developing a New Kind of Culture Within the Organization	1
Creating an Enterprise-Wide Knowledge and Learning Strategy	2
Crafting a Strategy for Gathering, Storing and Sharing Knowledge	2
Fueling Constant Innovation through Customer Feedback	4
Developing and Integrating a System that Promotes and Rewards Knowledge Sharing	5

Foremost on the minds of these leaders was the need to develop a new kind of culture within their organizations. They sought the key to creating an atmosphere of learning and knowledge sharing. This is significant for several reasons. First, it acknowledges the need to shift the entire behavior of an organization, rather than just adding rules and procedures to support knowledge in a rather superficial manner. Second, the use of the word "culture change" demonstrates a willingness to commit to instilling fundamental change at every level of the organization.

Business leaders are of one voice in their belief that their KMOL initiatives will only be successful if there is general buy-in at all levels of the organization. The recognition of the respondents that a need exists for a fundamental shift in culture reinforces the call for a commitment in all facets of the organization. The significance of respondents to develop a learning and knowledge sharing culture is clearly indicative of the symbiotic nature of the firm's organizational learning and its knowledge management. Both are most effective when brought together as part of one initiative. Finally, this leads us to the conclusion that an integrated KMOL strategy that encompasses meaningful culture change is the most effective vehicle for the transformation of organization at a time when the emergence of e-business is rapidly creating organizational obsolescence. In fact, the effective implementation of KMOL is the best way to reinforce organizational readiness for e-business.

Two factors tied for the second-largest concern of the survey respondents. Creating an enterprise-wide knowledge and learning strategy was equal to crafting a strategy for gathering, storing and sharing knowledge. There is a subtle, yet crucial, difference between the two. To create an enterprise-wide knowledge and learning strategy is to plan an overall method and scheme that will evolve the very nature of the firm. As illustrated by the case studies in this book, the most successful change comes from well-defined frameworks, a planned strategy and highly focused execution. This approach entails an overall program design and structured implementation of that plan. Part of the successful KMOL story includes a sub-plot that addresses the method for gathering, storing and sharing the knowledge of the organization. But it is even more important that the strategy address the key business challenges facing the organization. This is what creates relevance, adds value and leverages performance.

It is understandable that the respondents would be concerned with the basic management of what the organization knows, both explicitly and implicitly. The knowledge that consists of forms, documents, reports, projects, etc. is easily transmitted and organized into an electronic format. A database, an intranet, or a network server serves as tools of managing the tangible information of a company. But this is only the beginning. In fact, these tools can only make information available in a way that will more readily turn in into knowledge. Let's be clear! Knowledge is the ability to take effective action. There is still a large gap between making information more readily available and people or teams taking more effective action . This gap is most effectively covered by providing processes where people can validate this information with credible colleagues whom they trust. This exchanges that can then take place both validate and give meaning to the information. This generation of knowledge can only really take place through relationships. We need to leverage technology to both disseminate information as well as provide "electronic vessels" where these fuller exchanges can take place. It is through these exchanges that both we can bring to bear both the tacit and explicit dimensions of knowledge. This is how we combine both information with the experience and expertise that reside in the minds of those with whom we work. This presents a key challenge: it is not possible to leverage knowledge where people don't see that they can succeed only if they collaborate and learn from one another. Working through this level of interdependence will require fundamental change to behavioral patterns in most organizations.

Many of the respondents wanted to know how to develop and integrate a system that promotes and rewards knowledge sharing. It is unlikely that incentives will be effective in bringing people to share knowledge when taking into account that a KMOL strategy best succeeds when the entire nature of the organization changes. Many employees are often fearful of divulging their knowledge. They worry that sharing what is in their head will sacrifice the very thing that adds distinctness to their contribution and what they can achieve for the company. These are legitimate concerns if organizations do not change the way in which work gets done and objectives are achieved. For instance, structuring highly purposed cross-functional work teams to tackle projects with tight deadlines will compel everyone involved to use the knowledge tools available. Otherwise they will fail. Those who chose not to take part and hoard their knowledge in this context will make themselves irrelevant in very short notice. This is how every contributor comes to believe that sharing knowledge will increase their own value while making their team and their organization successful.

Third on the list of concern for the survey respondents was how to fuel constant innovation through customer knowledge and feedback. Many successful KMOL programs are initiated to generate more integrated and more relevant solutions for the customer in order to reach more customers, enhance their perception of value and widen the array of solutions they purchase. This is only possible by interacting closely with customers, learning from them and responding with agility to the evolution of their needs.

Finally, survey respondents wanted to know how to assess the cultural barriers to creating a learning organization within the emerging global economy. While it is imperative that people be able to overcome cultural differences, the gradual lowering of national boundaries, the need to look at the business from a global point of view and the intensity of business networks bring a greater propensity for misunderstandings and conflicts. It is not easy to bridge cultures that are worlds apart. A new economy has emerged in which the world is now a smaller place. Technology and its impact on shipping, transportation, communication relays, monetary systems, transport, tariffs and other factors affecting logistics have conspired to shrink the "time and place" of the global context where business takes place. Cultural differences, however, are not as easily addressed. Overcoming differences between societies and communities remains a concern worldwide.

Major Findings

Beginning in the year 2000, we talked to many of the best practice companies in the field of KMOL that we studied in the 1999 survey. We asked these companies and organizations to share the approaches, tools, and specific strategies that made their KMOL program a success. It was our intent to obtain these stories from a variety of industries, as well as include firms that ranged in size, age and where they are in the business cycle.

Distinct Business Drivers

While the KMOL challenge may seem altruistic, specific goals and objectives drove the successes of many of the best practices in this field. Ernst & Young had four distinct business drivers that maintained the focus of their program. AT & T had specific market-share and profitability goals. The World Bank made knowledge sharing part of its overall mission statement.

Total Commitment at All Levels of the Organization

Nearly all of the companies in this book acquired total commitment at every level in the organization. Buckman Labs then-CEO drove the KMOL initiative, making personal calls to associates to ensure that they were getting the most out of the KMOL program. Hewlett Packard, rather than initiate from the top-down, instilled its KMOL program at all levels. Microsoft garnered support from entry-level employees all the way up to its major stakeholders.

Building Communities

One of the most important factors critical to success was the creation of communities within the organization. Many of these groups were virtual, with almost all contact occurring online. Shell Oil developed communities of practice whereby employees could tap the well of like-experiences, plans, codes and other information important to a project, all within a matter of hours. Buckman Labs and the World Bank also constructed forums and virtual communities, substantially cutting costs normally associated with learning across distances.

Rewards & Incentives

Another common thread running through the best practices of KMOL is how they addressed rewarding and motivating employees for sharing knowledge and learning by making it an inherent part of how work was getting done. Each organization found innovative ways to enhance the continued support and reinforcement of commitment to the KMOL strategy. Hewlett Packard had its Knowledge Masters Award. AT & T presented those who participated in the successful application of new knowledge with a "Rising Star" recognition. Buckman Labs even treated the most frequent participants to knowledge exchanges to a weekend retreat.

Company	Industry	Employees	Revenue
AT & T	Telecommunication	151,000+	$ 64 billion
Buckman Labs	Pharmaceutical	350+	$ 158 million
Ernst & Young	Consulting	30,0000+	$ 1.8 billion
Hewlett Packard	Computer Hardware	85,000+	$ 42 billion
InFocus	Manufacturing	645+	$ 390 million
Massachusetts General Hospital	Healthcare	13,000+	$ 200 million
Microsoft	Computer Software	34,000+	$ 19.5 billion
Norske Skog Flooring	Manufacturing	6,000+	$ 2+ billion
Shell Oil Company	Petroleum Oil	20,000+	$ 13 billion
The World Bank	Finance/Banking	10,000+	$ 30 billion

An Approach to the Knowledge Management & Organizational Learning

Each case study looks at the process by which the organization effectively and successfully carried out a knowledge management and organizational learning program. This five-step process includes the following phases:

1. **Assessment**
2. **Program Design**
3. **Implementation**
4. **On-The-Job Reinforcement**
5. **Evaluation**

1. Assessing the Status Quo: Determining the Best Method for Change

In many of these best practice case studies, the need for adopting a KMOL program arose as an obvious dilemma. Many of the groups dealt with large volumes of information, a huge customer base, and thousands of employees. They began to understand that they could be overwhelmed with what they had. Worse yet was the fear of being left behind with what they did not possess – a well-organized, highly informed work force that had accurate and effective access to the organization's wealth of knowledge. These groups varied. Human resources, consultants, sales and marketing, sales training, information services, senior executives, and in some cases, the entire company, were often part of the initial pilot program.

Tools of assessment often included scrutinizing hard facts and numbers from within the organization. The need for change based upon analytical output was well established in the case study presented by the Sales and Marketing Group of AT&T. AT&T took a hard look at what the market was – and was not – by detailed analysis of earnings statements and sales reports. AT&T, in assessing its then-current business strategy, dared to conclude that it was outdated and ineffective. This honest assessment had to be met with a shared goal of AT&T's vision to empower its sales force in continuing to remain a global market leader.

Other tools of assessment are used after the initial diagnosis that a business is in need of managing what it knows. Microsoft knew that it had to create a system to manage its internal data and its employee knowledge. In order to understand what would be most effective, it had to find out the user's needs, as well as the type of information that would need to be used. Microsoft conducted a stakeholder survey, seeking feedback and asking questions on how to most effectively create a knowledge framework.

2. Program Design – Preparing for the Future

In each and every one of the successful KMOL change initiatives, there was a specific program designed to fill the gaps that existed in the status quo. Within each company, there existed a shared vision as to the goals of their programs. Many organizations turned to thought leaders for guidance in understanding how to stay true to this vision and still succeed. Ernst & Young drew from John Kotter's *Leading Change*[1] to develop a successful plan to persuade senior leadership to buy-in to its program. Massachusetts General Hospital required several pre-readings of thought leaders in each of its leadership seminars, relying heavily on principles expounded in previous books and seminars.

Many of the best practice companies listed one of the biggest challenges that influenced their program design: being able to understand and map out the problems and solutions to their needs. In essence, they wanted to *see* the problem, rather then attempt to visualize the abstract principles that the dilemma might entail. The designers needed to understand, from a human perspective, the impact of their design.

3. Implementation – Creating Communities of Practice

Tools and methods of implementation were both conventional and unique. Many of the best practice KMOL organizations refer to a variety of learning approaches where more structured learning experiences complemented efforts to create a continuous learning culture in their organization.

There were noted examples of implementation involving "communities of practice," which sought to engender more bandwidth for the exchange of explicit and tacit knowledge. Other names strongly associated with this term are cross-functional teams or cross-boundary groups. Whatever the name, a strong factor of success in implementing a KMOL initiative was often to create strong community ties in small groups, sometimes in person and sometimes in a virtual world. It was in these close-knit groups that continuous knowledge was passed back and forth between members of the group, as well as between one group and another. This is, in essence, a small-scale model of the worldwide web in action.

One of the strongest examples of a community of practice is contained within Shell Oil's Deepwater project. Richard McDermott, contributor of the Shell chapter, explains the elements and procedures of one of these communities:

> 1. Conduct regular forums for community members to think together, share ideas, help each other. The design team expected that these forums would stimulate innovation and build collaboration across teams.
>
> 2. Systematically find and collect the best practices, both inside and outside of the organization, organizing that information in a meaningful way, and quickly disseminating it through community forums and knowledge bases.
>
> 3. Create and manage its own knowledge base within and across skill groups. Each community was expected to decide what to document and what the level of detail would be within the documents. The community would also be responsible for organizing and evergreening the information contained in it.

While not all communities of practice are designated as such, similar formats have provided excellent examples where knowledge was leveraged though interaction. Buckman Labs created online, virtual forums in the early 1990s. These forums eventually translated into close knit communities of learning in differing disciplines throughout the company. In fact, many organizations have modeled their own forums and communities based upon the Buckman model.

The World Bank participates in nurturing communities of practice on a grand scale. Over a fifteen-year period, informal professional communities developed into 120 thematic groups, staff members who organize around common themes, such as environmental issues and childcare. These groups meet on a regular basis to discuss issues of relevance and priorities regarding these issues.

4. On-The-Job-Support – Reinforcing a System of Culture Change

The implementation of an effective KMOL strategy will change an organization at its very core. The change begins a process of evolution whereby a company cannot turn back to its old ways, which failed to give people access to the full knowledge base of the organization. We have now shown that it is possible to provide this access through new work processes, teams approaches, technology and knowledge tools. Once this is demonstrated in an organization, the alternative is simply too ineffective and wasteful. The best organizational change creates a system of continuous learning and growth. People are rewarded not only for their immediate contributions, but also for the manner in which they participate in building the knowledge and capabilities of the organization. Many of the chapters highlight the use of a reward system, including Hewlett Packard, Federal Express, AT & T, and Buckman Labs.

Norske Skog Flooring, a Swedish manufacturing company, wanted its US sales force to quickly learn about its new product. To reinforce that learning, Norske disseminated learning "work mats" that illustrated the product. Continually, employees participated in role-playing techniques to develop knowledge about the product through action learning. Constant ways to innovate learning were introduced to a more informed— and enlightened — sales force.

5. Evaluation – Measuring the Results of KMOL

Measurement is a constant challenge with the implementation of KMOL strategies. This is another of the depth of the change involving such a strategy. Many of the case studies refer to the need for measurement. We have yet to see the emergence of a robust measurement approach to support a comprehensive KMOL strategy. It is, however, incumbent on those who lead the KMOL effort to attest to its outcomes in the best manner possible. This is why the case studies vary a great deal in their approach to measurement. Sometimes, the results were depicted in a more tangible form than in other instances, depending largely on the nature and the breadth of the intervention. In many instances, the results of the program were measured in terms of the extent to which participants used knowledge management and organizational learning as part of their everyday work.

Tangible results are often correlated with the goals of the program that were created at the outset. For instance, one of the goals of the Massachusetts General Hospital Organizational Learning program was to decrease the time a patient spent between the Radiology Department and the Orthapaedics Department. "Patient through-put" time was decreased by 34 percent, showing tangible, quantitative results. On the counter-side, the adversary mentality that had existed between the two departments seemed to have greatly subsided – a result not measurable by statistic, figures or "bottom line" results.

At Hewlett Packard, significant progress was made in creating 70 learning communities globally. A tangible outcome of the program has been the development of a global knowledge repository that, when complete, will map out the entire company's knowledge. Hewlett Packard estimates that it has saved thousands of hours of manpower time and countless dollars in money savings. Use of a KMOL system is now an integral part of performance reviews, new-hire orientation and project management approaches. Knowledge management abilities are rated skills and competencies used for succession planning and for career advancement at Hewlett Packard.

Conclusion

The implementation of a comprehensive KMOL strategy will leave an indelible mark on the culture of an organization. The power of this strategy and its impact on performance will make it impossible to revert to old patterns that may have been effective at one point but no longer allow the organization to meet the challenges of the new marketplace. Productivity increases because people learn what they need to know on a just-in time, just-in-case basis. People no longer have to search for information: it is readily available to them at a touch of the keyboard. And when they need to put this information in context to apply it to what they have to do, colleagues who have done similar work in the past will help them do so by bringing the result of their own experiences. Those who are involved in these organizations become conscious of their interdependence: they acquire a much clearer view of a shared vision for the future. For many large companies, the future is here and they have invested a great deal to secure their place in it. Ernst & Young estimates that it spent nearly $80 million dollars on its knowledge management and organizational learning initiative. AT&T spends nearly $3 million dollars annually on its KMOL initiative. Obviously, it is less difficult for Fortune 100 companies to overcome the hurdle of budgetary concerns. The value of their investment is based on their belief in the strategy they have formulated and implemented. They use measurement wherever possible to verify their hypothesis.

Smaller companies tend to be more tentative about a knowledge management and organizational learning initiative. My experience tells me that organizations currently face very similar issues independently of their size or domain of activity. The business environment imposes similar pressures on all organizations. The organizations in this book offer a glimpse of benchmarks for KMOL strategies that apply just as well to small or large organization be they in the for-profit or not-for profit sectors. How people in the organization respond, participate, provide insight and feedback, and apply this system in their everyday work life are all key factors in success, no matter what the monetary cost. For instance, communities of practice provide a great tool for learning and knowledge sharing at a low-level cost. Writings by thought leaders are often published on the worldwide web, at no or little cost to the reader. The success of KMOL strategies will depend not as much on the level of investment as it will on the strength of the commitment of all those involved. The depth of the change required for any organization is such that without this level of commitment, the old patterns will keep re-emerging as obstacles. When they will have decidedly overcome these obstacles, KMOL strategies will set new and unprecedented levels of excellence for realizing the full potential of people and the organizations where they work.

---

[1] Kotter, John. *Leading Change*, Boston: Harvard Business School Press, 1996.

Hubert Saint-Onge is recognised globally for his innovative work as a practitioner of organisational learning, leadership development and knowledge value creation. As vice president for strategic capabilities at The Mutual Group, he is responsible for leveraging the firm's business through the systematic application of knowledge management and learning organisation principles.

Part Two:

1

ERNST & YOUNG

Utilizing KM/OL to develop a sales culture, globalize the practice, become an Employer of Choice and accelerate speed-to-market

GLOSSARY OF TERMS

Repository - also called KnowledgeBase; electronic container for knowledge, similar to a database but usually less structured

Knowledge Object - a discrete re-usable component of a document; e.g. a proposal document could have "resume" knowledge objects, "credentials" knowledge objects etc.; in a sophisticated KM environment the knowledge objects are individually tagged for easier re-use

Container - a generic name for anything that holds knowledge, electronic or manual, from a file folder to a highly structured database or KnowledgeBase

Knowledge Steward - a person whose job is to enable, encourage and champion the contribution and use of knowledge in the organization

Knowledge Manager - a person whose job is to accumulate and contribute knowledge from an assignment or business process to applicable KnowledgeBases, and to help co-workers find applicable knowledge in KnowledgeBases

Killer App - short for "killer application." the application of some technology or knowledge that transforms an organization's products, services, processes or delivery channels in a highly visible, dramatic and profitable way, so as to justify the investment in that technology or knowledge

Community of Interest - sometimes abbreviated to COIn; similar to a Community of Practice (CoP), but usually with less urgency, practical sharing of knowledge and workflow than a CoP; it is not uncommon for a small core CoP to have a larger halo COIn following the developments of the CoP and occasionally participating with it

Knowledge Behavior Curve - the dynamic shift of people's knowledge behaviour from intermediated (using a librarian) to disintermediated (doing one's own research and analysis) as comfort with the technology and value of the KnowledgeBases in-creases, and the counterbalancing shift from disintermediated to reintermediated (using advanced analysts and report writers) as the opportunity cost of doing one's own research rises and dealing with information overload makes do-it-yourself research unproductive

BACKGROUND & INTRODUCTION

Ernst & Young ("E&Y") is one of the world's largest integrated professional services firms and an acknowledged global leader in knowledge management. The firm has over 100,000 employees in over 100 countries, practicing in four service lines: audit and business advisory, tax and law, consulting, and corporate finance.

Since its pioneering knowledge management and organizational learning ("KM/OL") efforts began in 1994, the firm has since received at least a dozen awards for its KM/OL leadership. These include being named in the Top five world's Most Admired Knowledge Enterprises© recognition two years running. The firm's employees share a 650-person centrally managed Knowledge Organization (the "CBK—Center for Business Knowledge"), and have universal access to its knowledge-powered Intranet (the "KnowledgeWeb"). The firm is selling its consulting practice to Cap Gemini, but Cap Gemini has insisted on having ongoing access to the CBK and the KnowledgeWeb as part of the deal.

PHASE ONE: ASSESSING NEED

In 1994, E&Y had a KM/OL system that, as they describe it in self-deprecating terms, consisted of "two guys and a filing cabinet." Especially in its consulting practice, the firm was growing very quickly. It urgently needed a system to leverage its vast untapped wealth of best practices, proposals, experience references, marketing collateral and other intellectual capital. The firm's global management also saw the opportunity to use a robust KM/OL system to support its efforts to globalize E&Y's autonomous member firms.

Accordingly, E&Y established a Global Knowledge Steering Group ("GKSG"), consisting of the newly-appointed Chief Knowledge Officers of its US, Canadian, and UK firms. In addition, the GKSG included the global Vice Chair who was responsible for infrastructure, reporting directly to the global management committee. It had just drafted a business strategy called *Future State 2002*, whose four major focuses (development of a sales culture, practice globalization, becoming an Employer of Choice, and accelerating speed-to-market), dovetailed precisely with the potential offerings of KM/OL.

The four drivers of the need for world-class KM/OL at E&Y were (and still are):

1. **Growth:** E&Y needed to accelerate the development of new products and services especially in the e-commerce area, to replace "commodity" services and increase organizational growth;

2. **Cost and Speed to Market:** Both in pursuit of new assignments and in work delivery, E&Y needed to reduce cost-of-sales and reduce time to prepare deliverables;

3. **Customer Satisfaction:** E&Y needed to increase its depth of knowledge about clients and their industries — and about its own global competencies and best practices — to enhance customer satisfaction and increase "share of client"; and

4. **Learning Curve:** Due to the traditional high turnover in its profession, E&Y needed to offer its people access to learning materials and knowledge that would make them quickly proficient and productive in new practice areas, whether they were new hires or existing staff moving into new practice disciplines.

The GKSG, in its first meeting in 1994, hammered out a list of underlying principles for its new KM/OL system. It then set about designing a system that would improve performance in each of these four driver areas. They were able to leverage E&Y's intense customer focus to do this, but had to overcome three major obstacles:

· **Desire for Control:** E&Y's existing KM/OL personnel (librarians, researchers, analysts, competitive intelligence experts, database managers) were widely dispersed and their "owners" were reluctant to cede them to a centralized KM function;

· **Practice Autonomy:** The autonomy of E&Y's practitioners, while a key strength of the firm, would make it more difficult to introduce new KM practices and processes quickly, consistently and globally;

· **No Knowledge Culture:** In 1994, E&Y had just been through a huge change management program to introduce a Sales Culture. There was no immediate appetite for another major change program to convert knowledge hoarders into knowledge sharers.

One of the first tasks of the GKSG was to establish a Deployment Group to develop training, communication and internal marketing programs to address these issues. The GKSG also decided to *go slow* in introducing changes, starting by supporting just the consulting service line in the US, Canada and the UK. The changes would then expand to the remaining three service lines and seven additional countries once the GKSG had momentum and success stories to share.

The GKSG also recognized the need to completely re-engineer much of the pre-existing "legacy" knowledge resources, both human and technical. The process they used to do this is explained in the Planning & Strategy Phase, below.

E&Y's knowledge program assessment has focused, since day one, on five types of success measures:

1. Accessibility of the firm's people to KM/OL resources and staff (this measure category was later dropped when penetration reached 100%);
2. Rate of contribution of knowledge to the firm's repositories;
3. Rate of re-use of knowledge from the firm's repositories;
4. User-surveyed quality of knowledge in the firm's repositories and of deliverables of CBK staff;
5. Recognition of E&Y's KM/OL leadership by three groups: outside awards, E&Y's own people (unsolicited kudos), and university recruiters (becoming an "Employer of Choice").

PHASE TWO: PLANNING & STRATEGY

Building on a set of mutually agreed fundamental KM/OL principles, the GKSG developed a 5-step process to implement KM/OL. It divided its Center for Business Knowledge ("CBK") staff into six groups to manage the implementation:

1. **Strategy:** Development of a KM/OL strategy, future state vision, value propositions, and design principles (managed by the GKSG itself);

2. **Architecture:** Design and development of the knowledge architecture, access tools and content, both internal-source and external-source (managed by the CBK Architecture and Extranet groups);

3. **Infrastructure:** Design and development of the seven distinct) roles, knowledge network mechanisms and HR to support KM/OL (managed by the CBK Knowledge Services and Knowledge Networks groups);

4. **Culture:** Programs to achieve a Knowledge Culture, including training, internal marketing, thought leadership, communications, measurement and reward programs (managed by the CBK Acquisitions & Deployment group); and

5. **Innovation:** Programs to sustain change momentum and global leadership in KM/OL (managed by the GKSG itself).

2.1 Developing the Strategy

The design of this major change initiative drew heavily on the ideas in John Kotter's book *Leading Change*. Identifying the enormous opportunity that a comprehensive KM/OL program offered the firm created a sense of urgency. The program could be instrumental in achieving each of the four objectives outlined in Phase One (Growth, Cost & Speed to Market, Customer Satisfaction, and Learning Curve). This opportunity would commensurate the risk of allowing competing firms to advance their KM/OL programs ahead of E&Y's. For example, the firm's *Global Vision 2002* strategy envisioned the need and opportunity to increase revenues at twice the pace that the professional labor force was growing (See Exhibit One). This would force the firm to "do more with less" to meet its strategic objectives. Knowledge was seen as a key enabler to do so.

With help from the GKSG, E&Y's member firm CEOs regularly communicated the four objectives outlined in Phase One. They expressed how KM/OL was critical to their attainment at "town hall" meetings and in internal newsletters. By stressing the solution

EXHIBIT ONE: ERNST & YOUNG'S KNOWLEDGE GAP

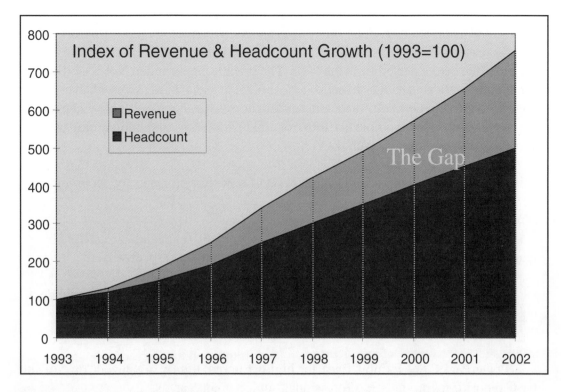

(knowledge) as well as the challenges, management successfully got buy-in from the 80,000 employees in the largest ten-member firms. These firms then began clamoring for additional databases and knowledge services. The newly formed CBK was ready to respond.

The firm assembled what Kotter calls a "Guiding Coalition" to lead the change. This group consisted of Chief Knowledge Officers, with a solid background in the firm's businesses and a strong appetite for innovation, in each of the firm's ten largest member firms. In addition, it contained executive sponsors in each of the firm's service lines who appreciated and could articulate to the field the importance of the KM/OL program and the need to invest both money and time in it. The executive sponsors, selected by the consulting practice leaders, were all very senior executives in the ten member firms who had already recognized the importance of KM/OL and were eager to do whatever they could to encourage knowledge sharing in E&Y.

Critical success factors in this process included global collaboration and interaction with other KM/OL thought leaders. Since KM/OL was such a new discipline in 1994, E&Y worked closely with other leading-edge firms to learn from their mistakes and vice-versa.

Guiding principles, including centralized management, standardization, ease of use, ability to migrate to evolving technologies, and ability to support practitioners 24/7 in remote locations, determined the design of the KnowledgeWeb technical and content architecture.

2. 2 Designing the Architecture

E&Y selected a combination of a Lotus Notes and Web technology platform, for pragmatic reasons. Practitioners spend an average of 4 days out of 5 at client sites, where they were often disconnected from the Web. The practitioners needed Notes' ability to automatically replicate changes to major repositories to users' hard drives when users *were* connected to the firm network, so that these repositories would be available when they *weren't*. Notes was also a simple platform for adding, deleting, and maintaining content, requiring no programming or Web skills.

The firm also decided upon a small, standard set of repository formats, or "container types." These ranged from:

· simple Small Document Libraries and Engagement Team Databases, used by teams in a small community of practice or work assignment respectively, to

· more sophisticated Large Document Repositories, with a comprehensive indexing taxonomy for finding relevant documents among tens of thousands of unfiltered "knowledge objects," to

· PowerPacks (See Exhibit Two), the highly filtered, tightly organized "best-of-the-best" repositories on specific, professional, subject-matter areas.

The architecture group designed these standard container types by selecting best practices from existing consulting services databases. They then generalized them into reusable templates. In a few cases, when there were either too many, or no, best practices, focus groups of practitioners were used to engineer containers from scratch. The firm then built a sophisticated architecture to draw contributions into these repositories, organize and maintain their content, measure utilization, and push content out to relevant users. The discipline required to organize and index over one million knowledge objects from all practice lines and participating member countries within this strict architecture paid off in many ways:

· Ease of training users how to find, and use/reuse, the firm's knowledge;

· Simple integration of external-source and firm-proprietary knowledge about subject matter;

· Consistency of quality of repositories and their content; and

· Ability to "replicate" knowledge from one area of the firm to another.

EXHIBIT TWO: POWERPACKS: STRUCTURED, FILTERED, "BEST-OF-THE-BEST" KNOWLEDGE REPOSITORIES

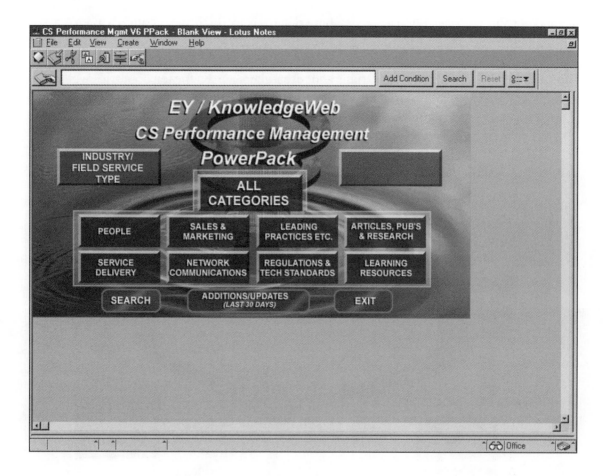

2.3 Designing the Infrastructure

E&Y recognized the need early on to completely reengineer its existing library and research/analysis infrastructure, and to give these employees new competencies. Librarians were, for the most part, experts in hard copy and external-source knowledge. They waited for the phone to ring and then obtained and delivered what was requested, no questions asked. What was now needed were knowledge professionals who:

· understood the firm's businesses and its clients' businesses;

· were comfortable with the technology and knowledgeable about sources of on-line content;

· knew as much about the firm's own internal knowledge as external-source knowledge;

· took the initiative to reach out and sell their expertise to their internal customers; and

· added value to "raw" library and database materials by distilling, synthesizing, analyzing, interpreting, packaging, and adding insight to them.

Two-thirds of the firm's 500+ librarians and researchers across the ten countries welcomed the change and rose to the challenge. The unwilling and unable, however, were identified early and counseled out or relocated elsewhere in the firm. The new roles are illustrated in Exhibit Three.

EXHIBIT THREE: CENTER FOR BUSINESS KNOWLEDGE ROLES

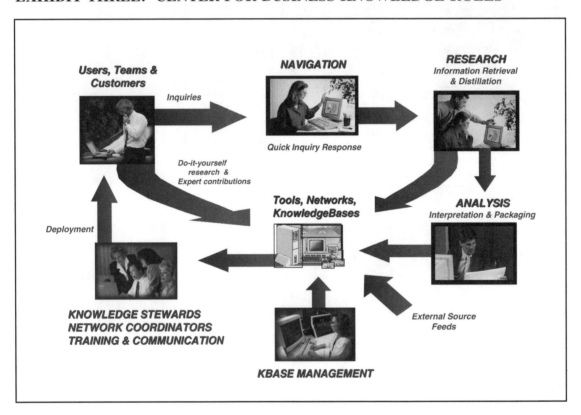

New knowledge roles and responsibilities were not limited to CBK staff. Many practitioners were designated to be Subject Matter Specialists, Knowledge Stewards, Knowledge Managers or Knowledge-Base Owners. Responsibilities were defined (and performance evaluated) for each role. *Every* practitioner in the firm was given responsibilities for contributing to and using the KnowledgeWeb. This was underscored by making KM/OL one of the four dimensions of the firm's Balanced ScoreCard, a key performance evaluation tool for all staff.

EXHIBIT FOUR: A BALANCED SCORE CARD EMBRACES THE KNOWLEDGE CULTURE

Growth & Profitability	Customer Management
• new clients new revenues improved margins	customer satisfaction customer market share customer retention
Asset Management process improvement employee satisfaction employee retention	Knowledge/Technology contribution use proficiency innovation

E&Y's resource guideline was, and still is, the "1 percent rule."

· Its annual investment in KM/OL, exclusive of hardware and basic software on users' desktops, was 1 percent of firm revenues (mostly salaries of knowledge and the cost of external-source databases).

· Additionally, the knowledge center's headcount was 1 percent of firm headcount in the firm's ten largest member countries.

2.4 Developing a Knowledge Culture

The task of creating a Knowledge Culture was planned and supported by significant investment and effort from day one. The details of the Knowledge Culture initiatives are detailed in Phase Three, Implementation.

PHASE THREE: IMPLEMENTATION

The implementation of the strategy, architecture and infrastructure designed in Phase Two occurred gradually between 1995 and 1999. It has grown and evolved to encompass all four E&Y service lines in the firm's ten largest countries, with few hiccups. Both the architecture and infrastructure has to be "tweaked" to suit the different needs of non-consulting service lines and non-English speaking countries. In 1999, the Global CBK formally assumed the responsibilities in all ten countries for all aspects of KM/OL architecture and infrastructure, which had until then been managed locally by member firm CKOs. The Global CBK also took over the technical and human resources in the countries that needed to carry out these responsibilities.

3.1 Architecture Implementation

As Web and connectivity technologies have improved, the firm has "Domino-ized" most of its Notes-based architecture. It has developed a succession of increasingly powerful Web-based navigation tools:

- **Knowledge Catalogue** (1995) - a simple "table of contents" searchable directory of the firm's 1000+ knowledge repositories;

- **Knowledge Search Engine** (1997) - a complete key-word index of over 1 million knowledge objects, with relevancy ranking and an ability to display retrieved objects in both native (e.g. Notes, Word or PowerPoint) and Web format;

- **Community HomeSpaces** (1998) - navigators that give members of a Community of Interest dynamic access to all of the knowledge, and only the knowledge, about the community's subject matter (See Exhibit Five);

- **Service Delivery Tools** (1999) - self-documenting software applications that take practitioners step-by-step through a professional sale, service delivery, or practice management process, and automatically extract the knowledge from the KnowledgeWeb that is relevant to each process step; and

- **Personal Home Page** (2000) - a completely configurable personal Intranet Home Page that links to all of the profiled news, repositories, communities of interest, service delivery tools, schedules and work-lists that the practitioner needs to do his or her job effectively, anytime, anywhere, completely on-line.

Legacy repositories have substantially all been conformed to the global standard architecture design and incorporated into the Catalogue, Search Engine, and Community HomeSpaces.

EXHIBIT FIVE: COMMUNITY HOMESPACES: WEB-BASED NAVIGATION TOOLS FOR COMMUNITIES OF INTEREST

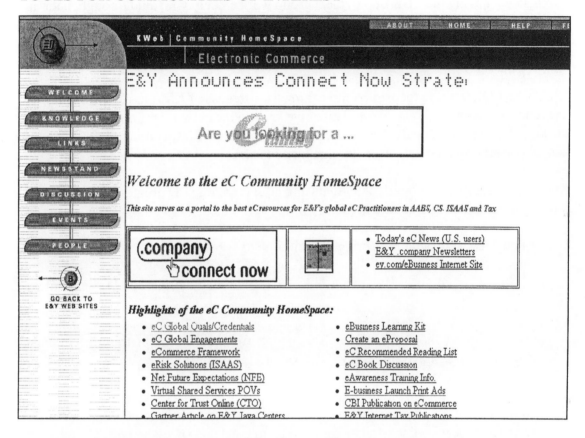

The underlying containers remain Notes-based (hence, easy to use and maintain). With the addition of these Web-based navigation tools, the KnowledgeWeb also has all the power of a Web-based knowledge environment, providing users with the best of both worlds.

3.2 Culture Change Implementation

E&Y's Knowledge Culture initiatives encompass training, internal marketing, communication, measurement, and reward mechanisms. These are all designed to reinforce the importance of making knowledge sharing an integral part of what everyone in the firm does. Ultimately, the goal is to embed "knowledge behaviors" into all core business processes so that knowledge sharing simply becomes, as one practitioner recently put it, "the way we do things around here."

The effort was sizable: about one-fifth of the total knowledge budget has been spent each year on these culture change initiatives. Since this effort focuses on end users, it is the most visible part of the CBK's activities to front-line practitioners. The effort was managed by having the CBK deployment group work closely with ,and through, national and local training and communication departments. The CBK provided curricula, internal marketing material and "train the trainer" sessions to these departments. The customization was left to localized needs.

E&Y's KM/OL training focuses on three things: awareness of KM/OL resources, how to use repositories and access tools, and effective knowledge network training. Training for the knowledge professionals (CBK staff plus practitioners with specific KM/OL roles described earlier) is separate from training for end users.

Knowledge training is currently integrated into all service line PD programs. Three training tools and techniques are used:

1. An entry-level curriculum to bring new hires up to speed;

2. The Global Deployment Hub to house KM/OL training materials and DTL modules; and

3. Business Unit training liaisons which are people from the CBK who train-the-trainers and help business units embed KM/OL modules into their training curricula.

Through these three training methods, over 80,000 E&Y employees have been trained since 1996, one business unit at a time. Each training started with a pilot group in each country and each service line to adapt the training to local and specialty needs.

The critical aspects of the implementation program have all been Knowledge Culture change aspects: communication, training, internal marketing, measurement & reward, and achieving external recognition for KM/OL achievements. It is a never-ending challenge. As new staff joins the firm, as knowledge behaviors evolve and change over practitioners' careers, as new KM/OL tools emerge, the programs needed to enable and encourage knowledge sharing must evolve as well.

The CBK deployment team leverages their own efforts by working with other customer-facing CBK groups. The CBK's researchers and analysts, for example, spend up to a third of their time on field assignments, and their work helping practitioners understand and use the KWeb (and the CBK's services) is an integral part of the knowledge deployment effort.

3.3 Lessons Learned from Implementation

The five elements of E&Y's KM/OL program that have had maximum user impact are:

· The development and roll-out of PowerPacks (the firm's first KM/OL "killer application");

· Evolution of the increasingly sophisticated access tools described above;

· The use of templates to standardize the design and streamline the preparation of CBK research and analysis deliverables (" 'productizing' the analysis service");

· The network program that supports knowledge-sharing across Communities of Interest; and

· The development of extremely sophisticated business analysis.

The Network program was successful, and critical to the KM/OL program, because it recognized that Communities of Interest need help to organize their knowledge and knowledge-sharing abilities. By making this facilitation role "someone's job," the firm has ensured that this challenging, 100-percent, internal, client-facing, knowledge-leveraging job got done, and was done well. This program, probably more than anything else, differentiates E&Y from other KM/OL leaders. It is the reason why E&Y has been singled out as one of the top firms in the world in knowledge sharing.

The critical lesson about KM/OL that E&Y has learned through implementation is the realization that a variety of different KM/OL programs are needed since different users have different "knowledge behaviors." At one extreme, many young practitioners, comfortable with both the technology and do-it-yourself research processes, are willing and able to use the full functionality of the KnowledgeWeb without ever using CBK research and analysis staff. At the other extreme, some older practitioners, and those for whom the opportunity cost of do-it-yourself research is too high, are prepared to engage the more senior CBK staff to produce final client deliverables with minimal intervention.

In between, many practitioners value the CBK staff's ability to extract and distill knowledge quickly and inexpensively. They prefer to do their own analysis, though, and interpretation and packaging of the results. The knowledge needs of users with these different knowledge behaviors are also different. As behaviors evolve, the knowledge content, tools, programs, and roles must evolve with them.

There have been two critical success factors in E&Y's KM/OL implementation.

1. Making the change evolutionary rather than revolutionary: People can only absorb so much change and new knowledge at one time, and the firm's service lines and people are only prepared to invest in KM/OL to the extent they could see early and continuous successes.

2. Focusing on Deliverables: The development of identifiable, valuable knowledge access tools, repositories, and research & analysis "products" has made KM/OL tangible to E&Y users and hence made it much easier to sell.

PHASE FOUR: REINFORCEMENT

E&Y continues to offer "lunch & learn" training in new KM/OL products. In addition, E&Y now offers an automated "assisted navigation" feature in its access toolkit that helps users find what they need online by asking and answering simple English-language questions. The goals now are to simplify tools and processes to make the use of KM/OL easier, reduce training needs, and handle information overload.

As a result of the above training, communication, executive sponsorship and internal marketing efforts, E&Y's culture has changed in two important ways:

1. Users now accept the need for and value of a centrally managed KM/OL function (attempts to hoard knowledge workers are increasingly rare); and

2. The majority of users are now active knowledge sharers (participation rates—those using and contributing to the KnowledgeWeb—have more than doubled to over 80 percent since 1996).

In addition, the "knowledge behavior curve" has flattened. More users (about 30 percent versus 20 percent in 1996) do all their own research themselves without KM/OL staff intermediation. At the other end of the spectrum, more users (about 20 percent versus 10 percent in 1996) now rely on KM/OL staff to do complete research/analysis in final format for delivery to clients.

E&Y's KM/OL strategy has benefited the firm in six ways.

1. Its Return on Investment ("ROI") in technology is much higher—the proportion of practitioners using their laptops for more than just e-mail has risen from under half to over 90 percent since 1996. The and size and use of the KnowledgeWeb have both more than quintupled in this period.

2. New staff has become knowledgeable — and hence productive in the field — much faster.

3. Many deliverables are built on templates or on deliverables from previous assignments, rather than built from scratch.

4. As testimonials and customer data indicates, E&Y clients, its people, and outside evaluators all see E&Y as a global leader in KM/OL.

5. Its clients see E&Y as more knowledgeable about their business, and therefore view it as a more rounded service provider.

6. Potential new recruits now perceive E&Y as an excellent learning environment to work in and hence E& Y is an Employer of Choice.

PHASE FIVE: EVALUATION

The four types of measures described in Phase One remain the firm's key evaluation criteria:

1. Rate of contribution of knowledge to the firm's repositories (number of new knowledge objects added);

2. Rate of re-use of knowledge from the firm's repositories (number of user sessions per day);

3. User-surveyed quality of knowledge in the firm's repositories, and of deliverables of CBK staff (users rate completeness, accuracy, subjective value and timeliness on a 10-point scale);

4. Recognition of E&Y's KM/OL leadership by three groups: outside awards, E&Y's own people (unsolicited kudos), and university recruiters (becoming an Employer of Choice).

By all four measures, the performance of the CBK and its KnowledgeWeb has improved consistently and significantly since 1995. At the same time, E&Y has also seen consistent and significant improvement in revenues, profits, revenue-per-person, margin, speed to market, customer satisfaction, and employee satisfaction and productivity—the Drivers for the decision to invest in KM/OL in the first place. Crediting KM/OL success with these improvements requires something of a leap of faith Other factors have undoubtedly played a key role in them as well. The strong correlation between KM/OL success and business success is compelling evidence that the firm's KM/OL programs and investments have given E&Y a handsome return.

Going forward, E&Y faces two main challenges in sustaining its "Knowledge Advantage." The next KM/OL frontier after Knowledge Sharing is Knowledge Collaboration—the leveraging of knowledge in a collaborative environment, rather than just person-to-person knowledge transfer (Exhibit Six). In Western society, people are motivated, hired, rewarded and promoted on *individual* performance. Work assignments (even those meted out by work teams) are to *individuals*. This raises the KM/OL ante from knowledge-sharing to knowledge-collaboration. It will require a quantum increase in effort, cultural change, improvement in supporting technologies, and KM/OL thought leadership. While E&Y is working with several leading-edge organizations to grapple with this issue, the challenge is daunting.

EXHIBIT SIX: THREE STAGES IN THE EVOLUTION OF KM/OL[1]

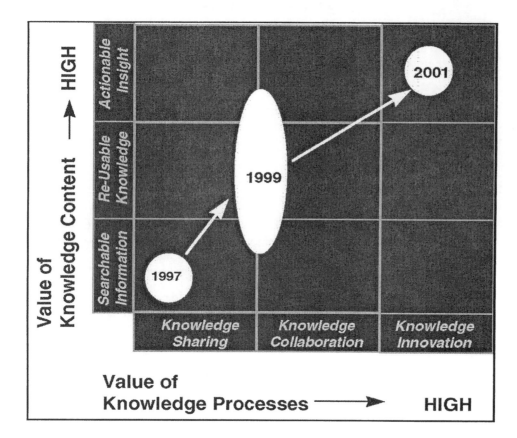

[1] Adapted from:The Knowledge Management Scenario:Trends and Directions for 1998-2003. Gartner Group OnLine - Knowledge Management Series, A. Cushman, M. Fleming, K. Harris, R. Hunter, B. Rosser, March 18, 1999

E&Y's second challenge is to develop even more sophisticated KM/OL tools and products to stay on KM/OL's leading edge and not be content to rest on its laurels. The firm has recently appointed its first global Director for Knowledge Innovation. The Director is working with both the firm's — and the world's — most innovative people. The aim is to make tomorrow's CBK and tomorrow's KnowledgeWeb as dramatic an advance in KM/OL as the firm's first, bold steps into the KM/OL arena were in 1994. Some of the innovations they are looking at include:

· Ways of codifying "stories," so that the KnowledgeWeb contains not only the assignment deliverable but the context that made it exemplary (E&Y is even studying how tribal cultures with no written language have kept their rich culture alive through story-telling, as inspiration for this project);

· Development of a Knowledge "Collaboratory" that will enable leading-edge KM/OL firms to co-develop and cost-share new KM/OL tools, products and resources, to mutual advantage; and

· Development of a new product development "Green Space" where E&Y's people, clients and colleagues can collectively electronically brain-storm, using new innovation tools to invent new products and services that meet identified and evolving client needs.

E&Y looks forward to solving these challenges, and sharing its "knowledge about knowledge" with clients, so that all can succeed in the knowledge-powered economy of the 21st century.

ABOUT THE CONTRIBUTOR

Dave Pollard, B.Sc. (Comp.Sc.), CA, has been the **Chief Knowledge Officer** for Ernst & Young in Canada since 1994, following twenty years as an Entrepreneurial Services practitioner and partner. Dave has responsibility as part of the Global Knowledge Steering Group for: developing the firm's Knowledge Strategy and Vision; design and deployment of Knowledge Architecture, Tools and Content; management of Research, Analysis, Navigation, and Specialist Network Services; and attainment of a Knowledge-Sharing Culture.

He is the new **Director for Knowledge Innovation** in E&Y's Global CBK. Dave's new role entails:

- meeting with CBK customers and helping them to anticipate and define their emerging knowledge, learning and new product needs,
- working with global knowledge thought leaders to identify and deploy leading practices,
- helping customers reengineer their existing knowledge processes and resources, and design new knowledge tools, to embed knowledge creation and use in E&Y's day-to-day business culture, and hence increase the value of knowledge to the firm, and
- helping to extend E&Y's world-class "knowledge enterprise" to engage customers, associates and other business partners in the firm in collaborative and innovative activities with each other and with E&Y's people.

Dave is also the **Global Corporate Finance Knowledge Coordinator**, working with the leaders of the firm's Corporate Finance service line to develop knowledge tools, processes and resources to meet the evolving needs of this service line. This provides strategic finance, valuation, litigation support, restructuring and M&A transaction services for clients.

Dave has chaired firm committees and focus groups on the Virtual Workplace, Internet/ Intranet strategy, and business innovation. He is a subject matter specialist advising clients and client service teams on knowledge management, business innovation and e-commerce. He has written and lectured on a variety of subjects related to knowledge management, innovation and the future of business.

2

HEWLETT PACKARD

An organizational wide program to share knowledge between projects, to learn from success and mistakes and to capture reusable material from engagements

GLOSSARY OF TERMS

1. **Critical Success Factor**: What must go right to meet the stated goal.

2. **Explicit Knowledge**: Knowledge that can be laid out in steps, procedures, words or numbers. It can be stored in a computer and accessed through a database or network.

3. **Human Capital**: The collective capabilities of an organization's employees including knowledge, skills, competencies, and experience. Human capital is the single source of innovation in an organization.

4. **SAP** (Systems, Applications, and Products in Data Processing) is the world's largest inter-enterprise software company and the world's fourth-largest independent software supplier, overall. SAP employs over 20,500 people in more than 50 countries to deliver services and provide high-level customer support.

5. **Structured Intellectual Capital**: Codified knowledge of the organization including solutions, models, processes, and procedures. Creation of Structured Intellectual Capital requires packaging and structuring explicit intellectual assets in a form that can be stored and shared widely to meet the organization's needs.

6. **Tacit Knowledge**: Tacit knowledge is based on experience and practice. Tacit knowledge is deeply rooted in an individual's action and experience, as well as their ideals, values and emotions. It is contained primarily in the heads of people.

BACKGROUND

Hewlett-Packard (HP), the No. 2 computer company worldwide, is a leading global provider of computing and imaging solutions, printing peripherals, software, and computer-related services for business and home. To fuel its growth, HP is restructuring itself as an Internet specialist providing Web hardware, software, and support to corporate customers. One of HP's major strategies focuses on capitalizing on the opportunities of the Internet and the proliferation of electronic services (e-services). To that end, the company has spun off its test and measurement equipment and medical electronics businesses as Agilent Technologies.

The company's more than 36,000 products are used by people for personal use and in industry, business, engineering, science, medicine, and education. More than half of HP's sales come from outside the US. HP employs 83,200 people worldwide, selling its products and services through 600 sales and support offices and distributorships in more than 120 countries across the globe.

Hewlett-Packard Consulting (HPC) is the solution-consulting arm of Hewlett-Packard that enables customers to integrate and optimize systems sold by HP and other vendors. More than 4,000 employees consultt with clients to ensure that customers get the greatest return from the products and services they buy from HP.

Both HP and HPC has been recognized broadly in the industry for excellence in knowledge management. HPC has been recognized as a best practice KM company by APQC (American Productivity and Quality Council) and HP has been voted by CEOs, CIOs and CKOs as a Most Admired Knowledge Enterprises for three years in a row (1998 - 2000).

ASSESSING THE NEED

HP Consulting came to realize the need for knowledge management in 1995. HPC's leadership inherently knew that there was value in better leveraging the organization's knowledge. Effective knowledge management became important in order to meet customer expectations for innovation, rapid execution, and global consistency. Clients expected that when they retained HP's services, their consultants would tap into the knowledge of the broader HP organization to solve their business issues.

To many of the consultants in HPC, sharing and leverage knowledge seemed "soft" and non-critical in their every day jobs. The first step was to ensure that the business case demonstrated a significant impact on customers and the profitability of HPC. A small team was chartered to interview clients and identify HP's effectiveness at leveraging internal knowledge and transferring it to client teams. Although the clients expressed satisfaction with the value they were receiving from HP Consulting, they felt that the depth of knowledge available to them was highly dependent upon the specific consultants assigned to their project. Moreover, clients felt that HPC consultants could do a more effective job transferring their knowledge to the clients' implementation team.

The results were reported back to HPC leadership:

> *"While some of our consultants may have doubts about the value of knowledge sharing and reuse to the success of our business, our clients have a different perspective. The feedback collected during the assessment reflects that our clients believe that the value and depth of HPC knowledge is highly dependent on the consultants assigned to their project. Our challenge is to deliver ever increasing new and innovative services in a consistent, high quality manner regardless of the consultants assigned to the engagement. To do this, we must rapidly leverage our experience from one project to the next and from one part of the world to another.*

The client feedback provided the important insights to the consultant community. Knowledge management would not only help them become more productive, but was essential to client satisfaction. People in the organization increasingly began to recognize that sharing knowledge between projects, learning from others' successes and mistakes, as well as capturing reusable material from engagements was essential to HPC's success.

At the same time, the focus on knowledge leverage created challenges in balancing innovation with reuse. A key goal of the organization was to continue to be seen as a product leader. From its inception in 1937, Bill Hewlett and David Packard felt that the company must "continually strive to develop products that represent true advancement." Consequently, HP Consulting management wanted to ensure that HPC struck a balance between the leverage and reuse of existing knowledge and experience with the development of leading edge solutions to meet clients' business needs.

In response to these business drivers, HPC developed an initial business case for knowledge management. The foundation of the business case was that knowledge is the currency of HPC's business. In the past, investment in managing knowledge was sporadic, bounded by organization structures, and focused on technology. The knowledge management team emphasized that HPC's ability to grow would be directly affected by its ability to manage knowledge efficiently and effectively across the entire businesses.

Moses and Knowledge Management

Realizing that the business case needed to be actively supported by senior management and that the effort would require a significant culture shift, the KM team looked for a metaphor that would depict the requirements to launch a successful KM initiative. The team used a parable of the biblical figure Moses to engage the sponsors in understanding their role. The goal of the metaphor was to demonstrate what was needed to make the initiative a success.

In this story, an involved and committed leader (Moses) had a vision (leading his people out of bondage into a land of milk and honey). He also had a high-level sponsor (God) who was able to remove obstacles (the Red Sea). Moses played an active role in leading the people to the Promised Land (taking the first steps into the parting waters of the Red Sea). He led the journey, rather than adopt the present-day management practice of simply checking on progress on a quarterly basis.

At the end of this story, the newly appointed VP and General Manager of HPC stepped forward and said, "I'll be Moses." This began a wave of support by the global leadership team that saw the KM initiative through its first few years. The VP/general manager kept his commitment by staying highly involved in developing the KM initiative, gaining and sustaining support from the leadership team, communicating to the organization about the importance of knowledge management, and working closely with the KM team.

THE VISION

The senior leadership team developed a vision for the HPC KM initiative:

> *"Our consultants feel and act as if they have the knowledge of the entire organization at their fingertips when they consult with customers. They know exactly where to go to find information. They are eager to share knowledge as well as leverage others' experience in order to deliver more value to customers. We will recognize those consultants that share and those that leverage others' knowledge and experience as the most valuable members of the HP team."*

HPC's leadership identified three measures of success for the program. These measures focused on sharing, learning, and reuse. Specifically:

1. **Sharing knowledge between projects**: In a environment of rapidly changing technology and skills, project teams would need to share their newly acquired knowledge with others working on similar engagements

2. **Learning from successes and mistakes**: Learning what worked, what didn't and how to improve on processes and approaches was essential to HP Consulting

3. **Capturing reusable material from engagements**: Minimizing reinvention of the wheel was a key factor in profitability improvement.

Over the next few years, the KM team collected stories that provided evidence that the organization was achieving these measures. Some of these stories were:

1. *Sharing Knowledge Between Projects*

   As a consulting organization, much of the knowledge of HPC is created on client projects. The opportunity is to learn from the experience of one project team to make the next project more successful. To accomplish this, a reflection session with the entire project team is held at scheduled times during the engagement. The purpose of these sessions is to identify knowledge gained by the project team that can be more broadly leveraged. Where possible, the knowledge is documented for reuse. However, much of the knowledge is too rich and subtle to incorporate in a document. So, the team also takes the person-to-person approach through Learning Communities, which provide forums for communicating the team's know-how and best practices. This experience reaches a broad network of consultants working in similar industries and with similar solutions. The value as one consultant said was:

"Because knowledge from one project is now made available to other similar projects, it save the time and expense of having to recreate the same basic documents and experience. This helps speed the flow of knowledge around the organization and enables us to provide more value to our customers in an accelerated manner. Bottomline, I'm not able to build and innovate upon a proven base of knowledge"

2. Learning from Successes and Mistakes

Knowledge management is not just for individual contributors. This was displayed by a senior HPC leader when he gathered his staff along with a project team for a review of a project that had not achieved its objectives. At the start of the session he put in place several guidelines:

- Everyone on the project team would participate in the meeting;

- Nothing would be put down in writing or leave the room without agreement;

- The people in the room were there to learn from what went well and what didn't;

- There would be no recriminations; no fault-finding.

The reflection session was focused on what the desired outcome of the project was, what actually happened and what accounted for the difference. Learning was summarized and an action plan for ways to avoid the pitfalls was generated by the team and then shared with other project teams dealing in similar environments.

This experience provided an environment of openness and trust and also showed the organization that senior management saw the value in learning from both successes and mistakes.

3. *Capturing Reusable Material from Engagements*

With each engagement, consultants were developing more effective ways to deliver a given solution. Consultants would often develop tools to assess the client's detailed requirements, or a template to capture design data. While the tools were oriented toward a specific client, most often, with a modest amount of effort they could be genericized and used by others. These tools could then improve the effectiveness and value of the solution in similar engagements with other clients.

THE STRATEGY

From the outset, HPC determined that the KM initiative would not be driven by technology. Instead, the KM team subscribed to a model that started with business results, and then identified the required actions and decisions to achieve those results. Once these were determined, HPC was able to define the knowledge needed to support the business. HPC began the KM effort with the end in mind, to ensure that the focus was on managing the most useful knowledge for the organization.

EXHIBIT ONE: PROGRAM DESIGN

Program Design

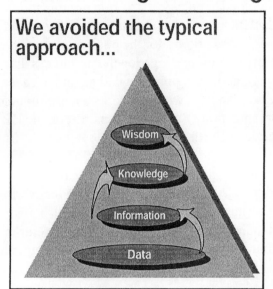

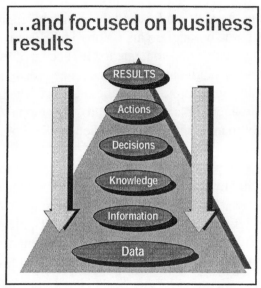

Source: The Performance Group
Bjelland & Co AS

HP Consulting

HPC leadership and the KM team designed a program with three objectives. The first objective was for all consultants to balance the reuse of knowledge with innovation. The second was to promote pervasive leveraging and sharing of knowledge. The final objective was to tightly integrate the sharing of knowledge into the work practices of the organization so that it became part of daily work, not separate from it.

At the start, the KM team recognized that the KM initiative needed to be evolutionary and adaptable to the changing needs of the business and the organization. They also recognized that establishing processes to easily share knowledge would be required to promote the behavioral changes needed.

Piloting Knowledge Management

The KM team decided to begin with a pilot that would foster learning by and produce understanding of the management challenges. They decided to engage a strategic organization business unit to understand the value and approach to knowledge management they would then take to the broader organization. They identified several criteria for the pilot: a group that was highly visible and strategic to the success of the organization; a high level of readiness displayed through having a business need for sharing and leveraging knowledge, and a leader that was strongly committed to the success of the pilot. The pilot would serve as a learning field for the broader implementation across the global organization. Based on these criteria, the HP senior management team selected the SAP practice in North America.

The SAP practice had a business imperative to transfer knowledge about a new and innovative solution from a small core group of experienced people to all SAP consultants in the North America. The ultimate goal was to ensure that this new solution could be delivered across North America in an efficient and predictable manner that produced both profitable returns to HP and highly satisfied clients. Attainment of that goal would enable the practice to build its client base and its internal consulting resources.

The SAP team had previously attempted to capture and share knowledge without success. Documents had been captured using a Lotus Notes database. The database, however, was rarely used. No process existed to enable the consultants to update the material to keep it current. The SAP practice leader became frustrated and disappointed with the lack of participation on the part of the consultants. The KM team used this experience to try a new approach to sharing and leveraging knowledge. A pilot project was launched within the SAP practice called Project OWL (Orchestrating Wisdom and Learning).

The goal of Project OWL was to demonstrate the effectiveness of knowledge management both to the consultants and the organization as a whole. The project was designed to develop a committed core consultant group that would identify, share, and leverage knowledge for the benefit of others in the organization. This group would then become advocates for the value of knowledge management.

Project OWL began by assessing the challenges to knowledge management and decided to focus on training, change management and process redesign as primary elements of the pilot. One of the first steps was to identify the knowledge that needed to be shared. The team began by creating a Knowledge Map with the help of several experienced consultants. The Knowledge Map helped determine what knowledge was needed to sell and deliver the new SAP solution and to identify where that knowledge resided (people or repository). This process avoided the typical frustrating approach of sifting through mounds of information to try to find useful knowledge.

The Knowledge Map (K-Map) exposed valuable tacit and explicit knowledge sources that previously were only known to a few experienced consultants. By surfacing this information, and then implementing processes and capabilities to share this knowledge, the knowledge became readily available and had an immediate payoff to the North American SAP community.

While the team was very energized about creating the K-Map, they realized this was only the first step. Other changes would be needed, specifically in the behavior of the consultants. To help identify the desired behaviors and expose existing challenging behaviors, the SAP consultants participated in a five-day workshop that trained them on the new delivery approach and tools. Integrated into this workshop was training on Knowledge Management and its implication on behaviors, values and work practices. The workshop enabled the participants to practice this behavior through experiential learning. Exercises framed in the context of games were used to illustrate behaviors considered "dysfunctional" and to reinforce the new desired behaviors. The exercises served to show the value of sharing and leveraging each other's knowledge in a safe environment.

EXHIBIT TWO: A KNOWLEDGE MAP

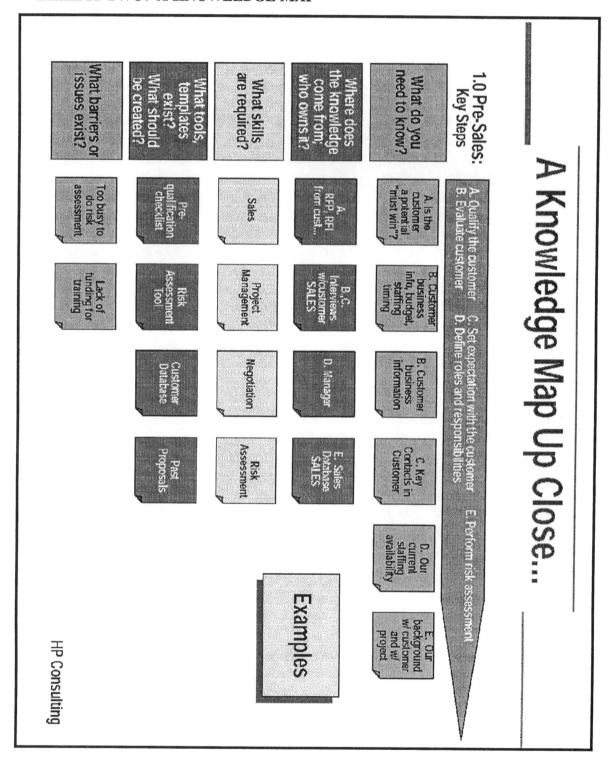

A Knowledge Map Up Close...

1.0 Pre-Sales:
Key Steps

What do you need to know?

Where does the knowledge come from, who owns it?

What skills are required?

What tools, templates exist? What should be created?

What barriers or issues exist?

A. Qualify the customer   C. Set expectation with the customer
B. Evaluate customer   D. Define roles and responsibilities
E. Perform risk assessment

A. Is the customer a potential "must win"?

B. Customer business info, budget, staffing timing

B. Customer business information

C. Key Contacts in Customer

D. Our current staffing availability

E. Our background w/ customer and w/ project

A. RFP, RFI from cust...

B., C. Interviews w/customer SALES

D. Manager

E. Sales Database SALES

Sales

Project Management

Negotiation

Risk Assessment

Pre-qualification checklist

Risk Assessment Tool

Customer Database

Past Proposals

Too busy to do risk assessment

Lack of funding for training

Examples

HP Consulting

The response from the consultants was far exceeded the expectation of the KM team. The consultants excitedly commented on the impact of the workshop:

> ***"The workshop had specific personal impact to me. It convinced me to work on changing my behavior, and helped me to see the value of sharing knowledge and learning from others. It clearly demonstrated that technical ability alone is not sufficient for success."***

> ***"We'll talk about the things we did wrong; we hope others will be just as honest with us. We're going to learn a lot from each other."***

At the conclusion of the workshop, the consultants were charted with developing a KM implementation plan. This plan resulted in a tailored program that met the SAP practice's needs for creating, sharing, and leverage knowledge within their business unit.

Substantive changes in behavior were also observed after the conclusion of the workshop. Learning Communities formed where experiences and best practices were shared; project teams consulted with each other to share their experiences in delivering this new solution to clients; solution documentation was gathered and made available to other consultants. Ultimately, these new behaviors enabled the SAP practice to expand the new delivery approach across the entire North American business and thus decrease clients' implementation cycles from 18 to six months.

AGENDA
INTEGRATED KNOWLEDGE MANAGEMENT WORKSHOP

Monday	Tuesday	Wednesday	Thursday	Friday
* Workshop introduction and objectives * Overview: the Accelerated Approach / Knowledge Management * How this is different: *The Four Hour House* Video * Client feedback / consultant input/ implications for work * Provocative ideas: changing values and behaviors * Reflection	* Reflections * Experiential learning: Trust * Experiential Learning: Teamwork * Learning styles * KM processes and roles (Knowledge Map update, initiating Learning Communities)	* Reflections * Experiential learning: conflict resolution * Experiential learning: Standing on each other's shoulders * A Day in the Life of a Consultant * Creating a new operating metaphor * Next steps: Action/ communication planning	* Reflections * The Accelerated Approach	* Reflections * How we will work together * WIIFM (what's in it for me) * Pilot planning * Group reflection /feedback * Recommendations

THE THREE-PHASED APPROACH

At the conclusion of the Project Owl pilot, the KM team collaborated with HPC leadership to chart the future course. Senior leadership was very pleased with the pilot results and gave the go-ahead for a full-blown global KM program. The KM team used their experiences and insights from the pilot to develop a three-phased implementation model that would be applied to a broad KM implementation across the worldwide organization. The initial focus of the global program would emphasize knowledge-sharing processes and behavioral changes rather than technology.

EXHIBIT THREE: A PHASED APPROACH

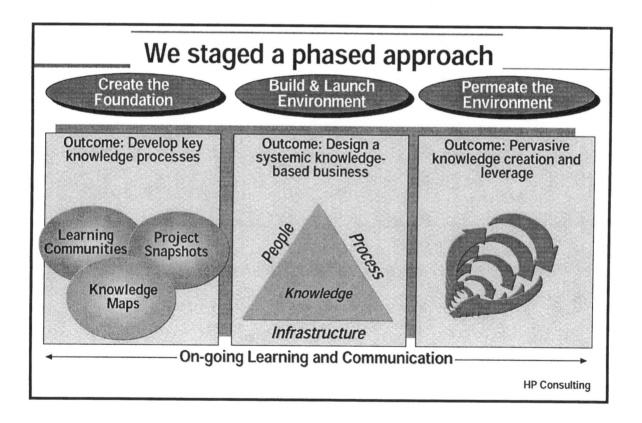

Creating the Foundation

The HPC knowledge management initiative began the global implementation with Phase I, Creating the Foundation. This phase involved three key processes: Learning Communities, Project Snapshots, and Knowledge Maps.

DEFINITIONS

Learning Communities are informal groups of people that cross-organizational boundaries and come together to discuss best practices, issues, or skills that the group wants to learn about. They may meet face to face or through conference calls.

Project Snapshots are sessions designed to collect lessons learned and collateral from a project team that can be reused by future project teams.

Knowledge Mapping is a process that identifies knowledge, skills, collateral and tools needed to sell or deliver a solution. Consultants with experience come together to build the map based on their experience and know-how. The map is used as a guide to what knowledge is important and where it can be found. It is updated as experience in the organization grows.

EXHIBIT FOUR: THREE PROCESSES

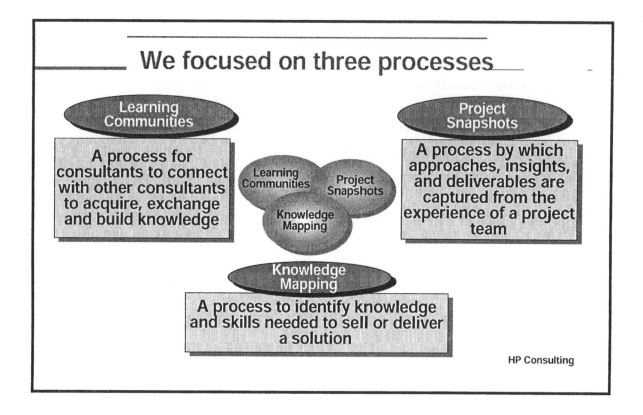

Learning Communities, in particular, began to quickly proliferate in HPC. This process enabled knowledge to be acquired and exchanged beyond an individual's personal network. It provided the consultants the opportunity to learn from each other. It also provided a forum for surfacing issues and discussing ideas. By allowing the participants to select the topics for the community sessions, the Learning Communities were assured of dealing with relevant, current issues and keeping user participation high.

Stories such as the following played a major role in motivating and sustaining enthusiasm for Learning Communities:

> During a team meeting, a consultant spoke up about a technical assessment he would be conducting the following day at a client site, and asked other participants for any experience or assessment tools they had used in similar situations. A participant commented that he had recently completed the development of an assessment tool and reviewed how it was successfully delivered in a client engagement. He then sent the assessment tool electronically to the consultant in need. The second consultant enhanced the assessment tool for his application, leveraging both the first consultant's experience and the tool to deliver the assessment to his client. At the next meeting, the second consultant shared his newly gained experience including what worked well, what he had learned, and what he would do differently next time. He made the enhanced assessment tool available to the team; both he and the first consultant offered to be contacts for additional information or mentoring.

As the larger organization began to adopt knowledge management practices, Project Snapshots soon received a wide following. Project Snapshots provided opportunities for project teams to reflect on lessons learned and identify collateral from current projects that could be used by future project teams. As the KM team facilitated Snapshot sessions, they realized that the key to successful implementation of Snapshots was to integrate the process into the project management work practice.

Knowledge Mapping was embraced by several of the solution development groups. These groups were chartered with developing new solutions that could be consistently and predictably sold and delivered to clients across the globe. The knowledge map proved to be a useful tool because it surface what knowledge was needed for a particular solution and where that knowledge could be found (person or repository). It gave further insight into the flow of knowledge and therefore helped in structuring the knowledge for reuse. A knowledge map was developed in two-day workshop with a cross section of consultants with subject-matter expertise from across the globe. These collaborative sessions provided a further benefit. During the mapping workshop, the participants formed new relationships that enabled them to form new personal connections for continued insights and learning after the mapping session ended.

Building and Launching the Environment

Phase II, *Build and Launch Environment,* broadened the scope of the KM effort to include measures, new roles and enabling technology. The goal of Phase II was to design and implement a holistic knowledge-based system.

The KM team chose to focus on three strategies. The first strategy was to broadly *implement and integrate the knowledge processes* developed in Phase I. Implementing and integrating meant embedding KM into the "core" work processes of consultants as they sold and delivered solutions. By integrating knowledge management into a core process, it would become a natural part of work and not an extra step.

The second strategy was to *build organizational capability* by developing skills, embedding knowledge management into the evaluation system, and providing rewards and recognition for outstanding examples of knowledge sharing and reuse.

In order to make knowledge globally available, the third strategy involved *implementing a repository* for the storage and access of explicit documented knowledge.

Integrating Knowledge into the Work

Early in Phase II, the team began focusing on integrating key knowledge processes into the core work of the organization. During this period, HPC was deploying to the worldwide field organization a significant enhancement to its project management (PM) methodology. This methodology provided the processes, tools, templates, and guidelines to effectively sell and deliver solutions to clients.

The KM team was convinced that the PM methodology was the logical place to embed the Project Snapshot process. As project teams complete the selling phase and move into the delivery of the solution, there is a natural milestone for reflection by the project team. Similarly, at the conclusion of the engagement, project teams should be reflecting on what went well, what didn't, lessons learned and specific tacit and explicit knowledge that could be shared with others.

The KM team began working closely with the project management methodology team to embed project snapshots into the newly enhanced methodology. They simplified the adoption by developing tools consistent with the PM methodology tools and integrating Project Snapshot training into the rollout training for the new project management approach.

As project teams began using the new methodology, they were expected to complete the two snapshots as part of the client engagement. The knowledge process became part of the core work and is now built into the engagement plan.

Creating New Roles

As Phase II was launching, HP Consulting was also undergoing significant change. The overall structure was being redesigned and new processes and roles were being developed across all business units.

The timing was now right for designing, testing and implementing new knowledge roles in the organization. The KM team evaluated the organizational needs and determined that several types of roles were necessary.

First, the team felt that a central group should to lead the overall program. Two types of roles were created: roles focused on providing knowledge management services to the field organization and roles focused on the development of processes and technology that would ultimately be deployed world wide. The *Knowledge Services Manager* worked closely with the geographies to plan their KM initiatives and drive the use of KM services and tools. The *Knowledge Architect Manager* was responsible for developing knowledge and technology architectures that would enable the use of the knowledge processes and provide easy access to the knowledge of the organization. Finally, the *Solution Development Knowledge Manager* role was heavily content based and included responsibilities for structuring, storing, and renewing solution content for reuse by the consultant community.

Second, it was understood that a central team could not, on their own, drive cultural change. Geographical knowledge roles would be critical to the permeation of knowledge management processes, measures, and tools within the organization. The *Knowledge Consultant* role was created to facilitate knowledge flow around the organization. These individuals were initially key to the implementation of KM in their geographies and solution areas, acting as a critical link between the field and the central KM team.

Finally, several roles needed to be created that addressed specific knowledge processes. These roles would initially facilitate knowledge processes while simultaneously building broader organizational competency in applying and executing the knowledge management capabilities. For example, the *Learning Community Lead* (LC Lead) role was designed to drive and sustain the learning community process within their subject domain. The leaders were consultants or managers with content knowledge and a passion to launch and maintain active participation in the community.

Technology and Content Management

As the interest in adopting knowledge processes heightened, the importance of technology in the overall knowledge management solution grew as well. In 1998, HPC launched K-Net, its knowledge technology solution.

K-Net is a structured, interactive electronic portal to HPC's knowledge that can be browsed and searched for content. It also includes structured solution knowledge that has a consistent look and feel, as well as project workspace, project document management, and a discussion forum. This tool helps guide consultants to the collective pool of organizational knowledge. K-Net was based on the software tool Livelink that is marketed by Open Text Corporation. Livelink was initially piloted in HPC Japan before the global team decided to embrace it.

The information technology infrastructure plays a vital role in supporting and promoting knowledge management at HPC. The simple and flexible technology structure allows consultants and managers to share and retrieve information at any stage of their project.

To evolve content management capabilities and ensure consistent content management practices, the KM team formed an HPC Standards Board. This board was chartered with establishing guidelines and standards for knowledge structures, service portfolio development, and collateral creation. The Board consists of a cross-section of individual in moderate to high-level positions in the organization with deep knowledge of the content management needs of the organization.

EXHIBIT FIVE: MANAGEMENT OF EXPLICIT KNOWLEDGE CONTENT

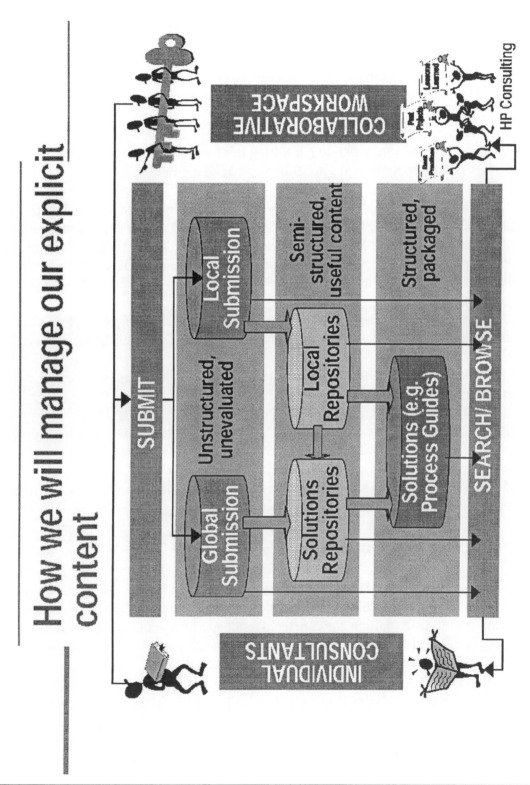

Reinforcement

As the KM program matured, it became important to recognize and reward individuals who were exhibiting the desired behaviors of sharing and reuse. In FY99, HPC created the Knowledge Masters Award to recognize and reward HPC employees who exemplified the highest standards of knowledge mastery. These individuals would be viewed as role models for sharing and leveraging knowledge and would share real life experiences with the broader organization.

In 1999, 182 nominees were submitted, resulting in 41 winners. Knowledge Master winners received HPC-wide recognition and an all-expense-paid trip or cash award.

The winners' stories were published internally and not only chronicled outstanding practices, but told of improved business results through the leverage and reuse of knowledge. Moreover, the stories reflected exceptional levels of expertise, teamwork, and a willingness to go contribute to the overall good of the organization. Some examples from the Knowledge Master's winners are:

· A knowledge mapping session led to the identification and packaging of solution material that was then delivered in a large banking engagement, resulting in $11 million in revenue.

· The reuse of existing materials and knowledge resulted in $10 million in revenue from five accounts.

· Selling HPC, intellectual material realized $180 thousand in revenue along with additional revenue for consulting services.

Over $50 million in increased revenue through knowledge management was identified in the first year of the Knowledge Master reward and recognition program.

Opportunities and Challenges

The HPC team tapped the well of cultural diversity throughout Hewlett Packard. It drew on people from other cultures within the organization as well as internal expertise on cross-cultural training and learning. In addition, the core team retained a cross-cultural consultant who understood the cultural differences in values and attitudes associated with sharing and leveraging knowledge. Cultural differences were embraced and leveraged. For example, the Japanese tend to be good at sharing tacit knowledge but less adept at sharing explicit knowledge. Americans are just the opposite. The outcome was that, in Japan, the focus was not so much on Learning Communities, but on building a repository to share documents. In North America, where tacit knowledge sharing was weak, the focus was on Learning Communities and Project Snapshots to get people in the mode of sharing experiences and best practices.

_____ A Knowledge-Based Business..._____

...deals with two types of knowledge:

- Tacit knowledge is based on experience and practice. Tacit knowledge is deeply rooted in an individual's action and experience, as well as their ideals, values & emotions
- Explicit knowledge can be easily documented, shared, and codified in words or numbers. It can be stored in a computer and accessed through a database or network

HP Consulting

Beyond cultural issues, the KM team also had address the perception that a "headquarters" group (based in the United States) was driving change across the organization. With a culture that valued decentralization and local control, the central team had to ensure that the local teams could chart their own course. At the same time, that KM effort needed to balance the desire for local control with the need for some global consistency.

This issue was addressed by "seeding" each geography with KM team members with strong personal networks and understanding of local culture who reported into the central team. These "knowledge consultant" positions were created as support roles to enable field teams to easily initiate KM activities and to encourage project teams and middle managers to use knowledge management as a tool to increase effectiveness and productivity. Knowledge consultants had credibility within their geography and were expected to understand how km could be positioned within the local culture and the business environment to provide benefits to organization.

Beginning in 1999, a new role was established that firmly placed responsibility for knowledge management in the hands of the local geography. The *Geographic Knowledge Manager* role was created as the focal point for each geographical entity's km implementation. This individual was responsible for identifying knowledge priorities and implementing appropriate knowledge processes and tools that would provide value to their local constituencies.

SUSTAINING THE KM EFFORT

As the KM team moved into FY2000, it shifted its focus to sustaining the momentum of the KM effort and evolving it to meet current and future business needs. The team identified three success factors to sustain momentum for the KM effort:

· Continued leadership guidance, support and modeling of desired behaviors

· Reinforce knowledge measures and performance management systems

· Measure progress and make continuous improvements to processes, tools and capabilities

Leadership Involvement and Support

As the KM community moves into Phase III, it recognizes the need to keep senior leadership involved and committed to the values and behaviors of a knowledge-based business. Since so many initiatives become the "flavor of the month", the HP Consulting KM team is committed to sustaining the effort and creating a pervasive knowledge sharing environment.

The team has identified key areas of focus for FY00:

· Identify a core group of KM sponsors who will help prioritize knowledge initiatives, set clear expectations for the organization and function as role models to his/her peers;

· Re-formulate the roles and responsibilities for sponsors;

· Incorporate knowledge-based measures into senior management roles;

· Collaborate with the HPC People Development to embed knowledge management training and education into executive development programs.;

· Keep key sponsors involved and informed of progress, successes and challenges

Reinforcement and Performance Management

While the Knowledge Masters Program was declared a success, sustained behavior change can only be realized through day to day performance management. All roles in the organization have embedded KM performance metrics. The performance evaluation system evaluates each employee on his commitment to managing knowledge and contributing and leveraging structured intellectual capital.

The team's focus going forward will be to educate senior management on the existing performance metrics and reinforce support for compliance. Once done, the team will work with the senior managers on communicating expectations, monitoring progress and making course adjustments to drive cultural change.

Measuring Progress

During phase 2 the KM team realized that the organization needed consistent and structured processes to measure and evaluate its KM efforts. Two development efforts were launched: the creation of knowledge maturity model and the development and execution of a baseline survey.

Knowledge Maturity Model

As other parts of HP developed maturity models, the KM team decided to adopt the approach as well. The Maturity Model measures a particular solution's maturity against five levels: ad hoc, repeatable, defined, managed, and optimized.

HP CONSULTING KNOWLEDGE MATURITY MODEL

Level	Attributes
Optimized 5	The organization's knowledge policies, practices, and activities are improved continuously using quantitative feedback from the process and from piloting innovative ideas and technology
Managed 4	Processes include detailed quality measures of knowledge management. The organization adjusts its workforce practices to motivate and support the development of team based knowledge competencies. Consultants' understanding of knowledge processes is measurable and consistent.
Defined 3	Knowledge requirements in core business processes are documented, standardized, and integrated into a standard process for the organization; gaps are identified. All engagements use the standard processes.
Repeatable 2	Opportunities to create, leverage, and share knowledge are explicitly incorporated into business and development plans. The process discipline is in place to repeat earlier successes on similar projects
Ad Hoc 1	The process for knowledge capture and reuse is ad hoc. Consultants depend heavily on personal networks and individual effort.

Adapted from the People Capability Maturity Model, CMU/SEI-99-MM-02

Baseline Measurements

The KM team also took a baseline measure of the organization's maturity in knowledge management. This survey, first administered in March 2000, will be conducted annually to measure progress over time and help central and geographic teams to plan their knowledge management initiatives. The key knowledge areas that will be measured are business and leadership, KM process maturity, people, technology, and culture.

Measuring the business value and ROI is an area that will get increased focus during Phase 3 of the KM implementation. Reward and recognition programs such as HPC Knowledge Masters provides both qualitative and quantitative measures of value from the consultants' own experiences and the baseline survey measures progress over time of achieving the desired culture change.

LOOKING BACK, MOVING FORWARD

The KM team periodically conducts snapshots to better understand what has been effective and what areas need improvement. As the team reflected over the past several years, it became clear that some periods were marked by rapid progress while others were notable for simply keeping the effort on the radar screen of the organization. As management changes and organizational change occurs, the team has to continually adapt to the new environment. As business pressures increased, the team had to find more effective and explicit ways to measure the contribution of knowledge management to the organization's bottomline.

EXHIBIT SIX: KM HISTORY CHART

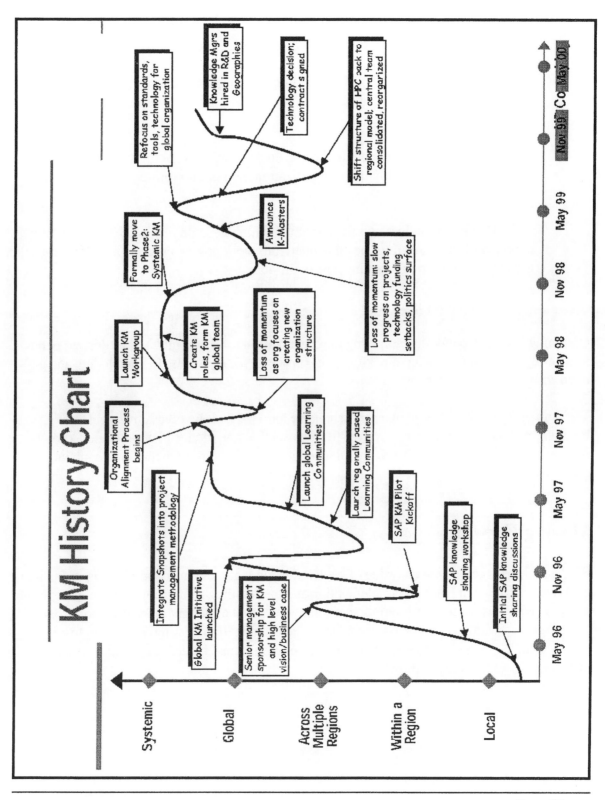

Lessons Learned

The KM team found that certain lessons had been learned along the way.

· KM must enable the business strategy by focusing on the critical business knowledge, recognizing that not all knowledge is equally valuable and measuring progress as well as results.

· KM must be embedded into the business strategy and core work processes. It must be embraced broadly in the organization; and is a bottom-up, top-down, and middle-out effort.

· Desired behaviors must be continually modeled and rewarded by leadership; knowledge processes must be embedded into work processes; and employees must be given time for sharing, learning; and codifying.

· Technology is an enabler, not a driver.

Obtaining results depends on energizing the organization toward achieving the desired behaviors through committed leadership, knowledge processes, easy access to knowledge, and an open and trusting environment.

The human side of knowledge management is the hard part—it involves creating a strong foundation where an organization moves from individual knowledge to organization knowledge, where it energizes itself to create knowledge sharing and reuse behaviors to tap its collective wisdom.

Moving Forward

HPC has clearly recognized the value of knowledge management in accomplishing its business goals and realizes that planning, implementing and maintaining a program is a time-consuming process. HPC has taken a long-term focus and realizes that although it has made some excellent progress toward becoming a knowledge-based organization, it still has a lot yet to be accomplished. The next step is to "permeate the environment" by creating a culture that routinely creates and leverages knowledge.

The success of knowledge management does not exclusively depend on the completion of the three phases, but on the iterative nature of these phases until knowledge, management has permeated all of HPC. During the first two phases, the KM team led the initiative to achieve overall organizational buy-in and adoption. As HPC moves into Phase III, leadership is being decentralized as the KM initiative scales up to spread and permeates across the enterprise.

EXHIBIT SEVEN: GEOGRAPHIC PERMEATION MODEL

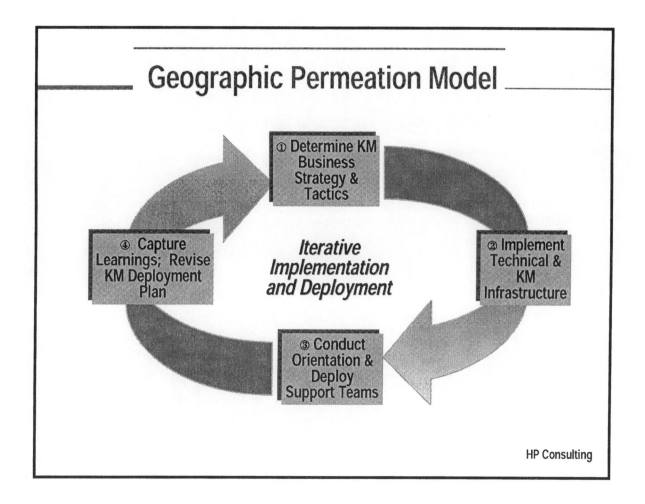

By driving new behaviors, HPC wants to help consultants develop new skills and know-how about creating and leveraging knowledge, as well as further integrate responsibility and measures into roles and performance management. Integrating the KM processes into the core business processes that cut across geographic boundaries will enable employees to leverage cultural differences, to enhance organizational learning and speed of implementation while still taking advantage of local knowledge.

ABOUT THE CONTRIBUTORS

Peggy Parskey
Global Knowledge Management Marketing Manager

Peggy Parskey is the Global Knowledge Management Marketing Manager for Hewlett Packard Consulting. In this capacity, Peggy is responsible for further advancing CPC's image in the knowledge management market place, developing relationships with external knowledge management professionals and bringing leading edge solutions to HP Consulting. During the past four years, Peggy led a worldwide initiative to integrate knowledge management processes, structures, culture, and technology into the organization design and operations of HP Consulting. In 1978, Peggy began her career in HP in finance working with product development and manufacturing teams. She joined HP field operations in 1981, delivering manufacturing implementation services to clients and then leading professional teams in the selling and delivery of integrated solutions to Hewlett-Packard customers. Peggy is certified in the field of Change Management and has extensive consulting experience assisting customers with large scale, multidimensional change programs both internally within Hewlett-Packard organizations and with external clients.Prior to joining HP, Peggy acquired a strong background in financial and statistical analysis within the financial services and oil industries. Peggy holds a Bachelor of Science degree in Mathematics from Simmons College and two Masters degrees in Statistics and Business Administration from the University of Chicago.

Marilyn Martiny
Global Knowledge Services Manager

Marilyn Martiny is the Knowledge Services Manager of HP Consulting, part of HP's Customer Service and Support Group. In that capacity, Marilyn is responsible for global knowledge services at HP Consulting including strategic direction, service planning and implementation and facilitating knowledge flows to improve organizational performance. In 1986, Marilyn began her career at HP in sales and marketing and she has developed several breakthrough programs for HP. Over the past 14 years, she has held various positions with HP, including a rotation assignment at Corporate to identify industry best practices for business process reengineering and driving large-scale organization change. Her first assignment at HP Consulting was to lead a strategic management consulting practice. In 1996, Marilyn was asked to launch a global initiative focused on implementing knowledge management at HP Consulting to enhance revenues, profitability, and client value. She is recognized across HP and in the marketplace as a thought leader in strategic consulting, organizational change and knowledge management. Prior to joining Hewlett Packard, she held management positions at Xerox Corporation and Wang Laboratories. Marilyn is a graduate of the University of California and has a Masters of Science in Organization Development from Pepperdine University.

3

AT & T

A transformation from chaos to organized knowledge communities that created a new flow of knowledge to improve process, products and profit

BACKGROUND

AT&T Corp. is among the world's premier voice and data communications companies, serving more than 80 million customers, including consumers, businesses, and government. With annual revenues of more than $64 billion and 151,000 employees, AT&T provides services to customers worldwide.

Backed by the research and development capabilities of AT&T Labs, the company runs the world's largest, most sophisticated communications network and has one of the largest digital wireless networks in North America. The company is a leading supplier of data and Internet services for businesses and offers outsourcing, consulting and networking-integration to large businesses. It is also the nation's largest direct Internet access service for consumers.

Through its recent cable acquisitions, AT&T will bring its bundle of broadband video, voice and data services to customers throughout the United States. Internationally, the AT&T/BT Global Venture — recently named Concert – will serve the communications needs of multinational companies and international carriers worldwide.

AT&T Global Services maintains the largest 2000 customers for AT&T. Global Services consists of only 7,000 sales associates and headquarters staff, however Global Services brings in over $10 billion in revenue for AT&T. IKE, the Information and Knowledge Exchange, Global Services' sales support intranet bridges the gap between the headquarters staff and the Global sales associates. This communications channel has improved the effectiveness of the sales force in supporting the Global customer base.

INTRODUCTION

In the later half of the 1990s, the Sales and Marketing group at AT&T faced many challenges in effectively supporting AT&T's Business Services sales associates. With new competitors, technology changes, and market share erosion, AT&T's leadership team realized the need for a new business direction. This need for a new business direction was becoming more obvious with technology changes and market profitability. AT&T needed to shift the sales focus towards the new technology markets and the leadership team needed a way to drive change throughout the massive organization. They also needed to ensure that a uniform message was being delivered to all associates to effectively compete in the rapidly changing business environment.

Distributing a uniform message across AT&T Business Services was only the beginning of the information exchange challenges. New products and services were emerging in the market every day. If AT&T was to remain a market leader, it needed to arm its sales force with all the information they needed quickly and effectively. The quarterly earnings indicated a dramatic shift in product and service profitability. The trend drifted away from traditional moneymakers, such long distance, towards new products and services, like data, IP, and wireless. Further, the sales funnel reports showed an increasing market demand for the new products and services. The existing business strategy was outdated and ineffective. Knowledge Management and Organizational Learning quickly became the 'buzz' words throughout AT&T headquarters. Executive support and intervention led to the creation of IKE©; the Information and Knowledge Exchange sales support intranet.

IKE© is one of the five largest sales support intranet sites in the world. Although intranets and corporate portals are the topic of the day, IKE© has in fact been in production since 1997. Since then, it's been changing and evolving continually – like all good web sites, it's never truly done.

Originally, IKE© was designed to provide sales information to 4,000 sales staff at AT&T Global Business Services. Its mission was also to rapidly, effectively, and uniformly communicate change from headquarters to the field. IKE© has now become the most important vehicle for executive communications within AT&T for Global Services sales associates and corporate headquarters staff. Today, IKE© handles 14,000 regular users throughout the company. It provides the sales teams, and other departments' staff, with customer and industry news, groupware, product news and collateral, presentations, contracts, and up-to-date information on sales or contract status.

EXHIBIT ONE: IKE HOMEPAGES

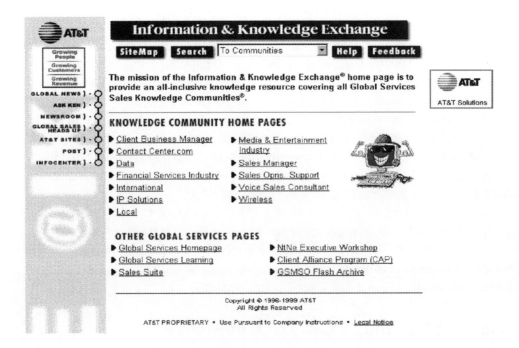

This case study covers the following topics:

· AT&T Sales Support and Corporate Culture before IKE

· Corporate drivers for Knowledge Management and the creation of IKE

· The evolution of IKE, realized benefits, the evolution of Knowledge Communities

· Lessons Learn from e-Enabling the Sales Force

· How these Learnings are being Applied to a new e-Business Initiative

BUSINESS CHALLENGE

Global Services is a small, elite group within AT&T Business Services that services the largest accounts for AT&T. IKE©'s mission statement is "to provide an all-inclusive knowledge resource covering all Global Services Sales Knowledge Communities." The business strategy focused on implementing knowledge management and organizational learning within Global Services. Implementation of such a radical paradigm shift was more likely to achieve success in a focus group. Most importantly, the objectives behind IKE included revenue growth and increased customer satisfaction. The Global Services sales force and customer base was an obvious choice for the focus group. Since it was the highest revenue producing sector of the company, the leadership team realized that the people in Global accounts were the best candidates to increase revenue and to maintain market share. Customer satisfaction and loyalty were essential.

If AT&T, its partners, and its customers are to remain successful, it needs to deliver solutions faster to keep up with the rapidly changing technological environment. To do that, AT&T needs to provide its sales force with a deeper knowledge and understanding of all its products and services to make quicker, better decisions.

Assessing the Stumbling Blocks to Knowledge

The system for acquiring knowledge, as it existed prior to the focus group, created stumbling blocks to the success of the team. AT&T sales associates were bombarded with e-mails from AT&T product and marketing managers for every service offering. These associates had no way of archiving this information for when they actually needed it. When the sales person did have a question on a service offering, they were often forced to call in to AT&T corporate headquarters in the hope that the product manager or offer manager would be there to answer their question. Often, the sales person was ready to close with the customer, but was hindered by stumbling blocks to acquiring essential information. The sales force knew that the hard parts of the sale were done, but to complete the sale, a contract or specific product and service-specific details were required. They couldn't understand why it was so difficult to get a timely response from headquarters.Transversely, the volume of calls from the field frustrated the staff at Headquarters. The product and offer managers couldn't understand why the sales people kept calling with the same questions and same requests.

The AT&T traditional sales training methods were insufficient. The range of products and services were growing at an incredible rate. The old methodology of training a sales person to be an expert on AT&T's full range of offers was becoming more impractical. For years, AT&T continued with the traditional sales training methods. These methods included making the classes longer and more condensed in an effort to fit all the information into one comprehensive course. Sales-person feedback questionnaires indicated the need for specialty courses surrounding each new product and service line. The range of products and services AT&T offered at the time was too much for one person to absorb in a single class. Global sales associates were geographically dispersed throughout the world, which added to the dilemma. Additionally, many of the AT&T product and service subject matter experts were centralized at the corporate headquarters in New Jersey. While AT&T always operated with the needs of its sales associates in mind, there were time and resource constraints to travel from city-to-city in order to train individuals. AT&T needed to capture the expertise that existed and leverage it for shared learning.

Technology was changing rapidly. Prior to implementing a knowledge management solution, AT&T used a database (My Partner) to store all content and brochureware. Using My Partner, a sales associate had to login to the system and was required to perform a download each time they wanted to obtain information. When the download occurred, if the sales associate wanted to save the document, it took up space and memory on their hard drive. Saving each document to the hard drive was not effective for two reasons. First, no one had a PC with enough memory to download all of the documents. Second, once the sales associate saved it on the hard drive, he/she would usually continue to use that version of the document for months rather than going back to My Partner to see if there was an updated version to download.

AT&T realized that the My Partner database was not the long-term solution for arming its sales associates with accurate and timely information. My Partner took sometimes weeks to update and there was no way of tracking if a sales person was downloading the most current version of the information they needed. A more productive and timely solution was essential.

To ensure success, the leadership team put together a plan to phase in the changes necessary for true Knowledge Management. Enter IKE©, AT&T's Global Information & Knowledge Exchange Intranet, rolled out initially in 1997.

PLANNING THE STRATEGY TO SUCCESS

Prior to the transformation to IKE©, content was pulled from a number of disparate sources. My Partner was the main data source for sales information, however, there were several other data sources to be added to IKE©. For example, there was an intranet site containing provisioning methods and procedures and a password-protected, database pricing tool to be converted to IKE©. The effort of identifying all of the required data sources to be added to IKE© was led by the Global services marketing team. The team had to contact each of the owners of these data sources to migrate the data to IKE©. The process took about two months in total. This process included gathering each data source and, more importantly, it also required buy-in from the data owners to allow access to the information via IKE©. The Global Services Marketing team was exploring new territory. They learned about technology enhancements and knew the sales teams were beginning to use the internet and intranet. Because the intranet was not a completely foreign concept to the sales force and would not be new system to learn were both additional "pluses" in the team's favor.

EXHIBIT TWO: DESIGN AND IMPLEMENTATION STEPS

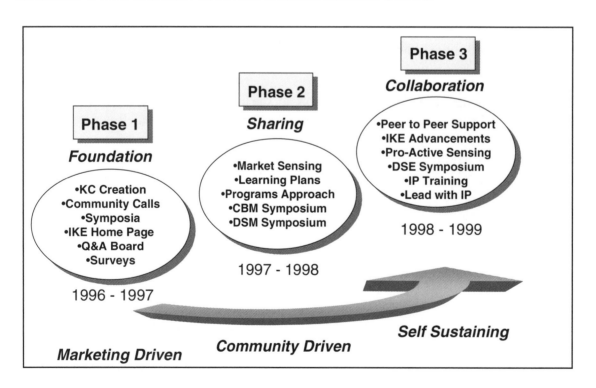

TRANSFORMATION

The plan anticipated the need for a significant investment of resources and dollars by the marketing leadership team during the first year or two. In Phase 1, the announcement of Knowledge Communities followed expensive, yet invaluable, symposia. AT&T flew in hundreds of people to each Knowledge Community Symposia to begin laying the foundations of 'communities' surrounding sales expertise. Although it was a great expense, it was critical to lay the foundation of community feeling, introduce the IKE Homepage, and drive the sales transformation.

The symposia were full-week sessions, conducted at hotels centrally located in the United States. The symposia were scheduled in the first quarter of the year. The agenda for each symposium surrounded issues in each sales discipline. The Knowledge Community leaders, the executive leadership, the subject-matter experts, and product or offer managers presented at the event. The presenters' role at these sessions was to define the desireed company direction of their particular service offering. They were also there to answer any questions presented by the sales force. A strong emphasis was placed on having fun and meeting others within the employee's community. The environment furthered the feeling of community as the attendees' families sometimes attended. This provided the opportunity for the sales associates to meet and interact socially after the learning sessions.

Before Phase 1, the sales associates had no focus groups. They held no sense of community within the organization. After the transformation, the foundation was set for knowledge sharing within Knowledge Communities. Sales associates now knew the leadership team, as well as the communication channel into headquarters. They established relationships within the sales force and began to form an environment of a self-sustaining collaboration among peers.

Like any social situation, the first days of the symposia required significant efforts from the leadership team and Knowledge Community facilitators to get active participation from the sales force. If the symposia had lasted less than a week, the effect would have been stifled. Towards the end of the week, many of the participants knew each other on a first-name basis. The foundation was laid for open communication. While not all of the sales associates took advantage of the opportunity to meet internal contacts within the sales force, they still learned about IKE©, the Knowledge Communities, and the proper channels to headquarters and the information they needed.

Exhibit Three depicts the Global Services sales force design before, and after, the transformation. Before the initiative, a national account manager was responsible for the customer relationship and had a team of sales executives and a technical lead to support the client. The teams had expertise in national account sales, but were not aligned in a particular community. They shared some, but not all, knowledge with like-sales titles in their branch office. After sales transformation, the Client Business Manager (CBM) function was established. Today, the CBM is now the Client Relationship Manager (CRM). Each knowledge community aligned with the CBM has an area of expertise and has a knowledge community of similar sales titles around the country to engage with and share learnings.

EXHIBIT THREE: SNAPSHOT OF BEFORE AND AFTER

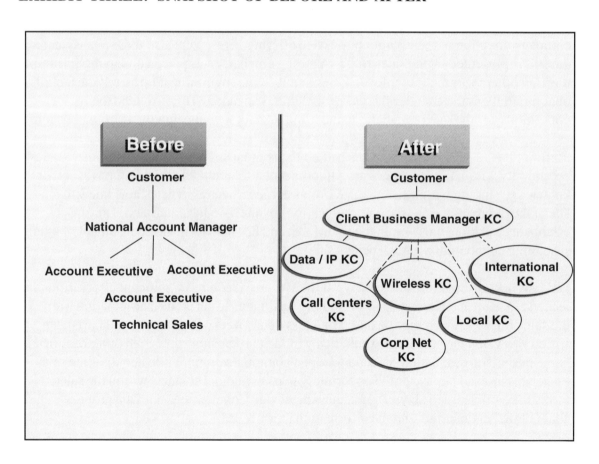

Knowledge Communities Become a Constant Reality

After a series of symposia, each Knowledge Community maintained the feeling of community through regular 'Community Conference Calls,' hosted by the newly staffed Knowledge Community Facilitator and his or her team. Each community created individually scheduled calls hosted by the KC facilitator, subject-matter experts, an IKE© representative, and special guests from the executive leadership team. These calls were intended to continue the feeling of community. The calls also created an open forum for questions and answers, as well as open discussion among the community members. These calls ensured that the leadership team remained linked with the sales force. The sales teams had the opportunity to voice their opinions and concerns on current issues, and the headquarters staff was able to gain a better understanding of what was on the minds of sales associates.

IKE© implemented Q&A Boards for each Knowledge Community that were monitored by each Facilitator's team. The Q&A Boards became the focal point within IKE© for frequently asked questions. The Q&A boards were also used as an option for a sales team member to get resolution to a problem that he/she had. Knowledge Community leaders were responsible for checking their boards several times per day, and they were expected to answer each question within 24 hours. The executive pressure to ensure a timely response gave the field a forum they did not have before. Within a few months, many Q&A Boards became self-sufficient. The sales force personnel began answering each other's questions.

Each Knowledge Community headquarters team acted as the liaison between the sales force and the various areas within headquarters. The sales force knew from the symposia that they could contact the Knowledge Community leaders when they had an issue that they could not resolve on their own. The Knowledge Community leaders knew that their job was to support the members of their Knowledge Community. Whenever the sales person could not find what they needed on IKE©, he/she would call the KC leadership team to determine where to find the information. These communications led to better organization of content within IKE©, as well as a more comprehensive library of information. Since the Knowledge Community leadership teams met monthly with the Executive leadership teams, there was better representation of the concerns of the sales force within headquarters meetings.

For the first time ever, the sales managers had sales experts in each discipline to engage for the larger proposals. Further, the sales staff had a single point of contact to assist with all their support needs from headquarters. The concerns, needs, and desires of the individuals within the sales force were being met more efficiently than ever before. The Knowledge Communities successfully channeled information between headquarters and the Global Sales Force.

EXHIBIT FOUR: THE NEW FLOW OF KNOWLEDGE

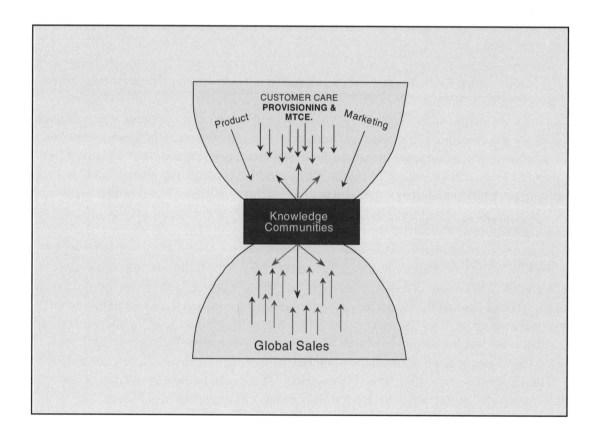

SHARING KNOWLEDGE

In 1997 and 1998, the sense of 'communities' grew stronger, and the need for marketing to be the driving force behind the Knowledge Management and Organizational Learning initiative subsided. Tracking the Q&A Board results was the first indication that the Knowledge Communities were beginning to share knowledge. Each month the number of correct questions answered by the sales force to the sales force increased. Knowledge Community conference calls began to change from being KC, leader-driven to sales-force-participant driven. Within the branches, the sales force began to bond themselves according to the Knowledge Community bonds.

The Knowledge Community leaders began driving results to meet the business-plan attainment goals set by the leadership team. To do this, each community had to develop a framework that would facilitate a functioning community. Each community had to define their team-member roles and responsibilities and truly understand the sales processes in order to develop competency models and training curriculum for the members of their community. This required linkages into the field, so they had to establish and reinforce communication channels with the sales associates.

EXHIBIT FIVE: KNOWLEDGE COMMUNITY COMPETENCY MODEL

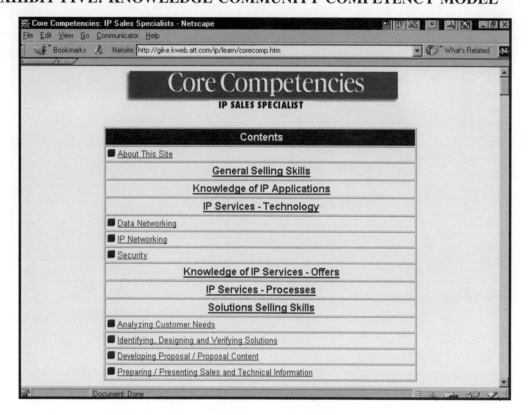

Through their homepage and community calls, the Knowledge Community leaders facilitated interactive communications exchange between sales members, marketing-to-sales, sales-to-marketing, and Knowledge Community-to-Knowledge Community. The homepage and community calls also provided ongoing learning for sales executives. Courseware, training materials, real-time competitive and offer information, continuous competency assessment, and sales force input were all accessible. The Knowledge Community Facilitators received valuable market sensing using community calls and a feedback button on IKE© for continuous improvement. Feedback ranged from individual comments related to web page structure and errors to editorial comments on the quality of marketing documents.

EXHIBIT SIX : Q & A BOARDS

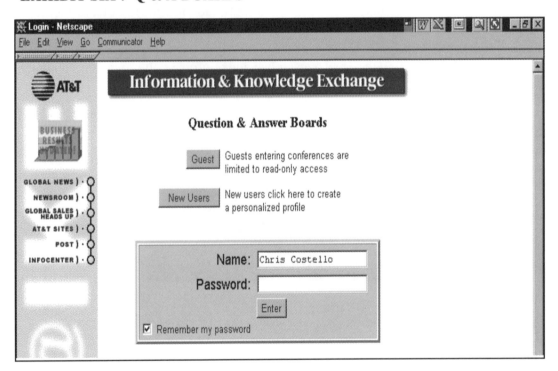

COLLABORATION & EVALUATION

From 1998 through 1999, the Knowledge Communities became self-sustaining, with active involvement from each community member. Each Knowledge Community facilitator continued hosting conference calls, as well as teletraining sessions, with high participation on both. There was a need for internal marketing and special hosts to encourage participation. Each call was generally focused around a host or main topic. The training sessions typically helped the sales force navigate the main pages within IKE© to ensure the introduction of the main collaboration and training tools within the sales support intranet. Each homepage Q&A board (See Exhibit 6) was managed by the knowledge community facilitator to provide answers to questions on the site. By late 1998, almost 40 percent of questions were answered by other community members. Strong peer-to-peer support and collaboration were forming in each community. Sales teams relied on IKE© and sometimes referred to the site during client visits. Clients began asking for demonstrations of IKE© and now ask, "how can I buy it?"

Critical Success Factors for Implementing IKE

1. Content management was critical! The number-one criterion for IKE© was that the information had to be accurate. If information was inaccurate or outdated, the user would be discouraged from returning to the site. The IKE© team learned this very early on via the feedback mechanism. The feedback tool was established for users to provide input to the team in charge of running the site. For example, if a sales promotion had expired and the documentation did not reflect an extension or end of the promotion, a sales person would submit to the feedback button on the site to inform the knowledge community information manager. The Knowledge Community information manager would then have to check with marketing communications and ask that they update their documentation. The team established a process where expiration dates were assigned to content and marketing communications was informed when content required updates. Updates were made to sales briefs, presentations, proposals, pricing, etc. on a daily basis.

2. A fast download time was essential. Many of the sales teams around the country worked remotely and used dial-up access to connect to the intranet. If a section of the site contained heavy graphics, the user would either have to wait for the site to complete downloading, or they'd get frustrated and call someone at headquarters for the information. The IKE© team formed templates and style guidelines for web sites and to ensure that the marketing team followed the guidelines. After the guidelines were established, sales teams enjoyed faster access to sites. For example, a sales person could download PowerPoint presentations quickly, with text only.

3. The site had to be intuitive and easy to navigate. The design scheme for IKE© was a similar look and feel for each community. If one were to visit a different community site, the navigation scheme would be familiar. For example, the CBM (Client Business Manager) utilized the CBM Knowledge Community page for the most part to gather information on RFP's or client strategy planning. From time to time, the CBM would require information from the Data Knowledge Community page. In surveys conducted, the CBM's sited the experience surfing a site other than the CBM page as an easy transition. The page layout and location of information was similar across all of the Knowledge Community sites.

4. Finally, implementing IKE© had to be a cost-effective measure. The team was challenged with creating a solution with no additional budget allocation. When Pat Traynor, the visionary and business leader behind IKE©, was challenged with this decision, she made the call to shift marketing dollars away from "white binder" production and moved the dollars to IKE©. Before IKE©, the marketing team spent significant time and marketing budgets preparing "white binders" containing product information kits or quarterly sales campaigns. Preparing and shipping these binders in the mail to each sales person in a branch was costly, because the information became outdated very quickly and frequent mailings were required.

Lessons Learned

The Global services team learned a great deal since IKE© was launched in 1997. Executive engagement was critical to the success of IKE© and the transition to knowledge management. The sales region leaders had to embrace the new sales model in order for sales transformation to be a true success. If the sales region managers were not using IKE© and not supporting making it part of every-day life for sales associates, adoption would have been much more challenging.

The knowledge community facilitator role was another critical element required for the success of IKE©. The facilitator is the glue that holds the community together. The facilitator is the team steward that leads the group and encourages collaboration and information sharing.

Obtaining feedback for improvement is also a must. For example, if a presentation is taking too long to download for a virtual office employee – the team can reformat the document in real-time and re-post it.

Measuring the Results

Managing content and ensuring accuracy of content is the single, most important factor in IKE©'s success. Keeping content up-to-date and easy to navigate is critical. The team initially underestimated the time it would take to manage content when IKE© was first implemented. It had to staff accordingly and to shift resources to make IKE© a success with thousands of documents to manage. This required establishing a sophisticated content management process. Here's how it works. A marketing communications manager creates a document. The Knowledge Community facilitator "screens" the document and tailors the message to the intended audience. The knowledge community information manager then scans the document to ensure it is in the appropriate template then tests the content to ensure download time is fast and is easy to navigate.

With newer technology available today, and with many businesses shifting to portal technology to manage communication, meta-tagging content is another important factor. Meta-tagging assigns properties to a document, such as author name, expiration date and/ or user community. By meta-tagging all content early, designers or administrators will save a great deal time on manual efforts when there is a shift in IT strategy to portal technology. One example that proves how meta-tagging can benefit information managers and users is the assigning of expiration dates to content. Once your content has been assigned with an expiration date properly, a rule can be assigned to the document that dictates what happens to the content on a determined date. For example, the rule can be set up to automatically notify the owner that the document will expire in defined number of days or the rule pull the content off of the site when it expires and automaticall notify the content owner.

Global services leveraged IKE© and Knowledge Communities as the basis of how we share information and gather feedback. Sales and marketing associates have come to depend on IKE© on day to day. Establishing Knowledge Communities was critical to continued Global services success. Sales associates keep coming back for the shared learning; they can get questions answered by experts in short order, download customizable proposals and presentations, gather industry information applicable to their client, and work on their sales competencies and learning plans.

Return on Investment

ROI was critical to quantifyto gain executive support. A great deal of time, training and influencing of business process change was dedicated to making IKE© and the establishment of Knowledge Communities a success in Global Services. The sales leadership team had high expectations that IKE© and the establishment of knowledge communities would dramatically increase sales associate productivity resulting in more selling time. The marketing team expected process improvements by moving to IKE© and knowledge communities. The financial leadership team expected cost reduction as a result of eliminating the My Partner database and lowering the usage of email which was very expensive at the time.

Productivity Enhancements

The Knowledge Community facilitator teams conduct quarterly surveys and compile sales feedback received via the feedback mechanism on IKE©. Surveyed sales executives have reported a 30 percent increase in productivity. Prior to IKE©, sales teams were pulling data from multiple sources and were bombarded with emails with no robust filing system to capture the information for a later date, when the material needed to be referenced. Sales associates claim that proposal development time has been cut by 50 percent as a result of having templated proposals that can be customized by the user.

Responses to complex information requests have been reduced from 40 hours to approximately four hours as a result of the accurate and timely content on IKE©. IKE© can be updated in real-time and usually contains all of the information and answers to questions that in the past, product management had to answer repeatedly via a phone call. General managers have reported they are less involved in escalations and issue resolutions by 40 percent. Most escalations occurred prior to IKE© because sales associates called a product manager for the answer and did not receive a timely response. One product manager returning multiple telephone calls to sales associate in Global Services was overwhelming and inefficient.

Process Improvements

IKE© is able to run statistics reports that track hits hourly down to document level, ensuring that employees are actually reading communications. Emergency publishing updates can be made in real time for breaking news and in near real-time for general updates. Feedback from sales teams is available via the feedback button and through quarterly surveys. This enhanced market sensing process was invaluable for the knowledge community facilitators and marketing teams. These process improvements have enabled the Knowledge Community information managers to make real-time improvements to information, enabled marketing managers to quickly respond to customer needs, and inform product and offer managers on how to tailor their product and service offerings based on field input.

Financial Impacts

Prior to IKE©, AT&T spent millions of dollars on employee communications via email due to the cost structure of email at the time. While e-mail is still used today, IKE© is the main source for obtaining information. The team has also realized significant cost savings with their intranet site by eliminating the My Partner database. Eliminating the My Partner system contributed to cost avoidance as it required significant time and manpower to maintain it. It was necessary to move to a more sophisticated system for cost avoidance and sales productivity savings.

Culture Change

IKE© provides a one-stop shopping source for Global services associates. To help drive users to IKE©, the Global services team eventually eliminated access to the alternate means of getting the information. The IKE© team implemented a phased approach to drive adoption to IKE©. The team sent out sales advisories in email, stating that My Partner would be shut down on a specified date and provided the URL to the IKE© site. The team also advertised teletraining sessions and asked the sales leadership team to make it a requirement for sales associates to participate in the training. When the former ways of accessing information were eliminated, the IKE© team experienced a high volume of calls until sales teams were comfortable with the new way of doing business. Feedback received from sales teams indicated that IKE© was much more efficient than email or My Partner, citing the ease of locating information and the ability to obtain the information in real-time (just a click away).

Today, instead of relying on email notification or sifting through a box of brochures in a sales branch, associates open up their IKE© knowledge community page for almost all of the information needed to perform their jobs. IKE© has created demand and expectation to receive information much faster and with context. Before IKE©, Global services distributed information to sales branches via US mail or in email where the information received did not necessarily apply to all associates.

Another culture change has been the interactive communications exchange that IKE© and Knowledge Communities facilitate. Global sales associates share valuable information, including learnings and best practices, virtually around the country. Sales team best practices are recognized and shared in a variety of ways. On monthly Knowledge Community calls, Knowledge Community facilitators will invite sales associates who have demonstrated sales excellence to share their solution with their peers.

Another best practice sharing channel is sales recognition programs. One example is "The Rising Stars of Global Services." This program offers sales associates the opportunity to share their solution sales among other community members. Associates that meet the criteria for the program submit their success story via a form on the "Rising Stars" web site. A team of "judges" reviews the submissions. The winners are recognized quarterly for their sales solutions. Associates receive an award for their accomplishment. Winners are also recognized by the sales leadership team. Their submission is posted on the web site so that other community members can learn from the sale and apply the solution with their clients. The sales associate's name and contact information are included with the write-up, so that other community members may contact them to learn more about the solution sale.

EXHIBIT SEVEN: INCENTIVES THROUGH REWARDS & RECOGNITION

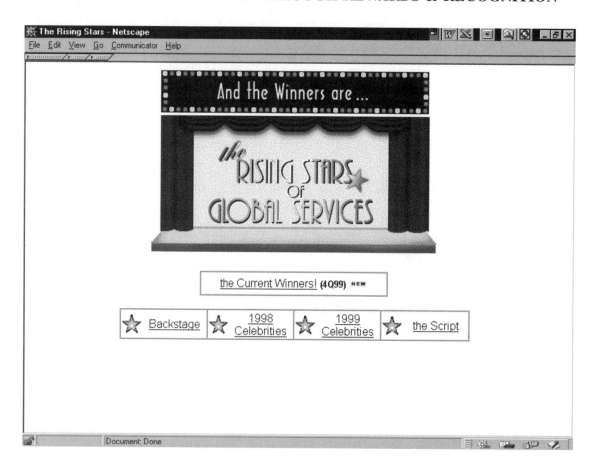

FOUR YEARS & GOING STRONG

The Knowledge Communities today have transformed into self-sustaining communities. Peer-to-peer support is common in each Knowledge Community. For example, if a sales associate is looking for a customer reference on a service offering, other sales associates will provide this information. If an associate requires assistance with an RFP (Request for Proposal), IKE© is not the only resource for information. Other community members often assist as well.

The marketing team also greatly benefits from IKE©. The Knowledge Communities provide continuous feedback loops, whereby users of IKE© submit feedback to the marketing team on various suggestions for the improvement of the site. The feedback is sent directly to each Knowledge Community facilitator for follow up and improvement. Another benefit for both sales associates and sales operations team: global sales processes have become much more automated, user-friendly and less time consuming. The IKE© team has created sales tools for inputting to sales funnels and reporting results. These results have a simple user interface and take minimal time to use. Sales associates can spend more time with clients and less time on manual processes. The sales operations team benefits from more accurate and timely information and an improved sales process.

THE FUTURE

Three of the team members involved in AT&T's Global IKE© intranet have since moved on to tackle a new knowledge management project – implementing a business to business portal application for AT&T Solutions clients. Pat Traynor, Chris Costello and Adam Flar will work in AT&T Solutions, bringing their experience to AT&T's customers.

Background

With enhancements in technology, and with many clients becoming web-enabled, there is more opportunity for one-to-one relationship management. There is now the prospect to share information with customers in a more meaningful and personalized way on the web. The Solutions e-Enabling Team has spent time with clients understanding their needs. The team conducted extensive market research on e-business. The team has also spent months investigating how new technology can further improve relationships with clients. The e-Enabling team has applied learnings from the implementation of IKE© in concurrence with researching customer needs. The team has taken these tools and coupled them with technology enhancements to address how to enhance the client experience on the web. The team has concluded the best way to improve communication with clients is through implementing and operationalizing client portals.

> *The definition of a portal, according to Yankee Group, is "A common interface that aggregates and delivers personalized material - both structured data and unstructured content to users throughout the extended enterprise."*

A portal provides clients with a "one-stop" approach to obtaining information from AT&T relevant to their account. It's like a personalized tool box, where the user has control over what tools are most useful for their needs – like a personalized "my AT&T." Many business units in AT&T have implemented client portals that are being used by customers today to obtain information and conduct transactions, such as paying bills on-line. AT&T Solutions currently provides clients with secure web access to information and many applications. The e-Enabling team is endeavoring to enhance the existing capabilities by adding more advanced portal technology.

> *E-business, according to the Garner Group, is "An Internet technology-enabled transformation that dramatically increases the efficiencies of current business processes, revolutionizes external relationships and redefines business on a global basis."*

How It Works

There are many different types of portal technology designed to serve varying business needs. In the case of IKE©, AT&T is in the process of turning IKE© into an enterprise information portal. The enterprise information portal will allow associates to customize information currently provided on their Knowledge Community pages. The portal will allow them to form their own pages, creating a view of AT&T information and sales tools best suited for their needs.

In the case of the e-Enabling team goals for AT&T Solutions, portal technology will be used to communicate with clients in an extranet environment. The portal will enable the client to obtain relevant information from AT&T that is personalized based on their company, their title, and what tools they require. The portal has a predefined set of permissions so that the user will automatically be provided with information relevant to his or her job function, as well as content relevant to their industry and specialty.

The user has the ability to customize the information that appears on their site through a personal profile. The personal profile is a menu page where the user indicates their information preferences by choosing from a menu of options. For the user, it is as simple as adding a check mark in a box, or selecting a topic, or choosing an application from a drop down menu. The portal technology also allows for the user to arrange how the information they've selected is arranged on the portal page.

Exhibit Nine is an example of a user experience in personalizing a portal page. A CIO of a financial services company enters the portal for the first time. The CIO is prompted for a login and password that she has received from AT&T. She types in her login ID and password. A message prompts her to click on "set up my profile" button. The client is presented with a menu of options to personalize her page.

In the client survey in Exhibit Eight, after the client selects their personal profile and clicks on the "submit" button, their page will be dynamically created based on the options and information they have selected. The client can go back and make changes to their profile at any time.

EXHIBIT EIGHT: CLIENT SURVEY

Section 1 – Product & Services
What products and services do you have an interest in?
    Networking and Professional Services
    Outsourcing
    E-Business
    Managed Network Services

Would you like to be notified when new information is available on this service?
    Yes
    No

Would you like this information pushed to your personal portal page or sent to you in email?
    Display on portal
    Email

Section 2 – News
What industry is your company in?
    Manufacturing
    Communications
    Retail
    Finance

News Interests in what area of country?
    Europe
    Asia
    US
    Australia

Section 3 – My Account
Application Selection
    Network Maps
    Network Monitoring
    Billing
    Contract

Section 4 – Favorites
Stocks
    NYSE
    NASDAQ

My Favorite Links – type URL here or search by category:
    Weather
    Industry News
    Research Companies

Submit

The portal can also be used as a collaboration tool between the sales team and the client. Group calendar is an example of a collaboration tool whereby the client and account team can view a shared calendar of service order due dates. The saels team and the client can use the calendar to advertise an upcoming seminar or register for a seminar on the site. A Q&A board is also a collaboration tool that allows the client to submit questions on the portal to the client servicing team. A client posts a question on the portal using the Q&A board tool. Notification is automatically sent to the subject matter expert designated to answer the question. In a pre-defined amount of time, an answer to the client's question is posted to the site. Q&A board functionality also exists on IKE© and has been very successful in assisting sales associates.

The client can also use the portal to conduct transactions, such as ordering new service or making a change to an existing service. Portal technology has security features built in so that the user will only see information if they have permission to see it. For example, if a client wanted to see a copy of their contract, only those designated with permission to see the contract will have access.

EXHIBIT NINE: PERSONALIZED PORTAL PAGE

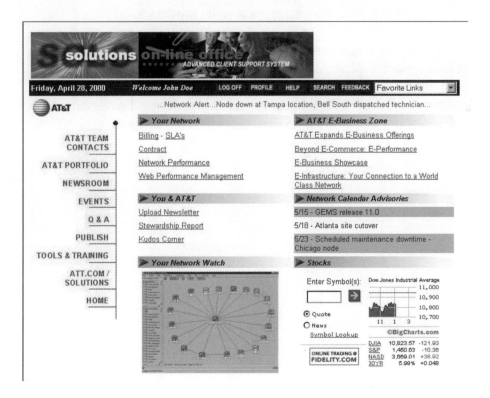

Critical Success Factors

1. The portal technology must be implemented and operationalized. This requires an initial investment to build the infrastructure. Also, planning time must be allotted to define the user groups that will be accessing the profile. Additionally, if existing content will be used in the portal, meta-tagging the content will take a significant amount of time to complete if content was not properly meta0tagged previously. Someone familiar with the contentwill be required to review the documentation to know which user groups would need to have access to the content to assign properties.

2. Business processes as they exist today will change – for AT&T and clients. Calling a toll-free number to ask a billing inquiry may take more time than simply obtaining the information directly from the portal. The user knows exactly what for what they are looking. Contacting the AT&T client team for a brief on a new service offering will not often be required, as the information will be easily accessible on the portal. For the AT&T sales team, sending out an alert e-mail each morning with the latest network update will now be a simple step to publish directly to the portal. Once changes in business processes occur, the portal will prove to be a tool to allow clients and account teams to spend less time and energy on manual processes.

3. Adoption of the portal will require continuous communications, training and collaboration to drive usage. The goal of the e-enabling team is to turn the AT&T Solutions portal into another success like IKE©. In order to ensure adoption, as learned when implementing IKE©, the user experience and ease of navigation must meet the client needs and the information must provide value to the user every time they visit the portal.

EXHIBIT 10: THE KNOWLEDGE INTERACTION

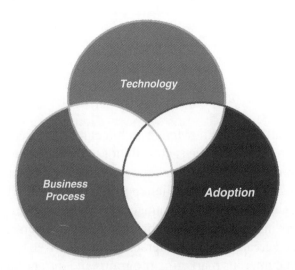

Knowledge Management, through the use of portal technology, will enable clients to find information more quickly, conduct transactions on the web, and drive significant expense savings for clients, partners and suppliers. As many companies are endeavoring to improve the customer experience, AT&T solutions is striving to revolutionize every aspect of its client experience through portal technology. It seeks to do this by utilizing several methods: simplifying client access to information; accelerating delivery; providing content relevant to user through personalization; serving up the information they are seeking out in real-time; and automating service ordering, purchasing, service delivery and billing.

ABOUT THE CONTRIBUTORS

Thank you to Pat Traynor, Vice President, AT&T Solutions e-business. Pat was the visionary behind IKE© and is helping build the foundation for communicating with our clients through business to business portals. Special recognition to Nancy Tubb, IKE©'s webmaster and Carolyn Tommie, IKE©'s original webmaster.

Christina L. Costello (ccostello@att.com) is knowledge architect for AT&T Solutions e-business services, based in Florham Park, NJ. She is contributor to the advancement of IKE©, AT&T's Global Information & Knowledge Exchange intranet and is currently managing the development of a business to business client portal initiative for AT&T Solutions largest client base. Chris has a knowledge management and marketing background and spent several years in business sales. Chris established a web presence for AT&T's toll-free service line and created the first interactive toll-free web site on att.com in 1997. Chris has created numerous marketing programs and intranet sites for global sales incentive programs, including the "Rising Stars of Global Services" program.

Chris is has been a contributor for many publications on knowledge management and selling techniques and presenter for several conferences in the area of e-business and knowledge management. Christina has a Bachelor of Arts in Communications/Journalism from Shippensburg University, Shippensburg, PA. Chris completed the Society for Organizational Learning Core Course at MIT.

Adam A. Flar (aflar@att.com) joined AT&T Business Services Global headquarters team in 3Q98 as the New Technology Director for IKE© (Information and Knowledge Exchange), responsible for bringing AT&T Sales Support Intranet into the 21st century utilizing state of the art technologies. After having successfully heading up the project, he has been promoted to AT&T Solutions to be the technical lead manager for the E-enabling team. His new challenge: e-Enabling AT&T for its' top customers.

Prior to AT&T, Adam Flar spent three years at Ariston Technologies, a start-up in Computer Memory Manufacturing; he joined as employee number one! Adam not only laid the foundations of the company, but he was the top salesman for the first 2 years. He opened and maintained accounts in Singapore, New Zealand, and Australia. The experience he gained in Sales had been more than valuable when it came to leading the IKE© project. Adam Flar has a Bachelor's Degree in Psychology from University of California at Irvine.

4

MICROSOFT

A taxonomy management system built to support information publishing and retrieval in a distributed content ownership environment, leveraging existing metadata and vocabularies and providing tools for local publishing systems and search interfaces

BACKGROUND

As the world's leading software provider, Microsoft strives to produce innovative products that meet its customers' evolving needs. In the Fiscal Year ending June 1999, Microsoft had a net revenue of $19.75 billion and a net income of $7.79 billion. It currently employs 34,751 Worldwide, 23,542 USA and 18,525 at its Puget Sound Headquarters in Washington State. In 1999, Microsoft was awarded the Most Admired Knowledge Enterprises (MAKE©) Award by Teleos (in association with the KNOW Network®), and ranked number one in three of the eight categories judged. Microsoft, like most large organizations today, faces the challenge of organizing and managing its own internal information. A key to achieving this organization is a knowledge architecture framework to focus content on business needs. One core part of a well-planned knowledge architecture is a taxonomy, which can be used to describe the content of interest to the organization. Building such a taxonomy can be a major project, both culturally and technically. Decisions about the scope of coverage, justification of the project, design of the taxonomy itself, and measures for success are all difficult and require careful planning and thought. During the past year, Microsoft Information Services has been leading a cross-company project that has resulted in a set of tools and a taxonomy that provide an extensible, central repository of vocabularies and metadata, which can be used across the company. This case study is used to illustrate some of these issues. It provides an example of one solution in an environment with distributed ownership of content and decision-making.

ROADMAP TO TERMS

Because many of the terms used in this chapter may be unfamiliar to readers, the following roadmap may be of use for reference purposes. Terminology in the area of taxonomies these days is somewhat slippery (a rather ironic situation, considering the purpose of taxonomies in the first place), so it is important to understand the context as well as the meaning of a term. This roadmap attempts to provide that context for the purposes of this chapter.

Taxonomy terms:

> **DOMAIN:** a sphere of knowledge, influence, or activity

>> **TAXONOMY:** a classification of elements within a domain

>>> **CLASSIFICATION:** the operation of grouping elements and establishing relationships between them (or the product of that operation)

>>>> **RELATIONSHIPS:** a defined linkage between two elements

>>>> **ELEMENT:** an object or concept

These are applied to:

> **ITEMS:** (aka resources) individual pieces of information

By the use of:

> **METADATA:** (aka properties, attributes) information describing types of data. Metadata can be considered a formula for describing an item; an abstract concept instantiated in schema, elements and tags.

>> **METADATA SCHEMA:** A specified set of metadata elements

>>> **METADATA ELEMENT:** (aka tag name) a label name for a class of metadata

>>> **TAG:** a metadata element, paired with a value

>>>> **VALUE:** a term authorized for description of an item under a specified tag

Which may or may not use values from a:

> **VOCABULARY:** selection of terms, classified or sorted

>> **TERM:** one or more words designating a concept

To create:

> **CONTENT:** an item and its associated metadata

INTRODUCTION

Knowledge management has become one of the most talked about disciplines in the last few years, as the rising tide of digital information sparks concerns about how to organize, utilize and prioritize the content now available at our fingertips. Users have moved from a perceived lack of access to information to being overwhelmed by information. How to organize and exploit all this in a way that increases productivity and helps a user to find what they need, when they need it, has become high on everyone's priority lists.

It is becoming increasingly obvious that one of the keys to achieving this organization is a knowledge architecture framework to organize content around business needs. Developing this framework is not a trivial task. Organizations everywhere are wondering where to start and how best to do it. This framework must encompass much more than the information itself-included are the tools and processes by which the information is created, used and stored, and the human interactions that surround the use of that information (Exhibit 1). All these pieces are critical to the success of an effort to exploit the riches we now have available to us.

EXHIBIT ONE: AN EXAMPLE OF A KNOWLEDGE ARCHITECTURE FRAMEWORK

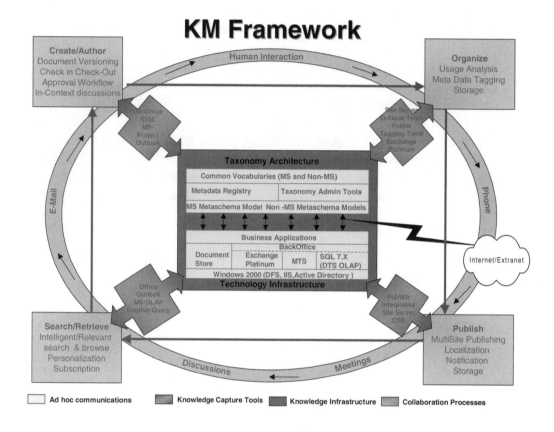

At the core of this framework lives a key piece of architecture that is enabled by a taxonomy describing the territory of interest to the organization. In most cases, the designers of information systems supporting the business needs have not systematically approached this area. This is not to say that there are not taxonomies of one sort or another in place for content sets that require organization in order to use them. Finance and human resource information are two common examples. But there is a larger chunk of information where the real growth is occurring: the files, web pages and multimedia objects that users create. These are of high value because they capture much of the knowledge being generated by the enterprise.

This semi-structured and unstructured information is what most organizations are wrestling with in today's environment. Not only is it difficult to navigate in and retrieve this content, but it is not integrated very effectively into the older, more structured information repositories that have been treated as separate containers in the past.

As in many large organizations, Microsoft intranet developers and users lacked a way to create, manage, access and link diverse vocabularies and associated metadata for the purposes of creating tagged content. In addition, they lacked a way to leverage the value of tagging when accessing that content through a search interface. It is a relatively easy task to develop tools to create, manage and access vocabularies and metadata schemas, but it is impossible to integrate the many existing vocabularies because of both the tremendous amount of work it takes to link them term by term, and because of incompatible data models. It is seemingly impossible. Yet, the need to pull them together, at some level, is critical to the successful management of Microsoft's internal information stores. It is only through this integration that cross-group content stores can be systematically linked to assist in the focused, targeted retrieval of information for users.

An example of the problem is illustrated by the many different product taxonomies that exist in the company. Different groups use a product taxonomy in different ways to organize their information store and retrieve information from it. This results in different term forms for a product like Excel (Microsoft Excel, Excel, MS Excel, etc.). Additionally, some groups might use hierarchy to capture product version. Another group might not even be able to support a concept like hierarchy in its data model. Finally, not all groups use the same tag sets to describe their data.

One possible solution would be to require everyone to use the same product vocabulary and tag set. This works in some cases, but does not always reflect the reality of end-user needs or of underlying systems. Another approach would be to link each term in each product-related vocabulary through Use, Use For, and Related Term relationships. This is very expensive to build and even more expensive to maintain.

A third solution, the one adopted by Information Services at Microsoft, was to create a metadata schema registry. The registry is a central repository of existing metadata schemas, with links to the vocabularies associated with the schema elements (or tag names). Within this registry, those elements that have equivalence can be mapped together to provide cross vocabulary access to content which uses these elements. For example, if one group chooses to describe a group of terms related to "Products" with the tag name "product," while Information Services uses "products and technologies" for their tag name in this area, the partial equivalence of these two elements can be established in the registry. The following case study uses this effort to extract some lessons and guidelines for those attempting such a project, using examples from the experiences of Microsoft's Information Services..

NEEDS ASSESSMENT

The first step in beginning such an effort is no different than in any large project. The purpose and scope need to be defined so that support can be obtained from the right stakeholders. Part of this process is, of course, justifying the project. This can be a difficult thing to do since much of the work necessary for success in a large-scale taxonomy project is cross organizational. Individual segments with budget authority may not see the value or need for such a service in their realm.

Historically, such projects have usually been driven by system requirements. A database needs to have its data defined precisely in order to serve its purpose of storing and manipulating the content for which it is built. There is a known cost for developing such models. That cost is built into the project budget and considered to be part of the development cycle.

With the taxonomies described in this chapter, however, there are no prior requirements driving a discrete project. It is far more likely that this will be a result of a perceived need (or actual pain) around inability to find what is wanted when looking through the huge stores of information available to users. Translating this into business drivers requires more than just saying the problem needs to be fixed. There have to be measurable outcomes that are expected from the implementation.

Unfortunately, these outcomes may often be far down the road and outside of the normal planning cycles that drive most budgets. The end result may be that a global project is not achievable, but a smaller project might be. If the smaller one can be justified to satisfy business needs, that may be used as a seed for a larger one at a later time. The important thing in this case is to think largely, even if implementing in a smaller space. The model then can be extended and reused at a later date.

Focus on User Needs

One of the first decisions facing anyone approaching the challenge of building a taxonomy is understanding the needs of the users of the system. These needs will determine both the content domain and the feature sets supported by the taxonomy. Because so much of our information has moved into the electronic world these days, it is often a greater task to determine what will be excluded than to determine what will be included. Because an enterprise taxonomy can be used in so many different ways, it is important to be clear about the requirements of the primary user audience, and set boundaries based on those requirements.

There are many ways of gathering this information, from user surveys to focus groups to individual stakeholder interviews. If there is a portal site or other central access point to information in the company, this can often be a rich source of information about user behavior and patterns. This can help focus further inquiry. At Microsoft, Information Services manages the internal portal, MSWeb. It was thus possible to mine the customer surveys that had been used to create the organization of the portal site, as well as feedback from users and usability studies done on the site in the recent past. (Exhibit 2)

EXHIBIT TWO: SAMPLE SURVEY QUESTIONS FROM MSWEB STAKEHOLDER SURVEY

MSWeb Redesign Information Goals and User Assessment Sheet:

1.   List the top five most important information services/or products under your area that you think most employees need to know about? What is the business impact of employees not being aware of this information?

2.   Are there additional services and/or information/products within your area that would benefit from increased exposure? Describe the potential business value from employees having a better awareness or understanding of this information.

3.   What types of content/information do you think is missing from MSWeb? Why is it important that this information be included?

4.   In reviewing the current list of shortcut options, circle and rank the top 20 items you think would be critical to have on the top level of MSWeb.

5.   In reviewing the current list of Workplace Services, comment on items you think are missing, do not make sense within their categories, or that are unclear to users.

6.   In reviewing the current list of MSWeb Lifestyle topics, comment on items you think are missing, do not make sense within their categories or are there are unclear to users.

7.   In looking to find information on MSWeb, what do you find difficult?
      a.   Can you give us a specific example(s):
      b.   How does this affect your ability to do you job?

8.   What do you find easy to locate or do on MSWeb?
      a.   Can you give us a specific example?

9.   Do you expect MSWeb to be one of the primary places where you could go to find both internal and external daily news related to Microsoft?

10.   Have you ever used the current Event Calendar on MSWeb? What type of events from your area would be important for the rest of employees to know about via the Calendar?

11.   Do you find that lack of contact information, source data, or running into broken links on the intranet hinder your getting your job done in a productive manner? If so, how?

12.   In reviewing the current top-level MSWeb page, please provide any other general feedback about the MSWeb site.

Analyze Existing Content

A sweep of the content that is being considered for inclusion in the taxonomy may also provide rich information about how that content is currently being organized. Areas where users and designers have already created some local metadata or other content organization schemes can be ascertained. In a large organization, this may be a mammoth undertaking. Because Information Services provides the central search crawl for the intranet inside Microsoft, this index was used to extract information on tag names being used and the values within those tags (Exhibit 3). A similar process could be done by a one-time crawl of the content of interest with a search engine, and extracting the tag names and their values from the resulting index. Alternatively, for a small content set with a known number of producers, the information could be obtained from visual inspection of the content itself, or through a survey of content owners. However it is collected, having this information at the outset of a project provides a snapshot of the current state of metadata use. This can later be used as a benchmark for defining adoption rates and use patterns of the tag names and vocabularies in the taxonomy.

EXHIBIT THREE: SAMPLE OF TAG AUDIT

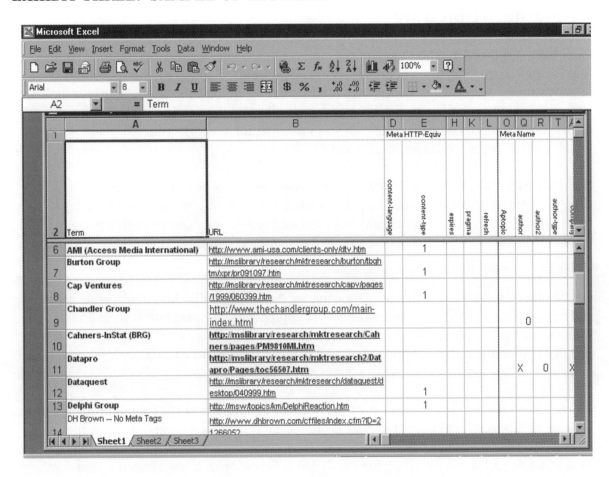

All of this information provides a way to understand the users. It also builds knowledge of the content in the domain that is being considered for the taxonomy. It further may well drive decisions about the boundaries of that domain. In some cases, it may become apparent that local needs mandate that portions of the organization require a different approach. The overall scheme may need to accommodate that variation. This initial study will provide a roadmap and guide to the remainder of the project, so it is important that it be thorough and systematic.

PLANNING

Define the Architecture

Once the groundwork has been laid for the project, the intellectual effort of defining the structure for the taxonomy can be undertaken. Organizing and defining the metadata and their relationships to each other is the first step in this process. If you have been effective at gathering requirements from users and stakeholders and collecting the existing schemas used throughout the organization, you will have a rich set of information to work with. This is the base on which you can begin structuring the taxonomy.

Some decisions will have to be made up front, based on the scope of the project. If it is a fully supported, top-down effort, it may be worthwhile to invest the effort and time necessary to build a fully realized, object-based structure. Polyhierarchy, inheritance of attributes, extensibility to include previously existing or anticipated systems, and complexity are characteristics of this approach.

On the other hand, it may be that an associative model, where individual schemas are gathered and related through their elements may be more appropriate when support is local and resources need to be spread across many organizations. This will create a much more loosely coupled taxonomy, with the sharing occurring at the tag name and vocabulary level as opposed to the fully integrated model above..

At Microsoft, both of these approaches have been used. Information Services chose the second because of the need for a central integration of metadata from taxonomies wherever they might live. By allowing flexibility, local implementations could be captured and shared with other groups, while still accommodating the local needs. This approach is described in more detail below in the section on Implementation.

Establish the Metadata Elements

Whatever design approach is taken, a core set of elements needs to be defined and provided with a structure that indicates their relationships so that tools can be built around them for tagging content, and accessing the vocabularies that will need to be created to support multi-valued elements. In Microsoft's case, these elements were developed through cooperative efforts with the groups producing the content and Information Services.

By using the information collected from the tag audit, meetings with key content owners, review of external standards such as the Dublin Core[1], and providers of publishing and search tools, the list of potential shared elements was whittled down from the extensive pool of candidates to a relatively short list. This core set is shown in EXHIBIT FOUR. It is important to note that this is not an exclusionary list; all the elements or tag names that have local use are still available for those local content sets. They were just not judged appropriate for use at a global level as a result of the group selection process.

EXHIBIT FOUR: SAMPLE METADATA ELEMENT LIST

BASIC	IF APPLICABLE
Title	Events
Author	Geography
Date	Language
Description	Organization
Keywords	Role
Contact Alias	Source
	Products

Create Vocabularies

This can be one of the hardest parts of constructing a taxonomy. It requires the most care and detail. Its complexities are probably the least understood. Definition of metadata elements and vocabularies require both a broad and detailed view of the space being covered at the same time. The interplay between the two is an important part of the evolution.

The complexity varies greatly, depending upon the type of metadata used. Some types, such as descriptive information about content (author, title, date, file size, format, etc.) may have variants. The values for these elements can generally be defined on the basis of rules that describe format and content. A vocabulary is not necessary for these types of metadata, only a well thought out set of rules that provide consistency and completeness for the values that populate them. Most of the current standards for metadata focus on this type of element, providing good opportunities for standardization and coordination.[2]

Other types may require relatively short, flat lists of allowable values, such as those related to workflow or use (approval state, intended audience, etc). These can be difficult to define. The vocabularies associated with them generally are relatively short and unstructured and will require much less effort to build.

The most complex area is in the set of metadata that is used to provide subject access to content. In most cases, this has been relegated to the "keyword" or "subject" element, which is supported by a large vocabulary. It is often, however, uncontrolled. There can be a great payoff in selecting certain portions of the subject space and defining it more tightly so that the metadata in these parts can be used to enhance retrieval tools. Areas like geography, product names, organization names and customer names can all be defined fairly tightly and dealt with as a bounded set of terms.

Constructing vocabularies for these subject access points is not trivial, but it is a manageable process. The payback is usually rapid; segmentation of content by these broad categories can be used to guide users more quickly to likely sets of information in portal sites, or even to personalize content for types of users. Guides such as Aitchison[3] or the NISO Thesaurus standard[4] can be very helpful in this work by providing a process roadmap and explicit guidelines.

The broader vocabulary in the subject space is probably one which is best left to a team of experts who can build a rich set of terms over time that reflect the business concepts of importance to the organization. Attempting to cover all areas at the outset may prove too ambitious. Until content can be tagged with these terms, the payback will not be seen.

As discussed earlier, Information Services at Microsoft focused on a few core vocabularies to support the common metadata elements, and in some cases leveraged existing vocabularies that were already being maintained by other groups. This will be different in each organization, but the analysis should point out the appropriate direction to be taken.

IMPLEMENTATION

To support all this design effort, a set of tools is necessary. It may be possible to purchase a vocabulary and metadata management tool that satisfies your requirements. It may be more appropriate to build a tool that can be integrated with your publishing or content management system. Many document management systems and library systems have very good tools built into them for managing metadata and vocabularies. They tend to be internal to the system, though, and do not provide a way for other systems to use or access the terms.

Other possibilities include systems built specifically for managing vocabularies and metadata, such as Synaptica[5], Blue Angel[6], or Data Harmony[7]. These are rich, powerful tools, that can provide much of the functionality that most organizations will need to build out their taxonomies. In other cases, an organization may find that its internal needs are such that a tool needs to be built from scratch to support the design. This may be necessary to support an internal publishing system, or because multiple organizations with different systems need to have access to the vocabularies.

Whatever solution is chosen, the value of a taxonomy only becomes apparent when it is used. This requires content producers or some central resource to apply the values from the taxonomy to the content of interest. Where the structure is simple, it may be possible to automate some of the tagging based on known values, or by running an auto-categorization tool against preexisting content. A complex taxonomy will require some manual tagging.

Having authors do this tagging may seem to be the most logical solution; but long-term value may not be the greatest from this choice. Unless the metadata and vocabularies can be tightly embedded in the workflow of the creators, it is unlikely that it will be used. For high value content, it will increase consistency and accuracy if a central group is provided for tagging. The trade-off here is that it will take longer to make content available, since an extra step in its publication will be introduced by the tagging process.

Those with long experience in this area (major database providers such as Dialog, Lexis-Nexis, Dow Jones and large libraries that do cataloging functions) are good resources for information on approaches that work. It is important to think about this part of the process up front. Unless the taxonomy is used, your results will be invisible to the users and stakeholders.

Automatic vs. Manual Classification

In many cases, it may be virtually impossible to invest the resources required to physically tag discrete items. A good example of this is the e-mail traffic that flows in and out of most knowledge workers' mailboxes every day. A taxonomy can help even in these cases, since it provides a common structure, which automated classification tools can use to sort and arrange this content after the fact.

Products such as Autonomy[8], which use a preexisting category scheme to analyze and distribute content that has not been previously organized, may provide a "good-enough" solution in many cases. If the taxonomy being used for this automated classification maps to the one being used for manual tagging, integration of the two types of content becomes possible. Both then become available as resources to the user through common entry points.

The major point to remember is that neither a manual or automated system will work well without some sort of glue binding them to other content sets. A common taxonomy provides that glue. Efforts invested in constructing a taxonomy well will pay off, both immediately and in the long term, as additional content is added to the scope of coverage.

One Solution to the Problem

The solution adopted by Information Services at Microsoft was to create a metadata schema registry. The registry is a central repository of existing metadata schemas, with links to the vocabularies associated with the schema elements (or tags). Within this registry, those elements that have equivalence can be mapped together to provide access to content tagged with terms from different vocabularies . For example, if one group chooses to describe a group of terms related to "Products" with the tag name "product," while Information Services uses "products and technologies" for their term set in this area, the partial equivalence of these two tag names can be established in the registry.

Through the registry, publishing and search interfaces have the ability to provide direct access to multiple sets of tags, and use the associated vocabularies to accomplish the same results as their stand-alone vocabulary management systems provide. The reach is substantially farther, since any content tagged with the common vocabularies will be accessible at the time of retrieval, not just the local content. Users can be directed to specific vocabulary sets (and the associated content) based on their query or their role at any given time. As described in Exhibit 5, this can be through several mechanisms, such as a publishing tool, a search interface, or a browsing interface.

This solves completely the problems related to different data models and disparate tag sets, easing the intranet developer's task considerably in developing cross-company search functionality. It also addresses to some degree the problem of cross-vocabulary term relationships by establishing a set of relationships through the tag names grouped at the schema level. This opens the door for developers to offer advanced features like relevance feedback that will partially solve the problem of multiple, cross-vocabulary terms for the same concept.

An overview of how these components provide the foundation for improved use of the vocabularies and metadata schemas is shown in Exhibit 5. The implementation of this system was accomplished in three projects:

1) A metadata schema registry

2) A vocabulary management tool

3) A solutions kit for tagging and search developers

Although the focus of this effort was on Microsoft's internal information stores, the project was modeled on similar activity centered around Microsoft's BizTalk service[9] and the Open Information Model[10]. These initiatives, although externally focused on the world of e-Commerce, deal with many of the same issues surrounding taxonomies for internal organizational information. Distributed ownership of content, multiple metadata schemas, and integration of these varied elements are common themes. The desired end result in both situations is a way to provide common access to the information for specific business purposes. The theoretical and practical work done on these projects provided insight into some of the issues discussed in this chapter, and guidance on steps toward implementation of a solution.

Metadata Schema Registry

As discussed above, the metadata schema registry (Exhibit 5) links metadata schemas to each other on an element by element basis and vocabularies, or chunks of vocabularies, to individual tag names. The registry also provides the infrastructure for the other two components of the project. The relationships and associated functionality are exposed through a developer's toolkit. The toolkit includes documented calls that can be made into the registry and working examples of how the registry can be implemented by intranet search and developers of user interfaces.

EXHIBIT FIVE: METADATA SCHEMA REGISTRY

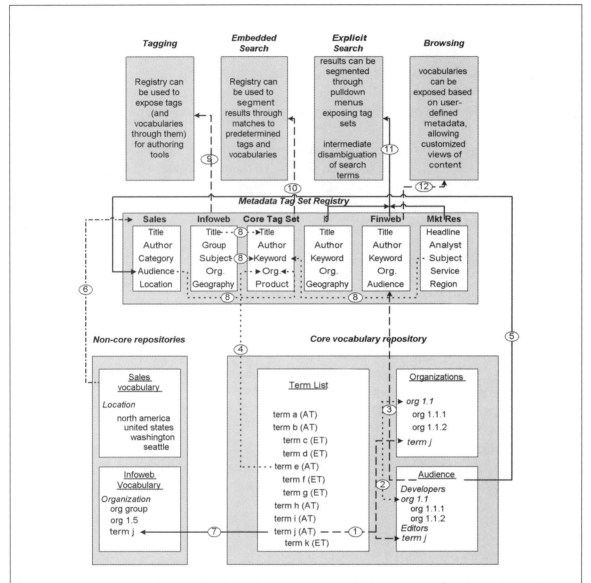

There are three layers of possible interaction between vocabularies, metadata tag sets and the search/publishing interface. Examples of these interactions are shown and described briefly below. Using a common data model for vocabulary construction allows the most powerful interactions between the layers. Any vocabulary registering its metadata tag set can, however, be exposed to a user at the time of search or browse.

Vocabularies using the same data model can:

1) Share vocabulary terms.
2) Share parts of vocabulary hierarchies.
3) Map entire vocabularies to metadata tag names.
4) Map parts of vocabularies to metadata tag names.
5) Expose their terms to non-KNAC vocabularies for reuse.

Vocabularies using different data models can:

6) Share metadata tag names with other vocabularies.
7) Share terms from KNAC vocabularies.

All vocabularies associated with metadata tag names can:

8) Be linked to equivalent tag names (and their vocabularies) through registry mapping.

All registered metadata tag sets can:

9) Provide ability to expose metadata tag names and associated vocabularies for publishing tools.
10) Provide ability for search to segment results through matches to predetermined tag names and vocabularies at time of query.
11) Allow exposure of metadata tag names before search as an advanced user interface, or during search as an intermediate query refinement assist.
12) Allow vocabularies and tag names to be exposed in whole or in part as browsing structures for content (as in Yahoo!).

Vocabulary Management Tool

The vocabulary management tool (Exhibit 6) is the means by which Information Services, and other Microsoft groups doing vocabulary development, actually construct the metadata schemas and vocabulary terms and relationships. It is built on top of a SQL Server database. It fully enables all associative and hierarchical relationships for both vocabulary and schemas. It provides the central management tool for the resources. These are exposed in the tagging tool and search interfaces enabled by the solutions kit (Exhibit 7).

EXHIBIT SIX: VOCABULARY MANAGEMENT TOOL

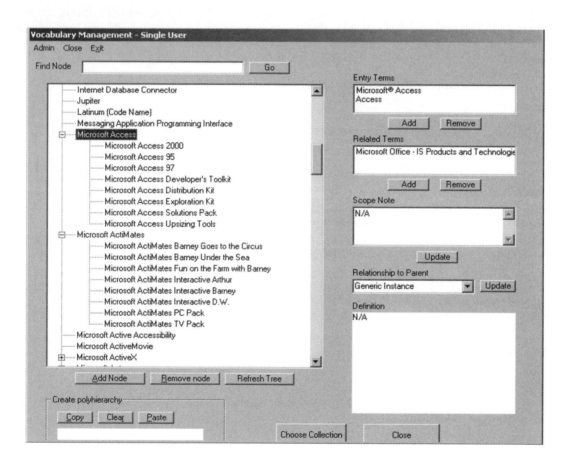

Solutions Kit

A set of specifications is available for those wishing to expose the vocabularies in their publishing or retrieval systems for adding value to their content. This is offered through a developer's toolkit (Exhibit 7). As use of the vocabularies for content creation becomes common, much more sophisticated retrieval systems will become possible. Use of the vocabulary will allow focus on the results of a user's specific needs.

EXHIBIT SEVEN: METADATA REGISTRY SOLUTIONS KIT

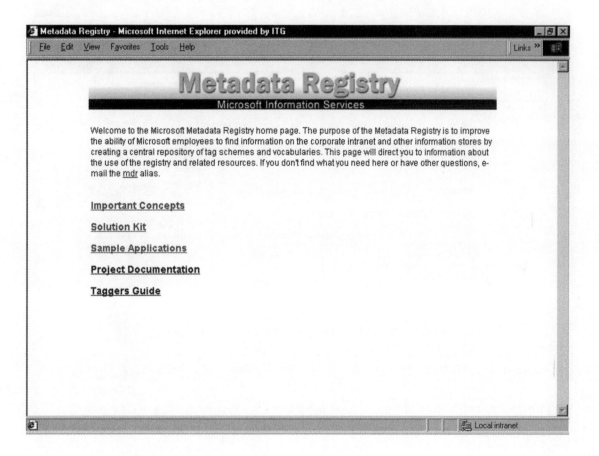

Examples of how this works can be seen today in MSWeb's search results page. Here, content that has been tagged with terms from the Information Services vocabulary is exposed in the Best Bets results. The associated terms themselves are displayed for further exploration in the Related Terms section (Exhibit 8).

EXHIBIT EIGHT: VOCABULARY EXPOSED IN MSWEB

SUPPORT AND MAINTENANCE

Change Management and Metrics

The final area that has to be addressed in construction of a taxonomy is the long-term maintenance of the system. This is often left out of the planning and budgeting for a taxonomy. It is a key part of the success. A taxonomy is not a static creation, but a living and breathing reflection of the organization and the environment in which it lives. Continual adjustment and refinement are necessary. Resources need to be committed to this function over time.

Change in the taxonomy also affects the content accessed through that taxonomy. Decisions will need to be made about how that will be done. Some can be accommodated by well-crafted vocabulary management tools that track changes in the terminology. A critical piece of the vocabulary management system built by Information Services is the identification of each term through a unique identifier, which allows others using the vocabulary term to always know when changes are made. This can be used to generate change reports, but also enables any systems built around the terms for publishing or retrieval to update automatically when those changes occur. The tool must also provide a way to link content which may have been tagged with previous terms to current terms. In other cases, re-tagging of content will be required, and resources committed to that effort must be determined on a case-by-case basis.

Metrics should be built into the taxonomy to help drive this change management process. There will also need to be a way to measure the success of the taxonomy through measurement of its impact on user behavior and improved productivity. Assuming the up-front work of defining these success measures was done with the stakeholders who approved the project, there will be clear areas where metrics need to be established and reported on a regular basis. These may be related to precision in a search engine, user feedback on ability to find material, customer satisfaction surveys, or any number of other key areas.

Defining these needs at the outset of the project is critical to successful results, since they will shape the design and direction of the entire effort. These measures will be the proof that success has been achieved, and the key to further efforts in the area of taxonomy management.

Issues

Although it may seem evident to information architects and those who have worked with content organization on even a small scale, the value of building a large-scale organizational taxonomy is not a foregone conclusion. There are several issues that work against the integration of metadata and terminology across an enterprise. These must be dealt with up front and on a continuing basis during a project. These issues are really outside the technical steps involved in constructing and implementing a taxonomy, but often turn out to be the critical drivers and roadblocks in the process.

Preexisting Activities may be Difficult to Embrace

A major hurdle in getting a large-scale taxonomy off the ground is discovering and coordinating already existing pieces. Most organizations have chunks of content that have been tagged with ad hoc schemas built to satisfy short term, immediate needs. Rarely will the metadata or the vocabularies used for these efforts be consistent. They may be embedded in work flows or tools built to take advantage of the tagging. This means that any attempt to build a taxonomy which will bring those content sets closer together must involve the owners of the content early in the process.

Because the principles of taxonomy design are not understood well by many developers, education is a key ingredient throughout the process. In many cases, particularly where the effort reaches across a large organization, it is unlikely that the participants will have backgrounds that lend themselves to rapid development of the taxonomy components. Players may come and go based on current interest or need as well. This means that individuals need to be brought up to speed quickly to avoid moving over ground already covered.

At Microsoft, this problem was addressed in two ways: through regular meetings with representatives of key stakeholders in the taxonomy effort, and through direct, ongoing one on one contact with individuals involved in implementing the taxonomy within each group. By providing two methods of contact, it was possible to address both policy issues and details at the same time, making sure that both areas were covered.

It takes Time to Build a Body of Tagged Content

A new taxonomy, even if agreed to by all the groups who have a vested interest in it, is not worth much until the common metadata elements and their values have been applied to the content through tagging or some sort of automated classification. This is not a trivial task in most cases since business processes and tools must be modified to incorporate the new taxonomy. Where existing vocabularies and tag names are embedded in publishing or retrieval tools, immediate migration to a new structure may not be feasible. Decisions about how to and whether to re-tag existing content and rebuild existing tools will need to be made.

This can often lead to frustration and impatience, since payoffs will take time to occur. Again, it is important to make sure that expectations are set ahead of time, and that communication about the status and progress of an effort is ongoing. Focusing on key areas that have implemented, with good results, can be helpful to show that value is being received, even if the overall project has not reached its final destination. Because a large project covers so many areas, it is important to make sure that something of value to each of the key stakeholders can be demonstrated in the short term. It is also critical to make sure that it doesn't seem as if no progress is being made toward the larger goals. The exposure of the tagged Best Bets in MSWeb's search results (Exhibit 8) is a good example of this.

Local needs take Precedence over Global Concerns

One of the most difficult challenges of doing a large-scale taxonomy is trying to accommodate local needs for content description with global needs. In many cases, there is no requirement for metadata elements that might be of use in integrating content across organizational boundaries at the local work level. Convincing groups of the value in using these elements may take a great deal of communication, education, and background work.

The converse is also true-a local group may feel that their elements are essential for everyone else to use. This group may try to press hard to get themselves included in a larger scheme when they may not be of value at that level.

One way around this dilemma is to design the taxonomy to allow extension for local elements without compromising those needed for cross-organizational use. It also may turn out that a local element is in fact equivalent to a more broadly used one, and can be subsumed or made equivalent in the taxonomy without losing its identity.

Funding Difficult to Obtain for Background Work

Much of the initial work necessary for a broad-based taxonomy in an organization tends to cross budgeting lines. It is often difficult to get funding to initiate the effort. This may mean that the organization is not ready to undertake such a project. It may make more sense to start with a local effort that does have funding. If success can be shown on a small scale, broader support may follow.

In order to gain support for a larger effort, it is often necessary to provide a proof of concept, which might be a simple effort to build out a portion of the larger taxonomy in a particularly critical content area that crosses organizational lines. At Microsoft, the use of the vocabulary for enhancing retrieval on the intranet portal was such an example. By applying the taxonomy to a small, well-managed set of hand-picked intranet sites, immediate improvements in search results could be shown (see Exhibit 9). As more content becomes tagged by participating groups, these results will be extended across larger sets of content.

In some cases, it may even be possible to use a commercially available set of content with attributes and vocabularies that can be re-purposed for internal use. An example might be a news source that is pre-tagged by the content provider and made available to users through custom profiles based on the tagging.

Attempts to solve a large-scale problem without good support will be doomed to failure-the ideal scenario is commitment from the top of the organization to support a distributed effort, with one group appointed the leader and coordinator of the effort. If this is not possible, be prepared to integrate multiple approaches, and compromise on the purity of your approach to gain a step forward. The solution may have to be a partial one that works as opposed to a perfect one that is not achievable.

EVALUATION

The basic reason for worrying about any of these issues is, of course, to improve productivity in the broadest sense of the word. As organizations increase in size, it becomes more difficult to find the right information for a particular activity. Taxonomies are created in the hopes of improving access to information, and reducing the cost of losing information that is of value to the organization. This means that the design and implementation of the taxonomy must be driven by user requirements, and shaped over time by the users' business needs. Ultimately, the payoff should occur in three areas- better access to high value content, better delivery of content, and better sharing of content by users.

Better Access to High-Value Content

Most organizations (and individuals in those organizations) are finding it more and more difficult to navigate through the geometrically increasing volume of information and applications available in electronic form. This is an interesting switch from the lament of only a few years ago about the difficulty of getting information electronically. Historically, content has been contained within delivery mechanisms built for the use of experts in retrieval, who often spent years being trained in the effective use of the tools available to them. The rise of the web has caused a major shake-up in this area, resulting in a challenge to the traditional business models surrounding information delivery and ownership.

In addition, as organizations become more aware of the rich resources available to them from commercial publishers of news and other electronic information, they are looking for ways to better integrate it with the huge amounts of information available from internal sources, ranging from messaging systems to highly structured databases. Each of these resources may have metadata associated with it, built to maximize the access to that particular resource. The real challenge then becomes finding a way to provide access to all these resources while still preserving the richness associated with each particular resource.

For instance, the Human Resources database within a large company contains a great deal of information about individual employees within that organization- their place within the structure of the company, personal contact information, historical information, etc. Integrating this information with, for instance, a messaging database, might enable a user to find out who has the answer to a particular question they are asking in an email, based upon organizational or job-specific characteristics. But in most cases, there is no way to link this information because the structure surrounding the content (the metadata) has no common linkage. Thus, no pathway to allow crossover from one resource to another exists.

The intent of building an enterprise taxonomy is to identify the areas where the most value can be obtained through this shared metadata, and to implement it in a way that provides increased productivity for the users of the system. By using common metadata elements and values to describe information in different stores, linkages between them can be established, and used to bring the information together for a user at the time it is needed. This can eliminate time lost searching for missing information, or actions taken based on incomplete information.

One of the key measurements being used in Information Services at Microsoft is the effectiveness of the vocabulary in bringing back relevant search results in the cross-company search engine. An example of the statistics tracking this success are shown in Exhibit 9. The increase in Best Bets (the most relevant material for a given query, tagged with the common vocabularies used in the taxonomies and presented at the top of a user's query) for the top search strings, and the decrease in the number of Best Bets for each query, is directly related to the implementation of the vocabularies and can be used as evidence of their success within a well-managed set of content.

EXHIBIT NINE: STATISTICS ON SEARCH RELEVANCE

Key measure	Q4 1999	Q1 2000	Q2 2000
Total number of registered sites	834	858	808
Average # Best Bets returned with 20 top search strings	3.6	2.75	4.35
Modal # BB with top 20	1	5	1
Median # BB with top 20	2.5	3	3
Percentage of all top search strings that return Best Bets	69%	85%	98%
Percentage of 50 top search strings that return BBs	82%	84%	98%
Percentage of 20 top search strings that return BBs	90%	80%	100%
Number of Best Bets sites marked as Authority sites	229	477	577
Number of BB marked as Hub sites	68	182	245
Number of all top search strings returning 10 or more Best Bets	18	12	5
Number of top50 search strings returning 10 or more BB	6	10	5
Number of top 20 search strings returning 10 or more BB	3	6	4

Better Delivery of Content

The flip side of providing better access to content is the ability to send content to users in a meaningful context. In an ideal world, a user should not have to look for information to accomplish a task they are working on, the information should come to them. The rapid rise and fall of so-called "push" technology underscored the difficulty of doing this a few years ago. As the vendors of these products quickly discovered, "push" is not worth much unless the information being pushed is part of a user's workflow and it helps them to do their work more easily.

A shared taxonomy is essential to this integration of work and content; but it requires careful thought about where and how value can be obtained. Enterprise-wide activities, such as self-help human resources tools, may need quite different metadata than a local work group publishing process. Systematic definition of the areas that provide high return on investment will help to focus the taxonomy building effort. Such definitions ensure that where content delivery is important, the metadata is there to support it.

There are layers of contextualization as well. These range from the departmental web portal site, which provides a project-centric view of information, to applications triggered by process steps in a workflow such as a travel approval cycle. All these layers interact and interplay through the metadata associated with content. A small improvement could have a large impact in the ability of users to use information in a context meaningful to them.

Information Services at Microsoft use query logs from the intranet portal, MSWeb, to track customer interest in topics. It uses this information to shape the direction of vocabularies in conjunction with the groups most affected by them. An example of the query log analysis tool used by the vocabulary builders for monitoring what is of interest and obtaining new terminology is shown in Exhibit 10.

As content sets begin to use vocabularies to assist with retrieval in narrower domains, this kind of feedback can be used to help refine vocabularies and identify new areas where terminology might be needed. Content can then be tagged to allow better segmentation for a particular set of users, and those users will be able to spend less time looking for results in their area of interest, just as the general purpose user can on MSWeb today.

EXHIBIT 10: QUERY RESULTS FROM INTRANET SEARCHES IN JANUARY 2000

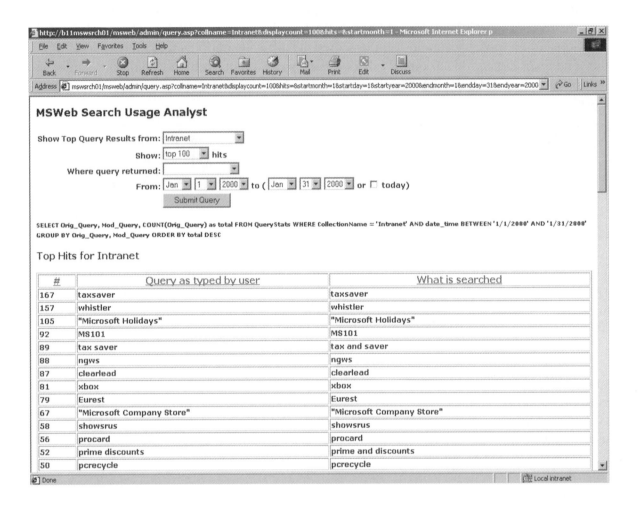

Better Sharing of Content

The third area in which a taxonomy can add value is in the sharing of information. As team-based efforts become more important and increasingly based on virtual interaction, sharing of content between team members becomes an essential part of the work process. Without good description of that content, it is very difficult to enable this activity.

The traditional networks used to share and distribute information are often rich sources of knowledge. Plugging new users into these networks is difficult without some entry points. The rapid deployment of collaborative teams, often geographically dispersed, requires a quick ramp-up of information sharing capabilities to meet schedules and make sure that all team members are operating from the same knowledge base. If elements of the shared knowledge can be captured in a common taxonomy, there is a better chance that new members of a team can take advantage of existing content. This can create a move towards a solution much more quickly because of it.

Whether this is done through manual tagging, or some sort of automated classification (which may be more likely in high volume situations such as these), a common agreement on structure is critical to enabling access to multiple content sets. This is the key to taking advantage of the value embedded in pre-existing information.

REFERENCES

1. "Dublin Core Metadata Initiative". <http://purl.oclc.org/dc/>. (5 May 2000).

2. Gorman, Michael and Winkler, Paul W., editors. Anglo-American Cataloguing Rules, Second Edition, 1988 Revision. Prepared under the direction of the Joint Steering Committee for Revision of AACR. Chicago: American Library Association, 1988.

3. Aitchison, Jean, Gilchrist, Alan and Bawden, David. Thesaurus construction and use: a practical manual, 3rd ed. London: Aslib, 1997.

4. Guidelines for the construction, format, and management of monolingual thesauri. ANSI/NISO Z39.19-1993. ISSN: 1041-5653

5. Synapse Corporation home page. <http://www.synaptica.com/> (5 May 2000).

6. Blue Angel Technologies home page. <http://www.blueangeltech.com/> (5 May 2000).

7. Data Harmony home page. <http://www.dataharmony.com> (5 May 2000).

8. Autonomy home page. <http://www.autonomy.com/>. (5 May 2000)

9. Biztalk home page. <http://www.biztalk.org> (5 May 2000).

10. "Open Information Model Version 1.0". Meta Data Coalition. August 1999. <http://www.mdcinfo.com/OIM/OIM10.html> (5 May 2000).

ABOUT THE CONTRIBUTOR

Michael Crandall is currently a Knowledge Architecture Manager for Microsoft Information Services. Michael has been with Microsoft since April of 1999. His current responsibilities include the management of the Microsoft intranet portal, MSWeb, and the search services and architectural design of the supporting infrastructure for the portal. He is also responsible for the development and deployment of a company-wide information architecture based upon integration of search tools with managed metadata schemas and associated vocabularies. Microsoft Information Services is working with key groups in the company to integrate their local taxonomies with the company-wide search engine, and provide a "gold standard" controlled vocabulary for common reference. Prior to that, Michael worked for the Boeing Company from 1986 though April of 1999. He started as online researcher in Defense and Space branch, moved to lead of the research group, then began working with electronic information delivery systems because of increasing customer requests.

Publications/presentationsinclude:

"The Portable Portal" Spring Internet World Forum, April 3-7, 2000. Los Angeles, California. Penton Media, Inc.

"Knowledge Architecture- Adding Value through Access". European Business Information Conference 2000, March 7-10, 2000. Amsterdam, Netherlands. TFPL, Ltd.

"Quantifying your organizational knowledge management to categorize, catalog, organize and personalize your corporate portal". Gaining Enterprise Momentum With Corporate Portals. February 7-9, 2000. San Francisco, California. International Communications for Management Group.

"Information Services Knowledge Architecture Initiative: A Case Study in Taxonomy Design and Implementation". In: *Korean Scientific and Technical Information Annual Conference.* Sponsored by KAIST/KIST. Seoul, Korea. December 2-3, 1999.

"Knowledge Architecture: the Role of Taxonomies, Thesauri and Indexing". New York Business Information Conference '99, November 15-16, 1999. New York, New York. TFPL, Inc.

"The Portable Portal". With Mary Lee Kennedy. Fall Internet World Forum, October 4-8, 1999. New York, New York. Penton Media, Inc.

"Users' Choice of Filtering Methods for Electronic Text". Special Libraries Association Steven I. Goldspiel Memorial Research Grant Report. Special Libraries Association, Washington, D.C. June, 1999.

"Creating a Company-Wide Vocabulary Resource". Intranets 99, April 26-28, 1999. San Francisco, California. *http://www.intranets99.com/presentations/crandall2.ppt* Aug 12, 1999.

"Site Server 3.0 Search and the Enterprise". Intranets 99, April 26-28, 1999. San Francisco, California. *http://www.intranets99.com/presentations/crandall.ppt* Aug. 12, 1999.

Role of the Technical Libraries in Boeing's Intranet. In: *Korean Scientific and Technical Information Annual Conference.* Sponsored by KAIST/KIST. Seoul, Korea. December 4-7, 1998.

5

THE WORLD BANK

This case study outlines the sharing of knowledge through communities of practice which is assuming a prominent role among World Bank's development partners because it allows rapid identification of global best practices and continuous learning opportunities.

"What we as a Development community can do is help countries – by providing financing, yes; but even more important, by providing knowledge and lessons learned about the challenges and how to address them."
-James W. Wolfensohn, President, The World Bank

UNDERSTANDING WORLD BANK

Created in 1944, the World Bank is an international financial institution and development agency. It provides lending and policy advisory services to developing countries to help achieve sustainable economic development. From a traditional lending institution, which until the late 80's, provided about $20 billion annually to its client countries for policy reforms and large-scale infrastructure, agricultural and education projects, the Bank has recently repositioned its strategy to address the broader issues of poverty.

The Challenge of Poverty Alleviation

With regard to setting the environment in which the Bank operates, James D. Wolfensohn, president of the World Bank, offered last March the following remarks to the National Press Club: *"Today we have 6 billion people on the planet. Three billion of them live under $2 a day. One billion, two hundred million of them live under $1 a day in what we call absolute poverty. Two billion of them don't have any power. One-billion-and-half don't have any water. One hundred and twenty-five million kids don't go to school. There are too many people dying due to lack of vaccines, and the world is showing an increasing inequity, not an equity, in terms of the disposition of the assets in what we call absolute poverty. And it's in this context that we come to the next millennium and the challenges that we face with one other very, very important component, which is that we're entering a new age of global development—not the agricultural revolution and not the industrial revolution, but a digital and electronic revolution, which will have enormous implications on where we go both in the world in general and in the developing world in particular."*

Confronted to this daunting challenge, the World Bank (hereinafter "Bank") now supports a broad range of programs geared to alleviating poverty and improving the living standards of the poorest people in the world **(SEE EXHIBIT ONE).** With about 10,000 employees headquartered in Washington DC and in 80 country offices, the Bank lends $30 billion annually through nearly 350 loans addressing human and social development and governance issues.

It is important to understand that the Bank is fortunately not alone in this battle against poverty. Bilateral agencies, regional development banks, and institutions such as government-sponsored development agencies have also reoriented their programs to address the same issues. During the last ten years, the private sector has also taken an increasingly important role in terms of its investment in developing countries. Ten years ago, the flow of private funds to developing countries was $30 billion. Today it reaches $300 billion. Therefore, the challenge for the Bank is no longer what it can do alone. It is rather how it can best partner with all the development actors to leverage its development impact. This has far-reaching implications for the institution. First, Bank clients who are also active players in the knowledge economy increasingly expect

Bank staff to provide advice based on the global experience of the Bank. Unless global knowledge and best practices are shared internally among staff, Bank clients may not want to finance their development through borrowing. Hence, internal knowledge sharing is essential even for the Bank's traditional lending business. Second, it is obvious that the Bank cannot fulfill its global mission of poverty reduction simply through its own loans and advice. Only by involving a very large number of development actors, informed by development know-how and best practices, can the Bank achieve its mission. Hence, external knowledge is essential for achieving the Bank's mission of poverty reduction.

Preparing the Organization to Share Knowledge

To respond to the challenge of internal and external knowledge sharing, the Bank established in 1996 an integrated, global organization co-located between Washington and major client countries. This matrix organization intersects six vertical geographical regions. These regions are responsible for project lending and country specific policy advice, with five crosscutting networks responsible for sector policies, quality assurance, learning and global knowledge sharing. Its organizational structure is illustrated below.

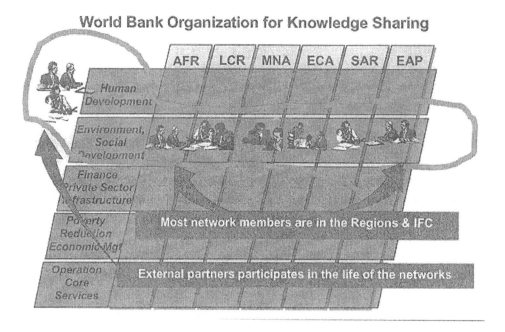

World Bank Organization for Knowledge Sharing

THE KNOWLEDGE-BASED ECONOMY

Due to the increasing globalization and the swift pace of technology changes, accessing knowledge is easier than it has ever been before. The rapid evolution of information and telecommunications technology is transforming the world economic structures and opening new opportunities for developing countries. With the collapse of distance and of the unit costs of computing, communications and transactions, developing countries can now access instantly knowledge that was still "brought" to them in a very fragmented manner in the not-so distant past.

As a result, a number of developing countries are attempting to enter global markets and to "leapfrog" outdated technologies. For example, India is taking a prominent role in software development. China is specializing in hi-tech manufacturing. The Caribbean is offering offshore data processing. The outcomes of these major and rapid transitions are impossible to predict, as multiple and interacting economic changes are occurring simultaneously. This fast changing environment also brings the threat of widening disparities in access to knowledge and information. Those countries, sectors, and organizations that will display agility and adaptability will much better succeed than those that cannot.

To cope with the pace of change, organizations are increasingly relying on communities of practice and networks to complement existing structures and capture and disseminate new ideas and know-how.

There is a growing body of evidence that information technology by itself cannot leverage knowledge. If organizational units, networks or communities do not already share their knowledge, or do not understand the potential benefits that others can draw from their own information, insights, experience and know-how, information technology is not likely to break the "silo" mentality. Without an information sharing culture, most knowledge management systems will rapidly become information junkyards. While increasing an organization's ability to nurture and support knowledge, communities will help in leveraging knowledge, global information systems should be designed to support the exchange of ideas and help capture the thinking process of these communities. Only then, the benefits of the technology will be felt.

Implications for Developing Countries

Considering development from the perspective of knowledge sharing brings new light to the development process. While global knowledge is increasingly accessible, 1.2 billion people still live in absolute poverty. Poor countries—and poor people—differ from rich ones not only because they have less capital but also because they have less opportunities to access knowledge. But developing countries can acquire knowledge as well as create their own at home. Forty years ago, Ghana and the Republic of Korea had virtually the same income per capita.

By the early 1990s, Korea's income per capita was six-times higher than Ghana's. Some surmise that half of the difference is due t o Korea's greater success in acquiring and using knowledge.

Approaching development from a knowledge perspective— that is, adopting policies to increase both types of knowledge: know-how and knowledge about attributes— can improve people's lives in numerous ways besides making more money.

·   Better knowledge about nutrition means better health, even for those with little to spend on food.

·   Knowledge about the transmission of AIDS can save millions from debilitating illness and pre-mature death.

·   Disclosure of information about industrial pollution can lead to a cleaner and more healthful environment.

·   Micro-credit programs enable the poor to invest in a better future. In short, knowledge gives people greater control over their destinies.

With communications and computing costs plummeting, transferring knowledge is less-expensive than ever. Why, then, isn't this transfer occurring as fast as expected? Because communicating knowledge involves not only taking advantage of new information and communications technology, but even more importantly strengthening the networks and communities of the civil society that are essential for any sustainable sharing of knowledge.

A New Framework for Development

If one considers the process of development not only from the traditional transfer of financial resources and knowledge from rich to poor countries, but rather from the perspective of fostering learning communities and networks who will have an opportunity to access and share knowledge, six essential dimensions should be considered.

1. **Adapting technologies:** Knowledge-sharing programs should be tailored to the needs and technological capabilities of users in developing countries. The technical design of such programs should be adapted to users with limited computer capacity, such as low-speed modems, so that their low-end technology does not become a barrier to access. The programs should use public domain software where possible, and should provide other means of access for those without computers.

2. **Building trust through participation**: People often fully trust only the knowledge

that they have helped to create. This implies that practitioners in developing countries should be allowed to participate fully in the authentication of know-how and particularly in the definition of the conditions under which such know-how can be adapted to the local environment.

3. Learning from the poor: People have abundant ideas and inspirations. There is an abundance of local know-how, including indigenous knowledge, which can be reinterpreted and reused elsewhere. Knowledge sharing systems in international organizations should be open and responsive to inflows from whatever source.

4. Connecting local practitioners across boundaries: Confronted with a problem, people learn best from others that have lived the same reality in their day-to-day life. Linking practitioners in developing countries across national boundaries will greatly accelerate the flow of high value knowledge and information.

5. Fostering global knowledge flows: The international community needs to function as an efficient connector and facilitator to promote the creation and dissemination of global knowledge to enhance the quality of life of the poor. Stronger knowledge partnerships among development assistance organizations are therefore required to ensure the seamless flow of information.

6. Fostering free information flows: Some countries use prohibitive pricing to preclude access to the World Wide Web for their populations. Approaches to limit access under whatever pretext – commercial priorities or political values or linguistic predilections – should be weighed against the enormous opportunity costs involved in interfering with the freedom of information. International organizations have to deliver a clear and consistent message to those governments limiting access to information and know-how.

KNOWLEDGE MANAGEMENT
AT THE WORLD BANK

To respond to the global poverty challenge described above, James W. Wolfensohn, the president of the Bank Group announced his vision of the "Knowledge" Bank in his opening address to the 1996 Annual Meetings with the world's finance community:

> *" We need to invest in the necessary systems, in Washington and worldwide, that will enhance our ability to gather development information and experience, and share it with our clients."*

The endorsement from the top executive of an organization to launch a strategic change initiative of such a magnitude, and with such implications in terms of its value and work behavior changes, was indeed essential to its future success. Without the benefit of a blueprint to implement such a change, the first steps of the newborn knowledge Bank were, at best, hesitant. A program director for knowledge management was appointed in the fall of 1996. A number of managers and Bank staff were unclear, though, as to the significance of this initiative on their daily work. Others perceived it to be the "latest flavor of the month, while still others were laughing at it as "star wars!"

The Bank sought to become a global development service institution, capable of offering to its clients and partners easy access to information on who knows what and where the best expertise resides. The Bank was assisted by external consultants who formulated a knowledge management strategy **(SEE EXHIBIT TWO)** and developed a set of criteria for implementation **(SEE EXHIBIT THREE).** It also benchmarked the best knowledge management organizations of the time and asked a cross-section of managers to develop a comprehensive "Renewal Program" **(SEE EXHIBIT FOUR).** The foundations of this program were the newly created Networks, a total revamp of the Bank's information technology systems and knowledge management.

Although some managers were slow to "get it," some staff were already "running" with it. The following story illustrates better than a long definition what knowledge management meant for these early adopters.

A Story about Knowledge Management

Confronted by frequent pavement failures on its highway network, the government of Pakistan asked the resident highway engineer of the World Bank country office for urgent technical advice to fix the recurring problem. The resident engineer was a seasoned professional with many years of experience in the field. He was aware of other highway maintenance techniques applied somewhere else in the world. His theoretical knowledge was not supported by practical experience. He was, therefore, inclined to respond that the same maintenance technique should continue to be applied but with greater attention to the quality of its implementation. He could however also understand the desire of the government to explore new technologies that could be better adapted to the local geographic conditions.

What typically happened in the past in such a situation was that the engineer would discuss the issue and try to persuade his counterparts of the wisdom of his viewpoint. Failing in this persuasion, he would request the World Bank headquarters in Washington, D.C. to commission a technical study carried out by a team of consultants. He would eventually get back to the government with the World Bank's official "position" on the technical issue, in the hope that this would satisfy his client. This could last for several months, undermining the government confidence in the technical capability of the Bank country office that is essential for effective collaboration with local authorities.

In this instance, as a result of the knowledge management program under way in the World Bank, what actually happened was quite different. From Pakistan, the engineer sent an electronic message to his colleagues in the Roads and Highways community of practitioners inside and outside the World Bank. This community had built up over time to facilitate the sharing of knowledge in this sector. Knowing that the "safe space" offered by the community will not jeopardize his technical reputation, he asked for urgent help to identify alternative maintenance schemes from the global experience of the group.

Within 24 hours, the responses came from a variety of sources around the world. These included responses from: a task manger working in Jordan presented the results of several years of applied research; from the Argentina country office where a senior highway engineer was writing a book giving an overview of experience in Asia, Australia and Africa, including the drawbacks and pitfalls of various technologies; from the Chief Executive Officer of the highway agency of South Africa who reported on his own experience with similar technologies; and from the New Zealand University.

From these various expert perspective, the resident engineer in Pakistan could see that the weight of international experience was in favor of applying a similar road maintenance technique to that already applied in Pakistan. So he was able, within one day, to go back to the government and start a dialogue on how to adapt the Bank's experience to their situation.

This illustrates the functioning of the World Bank's knowledge management system. Relevant know-how so identified can then be captured and entered into the corporate knowledge base so that it is accessible by all staff. Today, relevant parts of the system are already externally accessible so that clients, partners and stakeholders around the world are able to have access to the know-how of the organization.

The Evolution of the Knowledge Bank

By mid-1997, knowledge management began to take roots. A budget of $55 million (3 percent of the administrative budget) was decided for fiscal 1998, mainly through reallocation of existing budgets of business units. A small corporate knowledge management unit was created to facilitate, share and monitor knowledge management initiatives of Bank units. Finally, two governance decision-making bodies were put in place. At the policy level, a Knowledge Management Council headed by a managing director was guiding the overall knowledge program, and a Knowledge Board, headed by the program director for knowledge management, was discussing implementation arrangements and was providing a sharing platform to discuss success, as well as failures. Rather than being mandatory, implementation of knowledge sharing activities was left to the decision of the regions and the networks.

By fall of 1997, nearly 30 communities of practice had become active and almost all sector units were engaged in some form of knowledge sharing activities supported mainly by part-time staff. Each of the networks appointed a knowledge manager to coordinate their activities, and the first help desks opened for business. This promising start was not, however, without pitfalls. Local implementation strategies were often lacking solid definition and alignment with the corporate strategy. Because communities of practice were not hierarchical structures, the knowledge management budget was not always reaching them as intended. These communities, known in the Bank as thematic groups, were spending more time to build web sites and knowledge collections rather than engaging in sharing activities. Information technology specialists were developing a taxonomy and designing sophisticated systems to tag knowledge collections without sufficient inputs of the users. Finally, no personnel incentive had yet been developed to impact the old "silo" culture. Bank management decided nevertheless to allow a wide range of activities to continue across the board. This supportive attitude towards experimentation and innovation was critical to the development of ownership of the knowledge program among staff and managers.

By mid-1998, knowledge management was moving ahead rapidly on a broad front. The budget system had been fixed. Money was channeled to the thematic groups through the sector boards. As a result, the number of thematic groups jumped from thirty to over one hundred. Knowledge sharing was added to the set of values and behaviors against which staff and managers are evaluated annually. Finally, a consensus emerged from the networks to work on eight core activities **(SEE EXHIBIT FIVE):**

(i) building or strengthening thematic groups;

(ii) developing an on-line knowledge base on a common platform to make know-how accessible to all staff at headquarters and in the field;

(iii) creating help desks and advisory services;

(iv) building a directory of expertise;

(v) publishing key sector statistics;

(vi) providing access to transaction or engagement information;

(vii) providing dialogue spaces for professional conversations; and

(viii) establishing external access and outreach to external clients, partners and stake-holders.

The regions were also engaged in knowledge sharing activities through the development of standardized macro-economic databases, and the collections of country information and best practices. The lessons learned from these early days are summarized below.

The Eight Pillars of Knowledge Sharing

Drawing from the lessons of experience for launching a broad knowledge management program in a global organization like the World Bank, eight pillars were instrumental to support the Bank's initiative:

1.   Defining a clear strategy based on the business needs of the organization;

2.   Keeping small the central KM unit which oversees overall implementation;

3.   Making available a budget to allow communities to function;

4.   Supporting the development of communities of practice;

5.   Keeping information technology user-friendly and responsive to its users needs;

6.   Orchestrating systematic communications to explain what knowledge means and to keep every one informed;

7.   Introducing new incentives to accelerate the shift towards a knowledge culture; and

8.   Developing a set of metrics to measure progress.

Defining a Knowledge Strategy

Defining a knowledge sharing strategy that will be endorsed by senior management and front-line staff is a difficult, but essential, first step. The strategy should clearly articulate why the organization should share its know-how. It should address what the organization will share, with whom the organization will share, and how the organization will share. One critical element in the World Bank knowledge-sharing strategy was the public commitment made by its president to build a "knowledge" Bank. This decision to share sheltered the organization from lengthy discussions that typically surround the development of strategies in large organizations.

•   **Deciding why to share:** Given the characteristics of the global economy and the plummeting costs of communication and computing, the World Bank perceived that sharing knowledge would enhance its organizational performance and, therefore, its global impact on poverty. This was a business decision anchored on the realization that new opportunities offered were worth the shock of cultural and technological transformations it was going to introduce. Knowledge management was not undertaken for its own good. It was motivated by a decision to increase the speed and quality of service delivery, lower the cost of operations by avoiding rework, accelerate innovation, and widen the Bank partnerships to fight poverty.

•   **Deciding what to share:** The knowledge sharing program of the Bank is designed to share country and sector know-how, and global best practices and research in the field of development. The program would have been designed differently if the knowledge of competitive intelligence, processes or individual clients had been at the core of the Bank's business. The issues of the quality and authentication of what is being shared is addressed by the thematic group leaders.

•   **Deciding with whom to share:** The knowledge sharing vision of the World Bank is ambitious. It drives the institution to share its development know-how, both internally with staff at headquarters and in the field, as well as externally with clients, partners and stakeholders. Internally, the audience comprises the members of the thematic groups. The objective is to collect and make accessible the latest and best sector and country development knowledge that exists globally. This allows operational staff to bring higher quality advice to their clients, while saving time and costs. In itself, collecting, synthesizing and authenticating this knowledge is already an endeavor. External knowledge sharing poses further issues, such as the confidentiality of information given to the Bank by its clients and partners and copyright of documents. Additionally, for the Bank activities supporting the private sector, the protection of proprietary assets is also an issue of concern. Instead of developing constraining procedures to address these issues, the Bank is dealing with them as they arise.

· **Deciding how to share:** The Bank uses a multitude of different channels to share various forms of knowledge. For instance, a number of thematic groups are providing a mentor for each new recruit to quickly familiarize them with sector strategies, lending procedures and key professional contacts. Every staff member can also call a help desk where packets of information and referral services are available. Seasoned professional will attend and contribute to technical clinics (working lunches of one-to-two hours). They can also search the knowledge collections on the Intranet. Externally, knowledge sharing takes place virtually on the Web. It also is conducted face-to-face with clients and partners, either during field missions or during sector weeks organized annually by sector boards and their thematic groups.

Organizing Knowledge Management

The location of the central knowledge management unit in the World Bank has evolved over time. At the program's inception, it was attached to the information technology group because attention was primarily focussed on building a knowledge management "system", i.e. a repository of knowledge collections. When thematic groups gained importance, attention shifted to connecting people for accelerating learning and bringing the benefits of knowledge sharing to operations. To reflect this new orientation, the central KM unit was recently moved to the vice-presidency Operation Core Services. Whatever its location, the Bank knowledge management organization and functions is similar to what seems to emerge as a pattern among knowledge organizations, i.e.

·   a small central unit (five people) has overall coordination and facilitation responsibilities;

·   operational managers in the networks and the regions are responsible for implementing the knowledge sharing program;

·   thematic groups, supplemented by help desks, are the preferred instrument for sharing know-how; and

·   a governance body (knowledge management council) is responsible at the corporate level for the overall knowledge management policy formulation.

Providing a Budget for Knowledge Sharing

The decision to provide a budget for knowledge sharing tripled the number of thematic groups between June 1997 and 1998. This sent an unambiguous message to staff that the World Bank was serious in incorporating knowledge management into its operations. The knowledge sharing program receives an annual budget allocation of about 3 percent of the Bank administrative budget. Of this, less than 10 percent is used on technology. Two percent covers the operating cost of the central coordinating unit. The remaining, or nearly 90 percent, finances the thematic groups and the sector help desks that support the Bank's operations. These figures are at the low end of what other knowledge organizations seem to spend on knowledge sharing. Without appropriate funding, thematic groups could neither continue sharing knowledge at their current level nor survive since the community leaders and their members are all involved in day-to-day operations.

Nurturing Communities of Practice

In most organizations, building a repository of knowledge collections is easier than shifting the company's culture towards knowledge sharing. To successfully capture, share and leverage knowledge, an organization needs to facilitate and nurture human interactions between professionals who share a common interest or experience, who share common problems and whose interest is to identify solutions that will improve their work effectiveness. Without the benefit of a shared practice, people will constantly reinvent the wheel, deliver sub-optimal solutions to their clients, and miss potential efficiency gains.

At the outset of the knowledge sharing program, only a hand-full of professional communities was in existence. One of these, the roads and highway thematic group, had gathered informally over 15 years. Under the leadership of a visionary and curious minded engineer, the group had established an email distribution list where technical questions were debated, help was requested and, most importantly, where success stories were shared. Success stories validate the knowledge sharing concept and boost the enthusiasm and commitment of the practitioners. Nurturing the development of such communities became a Bank priority.

The networks encouraged their staff to organize around common themes such as environment or poverty, and sector priorities such as early childhood development or rural water supply and sanitation. Today, more than 120 thematic groups are supported by the Bank, without smothering their self-organizing drive lead by thought leaders (**SEE EXHIBIT SIX**). Beside budgetary allocations, various instruments have been developed to nurture the thematic groups.

Choosing a Technology for Sharing Knowledge

The "connecting power" of information technology often leads companies to believe that technology alone can leverage the know-how of their professionals and partners. Bank staff throughout the world can connect with their peers through email or the Web. They can also access electronically the knowledge collections of thematic groups to get the collective wisdom of their professional practice. From this, it is tempting to conclude that implementing a Web based technical solution to share knowledge is a no brainer. The reality did not match this perception. First, most of the knowledge of individuals is tacit. It resides deep in their minds and only a fraction of it is indeed explicit. Only the latter can be captured, synthesized and shared through the World Wide Web. Second, to effectively share this explicit knowledge, the information technology tool should be fast to access, user-friendly and easy to operate. It should provide classification and cataloguing capabilities to easily found and quickly retrieve knowledge.

The Bank's experience is that setting up such a system is not an easy task. It requires a collective vision of the organization concerning how knowledge will be shared. Many units have to be engaged from the onset in the development of the technology tools. Only this will ensure that the users' requirements are met, and therefore, that the system may have a chance to be used in the future. Besides information technology, other technologies drawing on the tacit knowledge of people are essential to consider. Widely available tools such as the telephone, electronic mail and video-conferencing play a central role in the Bank knowledge sharing activities. The combination of technology tools and human practices is likely to be more successful than programs that focus on one or the other.

Communicating the Values of Knowledge Sharing

In the process of communicating its knowledge management strategy, the Bank was fortunate to have the full commitment of its chief executive. The World Bank president held several "town hall" meetings with the staff to explain his vision. In 1998, the Bank published its annual World Development Report on knowledge and development. That year, it organized two Knowledge Fairs. It was there that thematic groups could, for the first time, display in a booth their knowledge sharing activities to the entire organization. They could illustrate the benefits of working together with concrete examples. The first fair took place in the lobby of the headquarters building in March 1998. It experienced thousands of visitors, including the Bank president and his senior managers. It generated an extremely positive response from the staff members, who could see and feel what knowledge sharing was all about. This first success lead the president to repeat each year the fair during the Bank's annual meetings, which are attended by more than 10,000 people from around the world.

Storytelling was used by the KM program director and some network KM staff to sensitize the organization to the kind of problems that knowledge sharing was meant to solve. Presenting real-life, problem-solving situations allowed each individual in the audience to recast the stories into his or her own contextual work environment. Suddenly, the highway knowledge sharing story was becoming relevant to the expert on early childhood education without even pronouncing the word knowledge management or attempting to give an elaborate definition of it. Storytelling turned out to be a much more powerful and effective way of communicating the values of knowledge sharing than using one of the typical complex definitions and diagrams found in every knowledge management book. Story telling was also used during the inception program of new Bank recruits.

Introducing New Personnel Incentives

Traditional vertical hierarchical models of organization tend to exacerbate the "silo" culture of a company and discourage knowledge sharing behaviors. In 1996, the World Bank decided to adopt a matrix organization to precisely promote the exchange of information and know-how between regional units that had been lacking. Although changing the organizational structure of the Bank was an important decision, it was not alone a sufficient reason to provoke the intended cultural change. A year later, the Bank made knowledge sharing an integral part of its formal personnel evaluation system. It did so by modifying the small number of core behaviors against which the performance of Bank employees is assessed. This sent a strong signal to managers and staff that the institution was serious about encouraging and rewarding knowledge sharing behaviors. Did this change produce an instant incentive effect? Not quite; some cynicism and posturing remained. It had to be supplemented by a series of monetary awards.

The Bank, to foster knowledge sharing behaviors, used annual performance awards that reinforced sharing behaviors. A President Award for Excellence was introduced to recognize outstanding team behaviors. A Development Market Place was organized to promote innovation and groundbreaking work with external partners. Seed financing was offered to the winning proposals. Finally, a pilot performance award was introduced in 1999 to reward cross-boundary work and client impact. It is expected that, over time, these incentives will accelerate the intended behavioral change.

Measuring Performance

Measuring the performance of an organization-wide knowledge sharing program is a difficult and sometimes ambiguous undertaking. On one hand, the return on the significant knowledge sharing investments needs to be evaluated. On the other hand, the evolution of behavioral changes throughout the organization should be measured. A set of metrics for measuring progress is essential to the sustainability of the knowledge sharing program.
At the outset of its program, the Bank focused mainly on measuring inputs (such as budget

deployment and recruitment of knowledge management staff) and activities (such as the number of help desks, communities, and knowledge collections available on-line). As implementation progressed, the focus was expanded to measuring outputs (such as the number of questions satisfactorily answered by help desks, the number of page-equivalent downloaded from the web, the number of knowledge databases and the usage of electronic tools). Outcomes, such as lending cycle times, the quality of services, staff and client perceptions are also measured(**SEE EXHIBIT SEVEN**). Measuring the overall impact of the knowledge sharing program possessed a unique challenge. Managerial factors, changes in processes, and the external work environment are simultaneously taking place with knowledge sharing activities. As a result, the causal relationship between inputs and impact remained, at best, unclear.

To overcome the shortcomings of traditional performance measurement, the Bank decided to subject its knowledge sharing program to two independent assessments. First, in February 1999, Larry Prusak, executive director of the IBM Institute of Knowledge Management, led an external panel of knowledge management experts to assess the relevance and efficacy of the Bank knowledge sharing program and to make recommendations for improvement. The conclusions of the panel were presented to the Bank senior management in April 1999(**SEE EXHIBIT EIGHT**). The knowledge management strategy of the Bank was found *"far-sighted in conception and sound in its fundamentals. It positions the Bank to play a key role in the new world economy of the 21st Century."*

This reassuring conclusion was affirmed in October/November 1999 by a benchmarking study of knowledge management programs in 80 organizations conducted by the American Productivity and Quality Center. In February 2000, The World Bank was recognized as one of the top-five knowledge management organizations in the US together with Chevron, HP Consulting, Siemens AG and Xerox. In June 2000, an annual sruvey of experts of Fortune 500 Companies also selected The World Bank as one of the top ten Most Admired Knowledg Enterprise (MAKE©) in the World.

Integrating Knowledge Sharing and Learning

Like many other organizations in 1997, the Bank was still organizing its training activities independently from the operational work units. A training department located in Human Resources was responsible for curriculum development and delivery. Training was an individual process with clearly defined starting and end points. As expected, the training activities were mostly ineffective. Training was delivered asynchronously with professional skill-building requirements. In addition, little cross-fertilization existed between various professional groups. The creation of the networks and the launch of the knowledge sharing program changed this situation.

Within each network, sector boards became responsible for mapping the skills of their staff and identifying knowledge gaps. Thematic groups started to offer regular study tours and informal learning clinics. As the communities organized, it became clear that professional training had to be completely reorganized. The training department was first absorbed by the group that had successfully trained Bank clients, mainly by using Bank experts as trainers, the World Bank Economic Development Institute (EDI). Later, the Institute, working in close collaboration with the networks, decided to transfer the training budget and the responsibility for course content development to the sector boards and thematic groups. EDI retained the function of facilitation and provision of logistical support. Today, knowledge sharing and learning programs are supervised by the same governance body, the Knowledge and Learning Council.

Providing Support to the Communities of Practice

Thematic groups are not intended to substitute for existing organizational units. Rather, the groups are to facilitate knowledge sharing and learning across regions and themes. By their very nature, thematic groups did not fit neatly into the Bank's conventional organizational structures and budgetary processes. Thematic groups did not conform to top-down decision making. Their membership was largely voluntary and based on self-selection, from a few individuals to several hundreds of practitioners. Some had been defined around very narrow themes. Others were cutting across a wide-range of topics and sectors. Only a few had the logistical and administrative mechanisms to deliver products or services in a consistent fashion. Given this extraordinary diversity, it is not surprising that specific arrangements had to be put in place to support their work and overcome early teething problems.

Other organizations had resolved the dilemmas of embryonic communities by injecting a cadre of "facilitators," "coaches," or "concierges." Whatever the name adopted, the functions performed included assistance in the processes of knowledge production, codification, synthesis, distribution and diffusion. Thematic groups needed a minimum level of structure and accountability to become the central instrument of knowledge sharing in the Bank. Their numbers also needed to be contained to ensure critical mass and to avoid the dilution of budgetary resources. A few network sector boards started to request a mission statement and work program to their thematic group leaders. An attempt was made to put in place a Directory of Expertise. The purpose was to identify the expert profile of the members and of their professional affiliation in each sector family. More needed to be done, however, to avoid "burning out" thematic group leaders who, in addition to their knowledge sharing and learning activities, continued to devote 70-80 percent of their time to their client countries.

The managing director in charge of the knowledge sharing program called several meetings with the thematic group leaders between 1998 and 1999 to identify means of supporting them and areas of immediate actions.

·   In areas, where the Bank was not at the cutting edge, efforts were directed to building up knowledge partnerships with outside partners.

·   Repeat activities such as data base entry, web site development, referral-type services and preparation of information packets were delegated to the help desks and sector knowledge coordinators who were recruited by the sector boards.

·   Knowledge coordinators were also asked to help thematic group leaders in researching and cataloging knowledge materials, and organizing learning events either inside the Bank or in partnership with external professional groups.

·   Networks undertook to disseminate quickly to the rest of the Bank information about their thematic group activities.

·   The procedures for obtaining funding for thematic groups activities were streamlined. Each sector board reviewed the alignment of thematic group activities with sector strategies and priorities.

·   A self-assessment tool was designed to encourage the candid feedback of members of the thematic groups (**SEE EXHIBIT NINE**).

·   Regular workshops of thematic group leaders were organized by the central knowledge sharing unit. This group encouraged the consolidation of overlapping thematic groups. It also created synergy and helped communication between thematic groups to help introduce good practices developed in other thematic groups.

·   A knowledge intern program was launched with graduate and under-graduate students to increase the research capacity of thematic groups.

KNOWLEDGE INTERN PROGRAM

Although there was a widespread perception that thematic groups added value to the work, the performance of individual thematic groups was felt to vary greatly. Since no data on the 120 thematic group was available on a Bank-wide basis, two networks undertook a survey of their 2000 thematic group members in December of 1998. The survey assessed the importance and quality of the delivery of knowledge products and services by thematic groups and help desks. The performance of key drivers, such as thematic group leaders and sector managers, was also assessed. The survey provided robust data to rank 19 thematic groups on several dimensions, showing the wide variations in this particular group of thematic groups.

	Survey Results	
	Percentage of participants who agree	
	TG is effective	**TG leader is effective**
Top third of TGs	72%	72%
Middle third of TGs	49%	48%
Bottom third of TGs	13%	20%

In general, even staff who agreed that a thematic group was effective, expressed dissatisfaction with their own ability to contribute to the TG's activities. The Bank's experience here was not unique. The uneven results shown are common to many organizations that have launched communities of practice. Their experience and related research shows that unless these problems are quickly resolved, the thematic groups will unravel. It was inefficient for thematic group leaders to devote time to day-to-day administrative, logistical, and communications tasks involved in making a community vibrant. Additionally, the networks had no incremental budgetary resources to recruit additional knowledge staff. The Bank then explored the opportunity to attract students from local universities in order to solve these issues.

Attracting Knowledge Interns

The Washington DC area is endowed with the presence of a large number of universities. The Bank had successfully run a summer intern program for many years. This program provided a paid opportunity for graduate students to improve their skills, as well as the experience of working in an international environment. Since the scope of work, its scale, and the diversity of cultures seemed to attract students during the summer months, a first challenge was to replicate a similar enriching experience year-round. The Bank was also facing another challenge. While summer interns are paid for their services, it had no budget left to attract students during the course of their university semesters.

A network advisor then had the idea to ask universities to build the time the students spent with the Bank into their course curricula, so that the students could earn course credits for their work with the thematic groups. This could only work if the knowledge intern program could offer a concrete learning experience to supplement the academic studies of students(**SEE EXHIBIT TEN**). He then contacted local universities to test the idea. Their response was overwhelmingly positive. During the course of discussion, Professor Elias Carayannis, Associate Professor of Management Service at George Washington University, proposed to create a dual TG and academic mentorship to further ignite student's interest. He also volunteered to serve as outside academic advisor to the program. This partnership turned out to be very beneficial to knowledge in the program. Universities readily offered to internally advertise this internship opportunity to their students.

On June 1, 1999, the knowledge intern program (KIP) was established. In their academic specialization, students were expected, under the overall guidance of thematic group leaders, to help:

- identify promising knowledge resources to capture;
- edit and present knowledge resources in a consistent institutional format and in a user-friendly way;
- establish and implement checking and vetting procedures within the thematic group, as well as help clean out obsolete material on the Intranet;
- carry out day-to-day administrative tasks;
- assess the knowledge sharing needs of thematic group members; and
- conceive tools for knowledge sharing appropriate to the thematic group.

Main Program features

A website was created to facilitate the students' application to the program. The list of thematic groups and a brief description of their work is available on the site. Students can either choose to express interest in working for a thematic group of their choice, or they can respond to the job description posted by thematic group leaders. Their applications are then routed automatically to the thematic group they have chosen. Thematic group leaders receive an e-mail notification that an application was received. They are asked to open the database displaying the CVs of applicants. Once they have read the application form, they indicate what action they wish to take by a simple click of a button, which indicates "accept," "reject" or "review." Interested thematic group leaders then contact the students directly. They discuss a mutually agreeable work program, work schedule and duration of the assignment. The student's academic obligations have to be taken into consideration, as well as the requirements from the academic advisor, who decides the number of course-credits the student will receive. The applications of students who have chosen a thematic group that has not an immediate opening for internship are sent to a general applications pool. This pool is open to all thematic group leaders to view. This ensures that students with promising backgrounds are not lost for the rest of the thematic group leaders' community.

Implementation Issues and Solutions

Within a week of posting on the web the knowledge internship program, 105 student applications were received. Within a month, the site had received over 30,000 visitors. The two Bank staff members who were managing the program on a part-time basis received dozens of e-mail queries and phone messages from eligible interns. Questions were taking up quite a lot of time and a lot of good will to answer. Also, figuring out email addresses or phone numbers of thematic group leaders turned out to be easier than expected for students interested in the program. Clearly, some adjustments had to be made to ease the life of overburdened thematic group leaders and to ensure the program sustainability.

A complete Questions and Answers window was added to the KIP website over the summer of 1999. Thematic group leaders were asked to post detailed terms of reference for their internships on the website. This was done in order to reduce the number of questions from casual browsers. The central knowledge sharing unit recruited an intern to answer queries, track applications, help thematic group leaders to locate suitable students from the database, and facilitate the recruitment of interns by the thematic groups. These measures were effective to keep the program running. By fall, students from outside the Washington DC area had also discovered the KIP website. Applications were now coming from universities from all over the United States and foreign countries.

Given the quality of applicants, it was decided to enlarge the recruitment of students outside of the Washington DC area. To avoid the travel and accommodation costs, as well as the trouble for obtaining a work permit for foreign applicants, students living abroad were allowed to work with thematic groups either in a virtual fashion or in the Bank field office of their country. Thematic groups that were interested took this opportunity via a literature search in a technical domain area. Today the roster of applicants contains about 2000 names of eligible students.

KIP Evaluation & Results

In December of 1999, 45 knowledge interns were asked to complete a web-based survey. The purpose of this survey was to provide understanding on how the intern program was contributing to the knowledge Bank. It was also designed to garner the perspective of the students. The survey results were then discussed at a workshop with the interns and the thematic group leaders. The surveys were answered anonymously and a mix of closed and open-ended questions was posed.

Survey Results

The majority of respondents had an internship assignment of three-to-six months. Surprisingly, only three interns were earning between three and five course credits for their work with the thematic groups. Although this was in contrast with the intention of the program, students explained that the additional tuition expenses that were required by their universities to obtain the internship accreditation were prohibitive. The richness of the experience expected from the knowledge internship with the Bank was, however, so attractive to them that they decided to work without compensation.

All the interns felt that they were applying what they had learned at the university. They recognized that they had gained valuable insights into how the practical work with thematic groups was complementing their academic studies. They had participated in the thematic group knowledge sharing activities, summarized project findings and best practices, populated databases and other information sources, catalogued knowledge resources and published them on the web, disseminated research findings, and undertaken research and technical studies. They also helped organize thematic groups learning events and produced newsletters.

From the open-ended responses, it is clear that the program more than met their initial expectations (**SEE EXHIBIT ELEVEN**).

The interns were also asked to propose ways to further improve the program. A majority felt that they should have received more detailed information about the Bank knowledge sharing program. They also indicated that more detailed information was needed about the precise role and functions of the thematic group for which they worked. They also asked for literature about the World Bank and its activities, perhaps to be given at their orientation day. Other advice to enhance the program included being able to communicate and interact more often with the other interns.

Full marks went to their various supervisors or mentors. All said that the supervisors and teams with whom they worked were very helpful, patient, shared views readily, and made the interns feel welcome. Finally, all respondents said they would recommend KIP to other students.

Seven-Month Follow-up Survey

Following the knowledge interns' feedback, a similar survey was conducted in February 2000 with the thematic group leaders. Since not all of the thematic groups had availed themselves to the KIP resources, the survey also sought to clarify the reasons of this apparent lack of interest.

Thematic group leaders confirmed that their students were doing the kind of work described in the intern survey. They also confirmed that the students were effectively supporting the work programs of their thematic groups and that their expectations of the interns were more than satisfied.

With regard to the recruitment process, there was agreement that the current process, which automatically routes application forms to each thematic group, was working well (mean 4.33). Suggestions for improving the recruitment and hiring process included the production of very specific terms of reference for each available internship, rather than asking students to express a general interest for one thematic group in the hope that a contract will materialize.
In answer to the question of "what would need to happen to enable you to hire an intern?" One-hundred percent mentioned a need for the provision of office space and time to supervise the intern. Fifty percent said that they could recruit more interns if they had sufficiently simple technical tasks that interns could handle. A third felt strongly that having someone else to handle the recruitment process would increase their intake of students. Additional time to recruit and time to supervise the interns was, in fact, a common thread in the write-in comments of thematic group leaders.

A large majority of respondents also agreed that the knowledge intern program was adding value and should be continued. Suggestions for improving KIP included having a general introduction to the Bank Group. Additionally, respondents suggested working closer with the student's academic advisor so those students have more time to work. Finally, doing more targeted recruitment and marketing of the interns to the thematic group leaders was also recommended

The key recommendations from the interns and thematic group leaders surveys are being acted upon. A revamped knowledge internship program is expected by June/July 2000.

EXHIBIT ONE:

Mission Statement -- "Our dream is a world free of poverty"

Our Mission

To fight poverty with passion and professionalism for lasting results.

To help people help themselves and their environment by providing resources, **sharing knowledge**, building capacity, and forging partnerships in the public and private sectors.

To be an excellent institution that is able to attract, excite, and nurture committed staff with exceptional skills who know how to listen and learn.

Our Principles

Client centered, working in partnership, accountable for quality results, dedicated to financial integrity and cost-effectiveness, inspired and innovative.

Our Values

Personal honesty, integrity, commitment to working together in teams—with openness and trust empowering others and respecting differences, encouraging risk-taking and responsibility, enjoying our work and our families.

The World Bank's mission is to fight poverty and improve the quality of life through sustainable growth and investment in people. It does this through five goals:

Pursuing economic reforms that promote broad-based growth and reduce poverty. The Bank will help countries to accelerate and deepen policy and institutional reforms to embrace growth, improve living standards, and reduce poverty.

Investing in people through expanded, more effective programs in education, health, nutrition, and family planning. This implies striving to reach the point where human capital limitations no longer restrain growth or keep people in absolute poverty.

Protecting the environment so that growth and poverty reduction can be lasting. The Bank will help countries reconcile the needs and aspirations of growing populations with the needs of the environment.

Stimulating the private sector so that countries can become more productive and create jobs. The Bank will help countries realize the potential of the private sector to promote investment, stimulate growth, and create jobs.

Reorienting government so that the public sector can efficiently undertake essential tasks, such as human resource development, environmental protection, provision of social safety nets, and legal and regulatory frameworks.

EXHIBIT TWO:

Knowledge Management Strategy

— Using our ability to bring together the world's leading practitioners with our many external partners to exchange experiences and innovations.

Reinforcing continuous learning

Bank staff are sharing their knowledge across organizational boundaries in communities of practice (thematic groups) to find the best know-how in or outside the organization. To get our clients better answers faster—and to improve the quality of their operations through continuous learning—we are:

- Making the Bank more open and transparent so that knowledge flows swiftly across internal and external organizational boundaries.

- Linking our internal and external learning programs with knowledge sharing, taking them out of the classroom and into the world.

- Putting budgets and personnel incentives in place to manage the full array of knowledge services.

Building client capacity and widening client partnerships

By reaching out to those who previously did not have access to World Bank services and know-how, we are providing the information clients and stakeholders need to do things themselves. We are:

— Building the capacity of countries to tap into global resources online.

— Developing the skills of clients to adapt the best global practices in knowledge sharing and management.

— Making our knowledge much more widely available through direct external access to our knowledge bases.

— Putting electronic collections of relevant information and knowledge about particular areas of activity—previously available only internally—on the Internet for all those interested in fighting global poverty.
  Our clients need access not just to the expertise of the individuals in a team assigned to them, but to the entire range of global experience on development issues—and they demand nothing less. That is why we are:

  — Adding to our wealth of cross-country know how and expertise by systematically capturing new country-specific experiences and indigenous knowledge.

  — Enlisting our clients, partners, and stakeholders in sharing knowledge for development by having them join thematic communities and inviting them to participate in global dialogues on development.

— Using our ability to bring together the world's leading practitioners with our many external partners to exchange experiences and innovations.

Reinforcing continuous learning

Bank staff are sharing their knowledge across organizational boundaries in communities of practice (thematic groups) to find the best know-how in or outside the organization. To get our clients better answers faster—and to improve the quality of their operations through continuous learning—we are:

- Making the Bank more open and transparent so that knowledge flows swiftly across internal and external organizational boundaries.

- Linking our internal and external learning programs with knowledge sharing, taking them out of the classroom and into the world.

- Putting budgets and personnel incentives in place to manage the full array of knowledge services.

Building client capacity and widening client partnerships

By reaching out to those who previously did not have access to World Bank services and know-how, we are providing the information clients and stakeholders need to do things themselves. We are:

— Building the capacity of countries to tap into global resources online.

— Developing the skills of clients to adapt the best global practices in knowledge sharing and management.

— Making our knowledge much more widely available through direct external access to our knowledge bases.

— Putting electronic collections of relevant information and knowledge about particular areas of activity—previously available only internally—on the Internet for all those interested in fighting global poverty.

Criteria for Establishing the Knowledge Sharing Program

In November of 1996, a panel of senior managers and Bank staff offered the following recommendations to launch a knowledge management system.

Category	Dimension
Leadership	Managing organizational knowledge is central to the organization's strategy
	The organization understand the revenue-generating potential of its knowledge assets and develops strategies for marketing then to external clients
	The organization uses learning to support existing core competencies and create new ones
	Individuals are hired, evaluated and compensated for their contributions to the development of organizational knowledge
Culture	The organization encourages and facilitates knowledge sharing
	A climate of openness and trust pervades the organization
	Client value creation is acknowledge as a major objective of knowledge management
	Flexibility and a desire to innovate drive the learning process
	Staff take responsibility for their own learning
Technology	Technology links all members of the organization to one another and to all relevant external partners
	Technology creates an institutional memory that is accessible to the entire enterprise
	Technology brings the organization closer to its clients
	The organization fosters development of human centered information technology
	Technology that supports collaboration is rapidly placed in the hands of employees
	Information systems are real-time, integrated and "smart"
Measurement	The organization has invented ways to link knowledge management to operational results
	The organization has developed a specific set of indicators to manage knowledge
	The organization's set of measures balances hard and soft, as well as financial and non-financial indicators
	The organization allocates resources toward efforts that measurably increases its knowledge base
Knowledge management process	Knowledge gaps are systematically identified and well-defined processes are used to close them
	A sophisticated and ethical intelligence gathering mechanism has been developed
	All members of the organization are involved in looking for ideas in traditional and non traditional places
	The organization has formalized the process of transferring best practices, including documentation and lessons learned
	"Tacit" knowledge (what the staff know how to do, but cannot express) is valued and transferred across the organization

EXHIBIT FOUR:

Knowledge Exerts from the Renewal Program

Retooling the Bank's Knowledge Base

Access to lessons learned and best practice is key to development effectiveness. Yet the Bank Group's knowledge is not always easily available to those who need it—inside or outside—when they need it, or in formats they find useful and accessible. As a result, the effectiveness of all our services suffers. To address this problem, the Bank needs to make a substantial effort to rebuild its knowledge management base—and utilize more fully its institutional comparative advantage in this area....

While the preliminary focus of the system will be on improving the effectiveness of Bank staff, its eventual goal is to meet the needs of both *internal* and *external* users....

The content of the system will depend on user interest and demand. To stimulate demand will require the establishment of: *help-desks,* with the capacity to answer queries and provide resource maps and information packets; *databases,* including terms of reference, consultants, lessons learned and key technical papers and reports; and *knowledge bases,* including sector strategies, tool kits, best practices, and think pieces....

It is important to emphasize that while knowledge management can be greatly facilitated by technology, the system is principally about people. The challenge is to harness the technology to link people together and to leverage its impact for development. That means both accumulating the right kind of knowledge—and also helping our clients build the capacity to use it.

In that sense, acquiring the right technology is the relatively easy part of the new investment required. The more difficult part is the organizational culture shift that must take place in parallel: from an individualistic mode of working and storing knowledge, towards a team-based, sharing mode. A sustained effort will be needed for this culture shift to succeed and much work needs to be done to develop the right kind of behavior. In the end, people will be the key determinant of success of the knowledge management system.

Various units will be involved in building this new system

The Networks will generally take the lead in developing the requisite knowledge bases, i.e. organizing operational staff so that the flow of global knowledge is facilitated. Each knowledge area will be led by a full-time knowledge manager and supported by subject-specialists and other operational staff who will spend part of their time building and maintaining the knowledge base – constituting "knowledge communities" in their fields of expertise. They will be assisted by help desk personnel....

Implementation of the system will be phased. Work is already under way within the HD (Human Development) network, with knowledge bases under construction and help desks in place. By the end of FY98, it is expected that half of all sectors will be active in knowledge management. The pace of further expansion of the knowledge management system will be decided on the basis of experience and demand from clients. It is anticipated, however, that knowledge management in all sector groups will be under way by FY99.

With the strengthened knowledge management system, the Bank will be able not only to provide new services, but also *higher quality services.* Lending will have a firmer foundation, which will lead to better development outcomes; and the advice offered by the Bank will be taken to a higher level. The knowledge management system will also result in:

Faster speed: client access to the Bank Group's knowledge will be accelerated and transaction costs lowered;

Best practice: the Bank's comparative advantage in providing international best practice will be consolidated;

Further decentralization: a better knowledge management system is critical for facilitating geographical dispersion – and thus constitutes a prerequisite for more effective decentralization and closeness to the client;

Stronger capacity building: genuine partnership can be facilitated through sharing of knowledge with clients and stakeholders, particularly in the poorest countries;

Better incentives for excellence: with knowledge generation and dissemination at the center of our development role, incentives for staff and managers to maintain their skills at the cutting edge and share their know-how will be stronger; and

Greater development impact: all of the Bank's products and services will benefit in terms of better information and analysis, design, implementation and feedback.

The development of the knowledge management system will be complemented by the following initiatives:

On-line communities: building on the successful IPA*net* experience, the Bank will develop electronic communities, with an environment for diverse individuals and groups concerned with economic development to exist side by side. Expert as well as non-expert users will be able to take advantage of the system—anyone with access to the World Wide Web is a potential participant.

World Development Report (WDR) on knowledge: The 1998 WDR will focus on the role of knowledge in development that should, in turn, contribute to the strengthening of the Bank's efforts in this critical area.

EXHIBIT FIVE:

Definition of Network Knowledge Management Activities

Activity	Definition
1. Community of Practice	A group of professionals, informally bound to one another through exposure to a common class of problems, common pursuit of solutions, and thereby themselves embodying a store of knowledge
2. On-line Knowledge	Availability of a well organized set of information resources responding to the needs of task managers through the corporate Intranet with appropriate classification and quality control in accordance with procedures jointly agreed between the Networks and the Information Solution Group
3. Help Desk	Referral services with dedicated staff endorsed by the Network providing personal support to task team with capacity to respond to substantive questions in the sector
4. Directory of Expertise	Availability through the corporate Intranet of accurate up to date information about staff member's background and areas of expertise
5. Key Sector Statistics	Availability of a set of indicators through the corporate Intranet related to sector and/or sub-sector performance
6. Engagement Information	Availability through the corporate Intranet of project, economic and sector studies, and research data and documents by sectors and themes, countries and task teams
7. Dialogue Space	Availability through the corporate Web of Lotus Notes databases for moderated substantive discussions among internal and external specialists in the sub-sector
8. External Access	Availability through the corporate Web of relevant development materials and best practices to external clients and partners

EXHIBIT SIX:

Key Attributes of Successful Communities of Practice

- Strong, respected, active and visible leadership – elected or co-opted by peers, not imposed by senior management;

- Pre-existence of a discussion/interest group or strong issues focus from a core group of staff;

- Clear business objectives and manageable set of activities;

- Good communication of KM offerings (through web site, newsletter, clinics, etc.) and links to external practices;

- Recognition by peers of the quality of work undertaken by the Practice, good communication, and substantive provision of information, and by management of the quality, innovation and team spirit exemplified by the community (Performance and Team Awards);

- Access to adequate and timely budgetary resources, and administrative support (help desk/advisory services, sector knowledge coordinators and knowledge interns);

- Clear understanding of institutional KM strategy, goals and values;

- Capacity to provide substantive advice in a non-threatening manner;

- Offering of learning and training opportunities, including mentoring of new members, based on an analysis of present and future knowledge or skill gaps;

- Community leaders are accountable before their sector boards for the quality and quantity of deliverables and for sound budgetary management;

- External professionals, including clients, are included in the activities of the community; and

- The community has developed a set of metrics to measure its responsiveness and value-added to the members.

EXHIBIT SEVEN:

Data Collection of Knowledge Management Activities

Data Collection for KM Indicators					
Data collection	**Respondents**	**Frequency**	**Sponsor**	**Method**	**Type of measurement**
Survey of Network Vice Presidents	Staff of Network Vice Presidents	Ad hoc	Central KM Unit	Survey	Open-ended qualitative response
Network knowledge sharing activity survey	Network Staff	Annual	Central KM Unit/ Networks	Survey	Quantitative
Focus groups from Networks, Task Teams, units	Network, Task teams, unit members	Ad hoc	Central KM Unit	Groupware implemented focus groups	Nominal; qualitative
TG Leaders (all Networks)	TG Leaders	Ad hoc	Networks	Survey	Some pre-coding
Client surveys	Bank clients and partners	Ad hoc	Regional management	Survey followed by one-on-one interviews	Quantitative and Qualitative
(All) Staff Survey	Bank staff	Annual	Bank Management	Survey	Nominal, ordinal; pre-coded

The Action Review of Knowledge Management was completed on April 28,1999, after a comprehensive stocktaking of what is occurring in knowledge management in the World Bank. Inputs were received from nineteen vice-presidencies. Interviews, focus groups, surveys, and discussions were conducted so as to incorporate the inputs of more than five hundred staff from all parts of the organization. The findings of the review reflect the consensus of the external advisory panel which was lead by Larry Prusak, Director of the Institute of Knowledge Management, and which included some of the world's leading practitioners, including Bob Buckman (Buckman Labs), Wendy Coles (General Motors), Carlos Cruz (Monterey Tech Virtual University), Tom Davenport (Andersen Consulting), Eric Darr (Ernst &Young), Kent Greenes (BP) and Brook Manville (McKinsey). The main points that emerged are as follows.

The Bank's knowledge management strategy was found far-sighted in conception and sound in its fundamentals. It positions the Bank to play a key role in the world economy of the 21st Century. The panel recommended that **management draft and issue a simple document (2-3 pages) re-stating the strategy in an authoritative form, and the principles it is based on,** and then disseminate this widely inside and outside the organization.

After reviewing all of the materials, the panel concluded that much had been accomplished in a short time without spending a great deal of money. Although some unevenness in implementation among units and groups remained, and some key implementation issues still needed to be addressed, the panel stated that, compared to other organizations, the Bank should be proud of what had been accomplished to date.

Among the action recommendations made by the panel below, four in particular stood out, as both essential to the success of the overall program and as likely to require strong management support to assure speedy implementation:

*"Thematic groups are the heart and soul of knowledge management in the Bank. An extraordinarily good start has been made in launching more than a hundred of these groups, which most staff agree are adding considerable value to Bank work. However for these thematic groups to achieve full interaction with task teams, to accomplish essential capture and distribution of know-how that is being generated in the work, to reach out to external partners, to enhance their value to external client, and to assure sustainability, the **thematic groups need additional facilitators/coordinators who can help the thematic group leaders energize and broaden their membership.***

*Although a large volume of knowledge resources has already been generated, most staff do not have easy access to these resources, owing to the fragmented way in which knowledge resources are being made available on various web-sites. We recommend therefore that **the Bank develop and implement a consistent, integrated web policy that meets the needs both of the institution and of business units and groups.** The policy should clarify what should be on the web, in what format, for what use, and who is responsible for content provision and infrastructure development, including internal KM, unit web-sites and external web.*

*For reasons of efficiency and effectiveness, the **Knowledge Management Board should be re-organized** to reflect the four major knowledge stakeholder groups (IT, content, **practitioners** and the **executive**) as well as have two **outside members** who can bring an external perspective to the group.*

*The Bank should develop **knowledge services for clients** that will enable clients to gain access to knowledge about knowledge as an economic factor of production, and to implement knowledge management for their own countries."*

EXHIBIT

Thematic Group Self-assessment Tool

Five factors are critical to effective thematic group (TG) work: Planning and Strategy; Clients/Partners Relationships; Technical Excellence; Resource Management; and TG members Involvement.

A self-assessment scoring mechanism allows a TG to graph results immediately. Each TG is free to decide which critical factor should be assessed A TG should be able to go through the full toolkit in less than 30 minutes.

Planning and Strategy				
Sub-categories	**Stage 1**	**Stage 2**	**Stage 3**	**Stage 4**
Mission Statement **Score 1/2/3/4**	No published mission statement	Mission statement published	Mission verified for alignment with sector strategy	TG verifies and update mission based on members and clients' inputs
Performance Targets **Score 1/2/3/4**	No key performance targets	Goal and targets established around the core work of the group	Goals and targets established based on broad sector objectives	Goals and targets established based on sector strategy and aligned to clients' needs
Work Program Management **Score 1/2/3/4**	Activities not organized into a work program	One year work program developed with inputs of members	Multi-year work program developed	TG uses plan to track implementation progress against milestones and self-corrects course
Activities link to results **Score 1/2/3/4**	Measurable improvements in quality are not due to TG activities	TG activities contribute to improvements made occasionally	TG members contribute to quality enhancement process when asked	TG self-regulates quality of members' outputs

Clients / Partners Relationship				
Sub-categories	**Stage 1**	**Stage 2**	**Stage 3**	**Stage 4**
Clients requirements Score 1/2/3/4	Client requirements are indirect through reports or other third parties	Requirements probed and identified with clients	Systematic process in place to appraise and update client requirements	Continuous evaluation to improve partnership process
Responsiveness Score 1/2/3/4	Responsiveness not defined or measured	Responsiveness defined as conformance with work program agreement	Client satisfaction is measured through surveys and/or groupware sessions	Clients are informed of responsiveness scores and participate in change design
Feedback Score 1/2/3/4	No formal feedback	Client feedback is sought systematically	TG activities are realigned on the basis of feedback	Problem solving and implementation solutions are developed with clients

Technical Excellence				
Sub-categories	**Stage 1**	**Stage 2**	**Stage 3**	**Stage 4**
Technical capacity Score 1/2/3/4	Technical skills of core group assumed to meet TG members requirements	Skill mix of core group formally assessed by sector board	TG leader identifies skill gaps and learning needs of the practice	TG leader develops and implement learning programs to fill skill gaps
Quality improvement Score 1/2/3/4	TG fills knowledge gaps of the members when known and as they occur	Knowledge gaps identified trough performance metrics and peer feedback	TG develops and implements quality enhancement and knowledge sharing plans	TG anticipates potential quality issues and knowledge gaps of new transactions
Best Practice Score 1/2/3/4	Best practice not formally identified	Ideas for technical improvement shared through informal discussions	TG identifies and communicates internal best practices	TG formally benchmarks its technical knowledge against *best in class*

Resource Management				
Sub-categories	**Stage 1**	**Stage 2**	**Stage 3**	**Stage 4**
Resource allocation **Score** 1/2/3/4	Allocation and management of resources done outside of TG	TG develops process for allocation and managing resources received from sector board	TG works with sector board to effectively allocate resources to priority areas	TG is actively involved in resource allocation across the sector family to meet strategic objectives
Workload management **Score** 1/2/3/4	TG is not involved in workload issues and work assignment	Input of TG leader is occasionally sought by sector managers on work assignment	Input of TG leader is systematically sought by sector manager to manage work program	TG leaders actively participates in sector board discussion on staffing issues and workload management
Membership management **Score** 1/2/3/4	TG membership is not managed	TG members' profile is draw and shared with the community at large	TG members' profile is regularly updated to reflect new acquired knowledge	TG formally offers orientation and mentoring programs to new members

Continuous Learning				
Sub-categories	**Stage 1**	**Stage 2**	**Stage 3**	**Stage 4**
Continuous learning **Score** 1/2/3/4	TG has no involvement in the design of training programs	TG develops training programs and learning events based on skills needed in the sector as identified by sector board	TG measures effectiveness of learning and outcomes. TG meets annual training and learning targets and update them as a result of changing environment	TG learning program expanded to a multi-year horizon to acquire and/or update needed skills to meet future business requirement

EXHIBIT TEN:

Examples of Knowledge Internships

HNP-Nutrition Thematic Group

Ms. X, from GWU served as a member of the team working on an assessment of the Bank's work in nutrition. She was involved with the inventory of work and an in depth portfolio review. Her initial commitment was from July 14-August 30, 3 days per week. Given the mutual interest expressed after this initial period , the thematic group leader renewed her position through the fall semester and re-defined her scope of work.

Fiscal Sustainability and Contingent Liabilities Thematic Group

Ms. X of American University concentrated on literature search and prepared Knowledge Management briefs. Her main contribution was in gathering the information available in the Bank and best practices in the private sector on dealing with risk, and in assisting in disseminating the information to thematic group members.

Energy Markets and Reform Thematic Group

Ms. X from GWU worked principally in the areas of data/information mining, and web page buildup. She started her 20 hours per week internship in early September 1999. To obtain course-credits for her internship, she prepared a proposal and presented it to her academic advisor and the thematic group leader.

Poverty-Community Based Development Thematic Group

Ms. X from American University provided more than 250 hours of internship services to the thematic group in return for approximately $500 course fee payable to AU for 5 credit hours. She started in the summer and continued through the Fall and Spring semesters of FY2000. The thematic group budget was used to pay for the course fee.

Adult Outreach Education Thematic Group

Mr. Y of American University is working virtually from the UK on adult education research.

Globalization Thematic Group

Mr. Y of George Mason University was hired to research information and analyze institutional issues of global foreign investment. Main tasks included reviewing the World Bank and IMF documents/publications on FDI policies for developing countries, contacting agencies (e.g. embassies) to update legislative information, and help maintain and upgrade FDI-related databases. Some data manipulation and clerical/administrative work was also required.

EXHIBIT ELEVEN:

Success Stories Provided by Knowledge Interns

During their internship, Knowledge Interns are requested to evaluate if their expectations of the Knowledge Intern Program are being met and to describe how their work with the Thematic Groups is supplementing their academic studies. The following are four excerpts from intern feedback.

"I have learned a great deal about enterprise reform in Chile, Venezuela, and especially Argentina and Brazil. I have discovered academic journal articles and books dealing with not just enterprise reform, but also macroeconomic policies of structural adjustment and stabilization in Latin America. The experience has been beneficial in many ways. I have more complete knowledge of said policies and their effects, especially certain cases and not just a general picture. I was able, with assistance from my supervisor, to formulate a structure with which to evaluate the overall results of enterprise reform. It has been extremely valuable for my academic work at the university. My knowledge of development terms has also grown as has my understanding of the general development problem in Latin America and the World. I have learned how non-governmental, especially multi-lateral organizations function."

"I am creating/ collecting/storing the kiosks for the International Coral Reef Initiative FORUM. These kiosks were related to different NGO's all over the world, Government bodies and Government agencies. I have collected/created / populated links related to organizations / research institutions and colleges that are implicitly involved in Coral Reef initiative. I have populated bulletins and other information related to Coral reef. I have formed a database of all the members signed up on the ICRI FORUM website. I have created a website for all educational information on coral reef's that might be connected to the ICRI Forum website. This work is enhancing my professional experience."

"I have studies about neo-liberal reform in Latin America and its affects on the economic, social, and political situation. My previous studies were very general and lacking in specific case studies. It has been helpful to brake-down the policies of neo-liberal reform into more substantive real-life policies and evaluate their success and failure. The difficulty has been bridging the gap between the actual case studies and the general evaluations by academics. I have tried to incorporate the knowledge I have gained here at the Bank with the knowledge I had acquired at the university with other academic materials to create a study that combined or compared the two results. What have been the results of enterprise reform, in general, on the societies in question. It is an area in which I learn something new everyday, and everyday I change my mind a little. It has been a wonderful learning experience."

"The courses I took at the Graduate school helped me gain theoretical knowledge of various practices and concepts in two fields, namely, gender and development and rural development. Now my work at the Bank is helping me enormously to gain practical knowledge of how gender is so much integrated in rural development. Therefore I am happy to say that my work is extremely supplementing my academic studies. It could not have been better."

ABOUT THE CONTRIBUTOR

Michel JL. Pommier (mpommier@worldbank.org or Mpom1946@aol.com) is a Senior Advisor of the Private Sector and Infrastructure Network of the World Bank. He is responsible for the development of the Network's communities of practice. Previously, he led the change management and knowledge management initiatives of the Africa Regional Office of the World Bank. He also spearheaded the business innovation and simplification programs of the World Bank from 1992 to 1994. He now centers his research and consulting services on Knowledge Management.

Michel conducted Knowledge Management seminars for MBA students and senior executives with the Chinese Academy of Social Sciences, UNDP, the National Institute of Health, George Washington University, USAweekend magazine, the Institute of Knowledge Management and the Theseus Institute. He founded the Knowledge Internship Program that links universities to businesses. He is on the advisory board of the World Customer Service Congress. Prior to coming to the World Bank in 1980, Michel worked in France at Suez Lyonnaise, the Institute de Gestion Sociale, Jacques Borel International and in Ivory Coast at SORECI and the Ministry of Planning. In these positions, he was deeply involved in a variety of large-scale organizational change projects. In the course of his career, he also had the opportunity to work in over 25 countries in Europe, the Middle East and Africa regions. He has a Master degree from the "Ecole des Sciences Economiques et Commerciales" (ESSEC) and his background is in business administration, strategic management, team development, performance measurement and Total Quality Management.

6

BUCKMAN LABS

Two decades of evolution to the next level of organizational learning and the next generation of knowledge sharing

BACKGROUND

Buckman Laboratories is an international, family-owned, specialty-chemical company with headquarters in Memphis, Tennessee, USA. For more than fifty years, Buckman has provided the world's leading industries with a broad range of specialty chemicals for the papermaking, water treatment and leather production industries.

Buckman Laboratories was founded in 1947 during America's booming post-war years. From the beginning, Stanley Buckman, founder, established his success by understanding his customers and stopping at nothing to achieve success for them. Stanley had a Ph.D. in forestry and microbiology and was fascinated by the papermaking process. Today, the paper industry accounts for a large percentage of Buckman's business. He did this by hiring as many PhD's for research and development and for technical assistance as possible. He also put in place a policy stating that **no idea** from any associate for a new product or service would ever be discounted by the company. Every employee was important – **every contribution was valuable and every single customer was precious to the company.**

Stanley's son, Robert Buckman, took over the company after Stanley's death. Bob honored the values of his father, but he also had dreams of an international company. He had a vision of a wireless economy – when few knew about the Internet and before the web even existed. Around 1978, Bob began to realize that Buckman Laboratories could not successfully compete with a product-driven strategy. He began to steer the company toward a "customer-driven" focus. He led the company toward concentrating on markets and customers saying, "Cash flow is generated on the front line with the customers. Associates (a term he prefers to employees) build relationships of longevity and trust - face to face with the customer - one individual with another, over a significant length of time."

INTRODUCTION

A push toward an international, more diverse, decentralized company became important to Bob as he pondered the future of Buckman Laboratories. He sought to expand globally, from the seven countries in which the company was then operating. These changes meant the recruitment and training of a very much larger sales force.

At Buckman, individuals called "runners" conducted exchange of information between the sales force, technical experts, and general managers of the various companies. These information Specialists would identify those who could answer requests coming in from anywhere – generally technical questions from the paper, water, and leather industries – field the requests to the experts in Memphis, gather a comprehensive, multi-disciplinary answer, and send it to the requestor via fax or telephone. This was the late seventies and very early eighties and the requests were paper-based, requiring weeks to receive, process and return and. It sometimes took longer for overseas requests.

In the mid-eighties, Bob began his search for an electronic network that would allow associates to request information and receive answers in a much faster manner. His goal was to have communication for everyone in the international organization –**instant** communications. He wanted to communicate best practices, indeed the total knowledge of the organization, immediately. Plans for organizational learning were at the seedling stage at this point, but they would come to the forefront in the early nineties. As Bob said: **"People who are consistently exposed to new ideas and who are learning are pre-disposed to embrace change. Change is inevitable and totally unforgiving."**

ASSESSING BUCKMAN'S NEEDS

In 1987, the company implemented the IBM network for e-mail, which unfortunately resulted in a system that was not very easy for associates to use. Every time someone moved from one country to another, he or she had to use a new user name and access code for just that one country. This was the beginning of e-mail for Buckman, but it had a long way to go to reach Bob's communications goals.

To gather a body of knowledge that would become Buckman's best practices, Bob began sending out the company's most knowledgeable chemists, engineers, and biologists. These experts had many years of experience in problem solving for customers. They traveled the globe, rushing from country to country, gathering information to add to what they knew and disseminating information to those who ask for it. But, as Bob said, "These PhDs could not move fast enough because by the time they had captured and disseminated a best practice, the customers had moved on to another area." Bob concluded that it was not possible to go up the ladder to an expert and then come back down again with answers. It was too slow and lost relevant detail in the process.

> *Most companies today gather information on the front line or from some other point of direct contact with an information source, such as the business press or industry connections. This information is then passed sequentially up the line, with each recipient adding his or her perceptive wisdom to make it 'better'. Finally it reaches a guru who gives the information the benefit of his or her 'infinite wisdom'. The information then either starts to travel back down the line or is deposited into the knowledge base of the company. Thanks to this cumbersome chain of communication, by the time the information arrives at the 'guru' the original source of the information would not recognize it. So it comes as no surprise that the guru's 'wisdom' is often neither correct nor appropriate. Far too much is lost during transmission among several different people. Instead, the goal was to let the person with the need for knowledge 'speak' directly with those with the latest and best knowledge. This eliminates the confusion of including 6 to 8 people involved in transmitting the question from the first person to arrival at the 'guru.'*

There were additional issues as important as the sharing of best practices that mandated the creation of knowledge sharing and, later, distance learning:

1)   The need for communication amongst the far-flung associates of Buckman's fast-growing international company;

2)   the need for access to communication – 24/7 for associates who were rarely in the physical office;

3)   the need to increase the speed of innovation. The percentage of sales of products less than 5 years old was and is the measure of speed of innovation at Buckman.

Access to Communication

On the need for access to communication, Buckman conducted a weighted average of the amount of time that its associates were at any one time in any of our offices. It found that people are in the office less than 14 percent of their available time. During 86 percent of that time, it was not known precisely where the associates were. They might be in any one of some 90 countries, they might be at home, they might be in a hotel room. **Bob Buckman said: "It was clear to me that the office was not the place where the business of the company was taking place."** Those words were far before their time but were prophetic of the workplace of what is known so far of the 21st century. Bob also began to think about ways to access what he calls the 'unconscious knowledge' within Buckman. He believed that the greatest knowledge base in the company would not reside in a computer database, but in the heads of Buckman's associates worldwide. He decided that Buckman needed to cut the umbilical cord, referring to the mainframe mentality that kept people tied to the Memphis office for information. Questions arose regarding how to address this need: What would take its place? How would Buckman's trans-national associates stay connected? How would they share their knowledge? How can associates function anytime, anywhere, no matter what?

Initial Conclusions and a Shared Vision

The answers to these questions came from an improbable incident. In 1988, Bob Buckman injured his back severely. His physicians confined him to two weeks in bed, flat on his back. While there, with a laptop propped on his chest, he was isolated from work and his associates. It was then that Bob began to think about what it really was he wanted in a communications/ knowledge sharing system and how he would he would design it. (Bob prefers the word knowledge sharing to knowledge management, saying that it is impossible to manage knowledge.) He realized that what he wanted was information, not just for himself but for all his people. He wanted a continuous stream of knowledge about products, markets and customers. He wanted it to be easily accessible. He knew that if he could give his associates complete access to information about the company – its customers, products, services, and capabilities then **nothing could stop them**. By connecting people through a network, Bob visualized a replacement of the depth of knowledge offered in a multi-tiered hierarchy with "the breadth of knowledge that is the sum of the collective experience of the associates." As he lay in bed, pouring over the ideas for a system to enrich Buckman's capabilities to share knowledge among all members of the organization, these are the things he realized he wanted the system to possess:

- It would make it possible for people to talk to each other directly, to minimize distortion.

- It would give everyone in the company access to the company's knowledge base.

- It would allow each individual in the company to enter knowledge into the system.

- It would be available 24/7.

- It would be easy to use.

- It would communicate in whatever language is best for the user.

- It would be updated automatically; capturing questions and answers as a future knowledge base.

On his return to work, he appointed a Chief Knowledge Officer, a young organic chemist with an avid interest in computer technology, to head a task force to develop this new idea of knowledge management – information with value for action.

It was now becoming clear to the company, as it had already been clear to Bob, that Buckman needed to design and implement a plan for knowledge management. In the mid-eighties, Bob and groups from IS (called KTD – Knowledge Transfer Department at Buckman), R&D, and marketing began to meet regularly to explore the problem. With the Chief Knowledge Officer and Bob's task force, things were really taking off. It was an exciting time for everyone because it was something that very few other companies had yet come to even consider. Certainly even fewer were at the formal planning and construction stage. Of course, there were people who did not buy into the new ideas immediately. Lots of encouragement and incentives were used to help people to become involved in the knowledge-sharing program.

The biggest problem in getting people to share what they know with others was that they felt if they shared what they know online, for everyone to see, they would lose their status as an expert. That is, he/she would lose the prestige of having everyone come to him/her for information on an almost daily basis. Asking individuals to give up their personal power for the good of the organization was the first and most difficult barrier Buckman had to overcome. Even now, in a recent Time magazine (April 10, 2000) article entitled *Workplace,* these words appeared regarding today's worker: "More connected equals less control. Power over anything – even a drawer – is everything.")

Implementation of the First Knowledge Sharing Stage

The system Buckman put into place originally was very easy to use and designed for Buckman by CompuServe. There were forums for every industry – papermaking, water treatment, leather preservation and production, paint and coatings, swimming pool products, and a general news bulletin board, a breakroom bulletin board (for non-technical, non-business postings) and a human resources bulletin board. People were encouraged to read and contribute to every forum. But at the beginning, most people were afraid to give up their knowledge to an electronic bulletin board.

Bob began to put into place incentives to encourage the involvement of everyone at Buckman. He also has disincentives for those who are reluctant to share. He read all forums daily and publicly made note of those persons who shared information on a regular basis. He also sent e-mails to people who did not participate, asking them if there was a reason why they felt they did not want to contribute to the knowledge base. The message was clear to everyone: either associates participate and contribute or there would be no further promotion or recognition. Finally, the grandest gesture of all was the 'fourth wave', a resort vacation of a week at an Arizona for the top 150 users of the system. All these efforts served to create camaraderie amongst those who had bought into the idea of knowledge sharing at Buckman and incited others to share more.

Assigning laptops for every associate was another strong incentive. Undoubtedly, the most powerful incentive of all was Bob's hands-on and involved attention to the system itself. He constantly listened to input on how to make the system better and acted on those suggestions. He talked to many groups, both within Buckman and with other like-minded groups – universities, government agencies, telling his story of the importance of knowledge sharing. And that's why, in 1996, Bob was named the Father of Knowledge Management by Delphi.

One goal of implementing KM/DL took precedence over the others. In fact, it was from this goal that all other objectives grew. Buckman Laboratories wanted to provide superior, instant, personal solutions to all customers. Bob wanted all associates to know the customer's business, as well as they knew their own. He wanted them to anticipate customer process improvements and change before the customers thought of it themselves. Buckman would become the company that ensured not only profit to its customers, but customer service that makes the customers workday as trouble free as possible. Of course, the company wanted to increase sales, especially sales of new products. Buckman also needed to communicate with each other, across the world, at a very fast rate of speed. While there were other objectives for creating KM/OL systems, the main one remained customer service.

The goal was to move the decision making process and support information as fast as possible to the front line, to the people who are in direct contact with the customers on a day-to-day basis. For many accounts, Buckman also became involved with the customer's customer. Account representatives and customer representatives meet with the customer's customer: for example, the printer using paper made at a mill Buckman supplies. The vision was to develop an absolute dialogue. Buckman tries to identify not just a problem, but a wish, which takes customer service to the next level. The mill's customers, who buy paper, might wish the paper were a little brighter. Buckman would never know of these requirements if we didn't go those last few steps further - to the end-user with the mill to find out what pressures our customer experiences from his customer.

> *One Buckman associate airs his views about what organizational learning and training have meant to Buckman associates and customers. "Through OL/ Training, we want to give our people the ability to assimilate the information, draw conclusions, make assumptions and solve problems by studying cause and effect. You can only do this when you have people with enough experience to understand what sequence of events took place and how they influenced each other. Training starts with the basics – lecture sessions covering paper industry terminology, performing standard tasks and getting acquainted with paper machines. Employees are then instructed in problem-solving, cause and effect, quality control charting and identifying and documenting results. Employees can also draw information from the company's extensive information system and Distance Learning Center as well. For some of our younger people, it's tough because it's so much information, but that's the idea of training. It's never-ending – where you were yesterday won't suffice today."*

LEVERAGING NEW TECHNOLOGY

The new technology conceived by Bob Buckman and brand-named K'Netix®, the Buckman Knowledge Network, leveraged new business for the company and new opportunities for its associates. Since 1992, at the inception of K'Netix, results have dramatically increased:

> Sales per salesperson are up 51 percent

> Sales per associate are up 34 percent

The Critical Elements of Soft (knowledge-based) Products Comprehensive Product Lines are a necessary first but people with skills and knowledge to give the customer, plus providing continual training and team-based problem solving are just as important. Buckman has both kinds of products: solutions for systems (chemistries) and solutions for people (knowledge, creativity, and team problem solving). Buckman has always valued communications, both internally and with customers. The company has always don two things to satisfy our customers: understand the customer's requirements for his system and meet and exceed those requirements. Via K'Netix, there are 1300 associates online at all times to bring to bear their collective knowledge on any challenge. There is computer-based training for all technical personnel as well as self development training. There are forums for every industry Buckman serves with technical 'sources' available all over the world. All knowledge in the international company is available to any of our customers anywhere at any time. Certain services can be accessed online as follows:

Customer Service

Technical Experts

Lab Analysis

Safety and Environmental Services

Product Development Teams

Problem-Solving Workshops

Change Management Seminars

Bridging the Gaps in Implementing K'Netix® and Distance Learning

From implementation of K'Netix to sustaining the program, it has been a long journey. A great deal of change has occurred from the time the company was founded. Many who were with the company in those early years are still with the company today, even as retired associates. There are many that have been with the company for twenty years or more. Those long-term employees, of whom Buckman has many more than the typical company, were difficult to bring on board in terms of knowledge management. Buckman's associates today are highly educated. Seventy-two percent hold a bachelor's degree or higher and speak more than one language. Buckman associates currently work in or sell to customers in over 90 different countries.

Bob Buckman put in place a human support structure to help associates make use of K'Netix (the knowledge sharing system). There are Sys Ops, systems operators who act as cheerleaders, monitors and nags. They monitor the bulletin boards and make sure all questions posted are answered quickly and completely. They also archive all the information in the system so that it is available in coherent, easy to access formats. Section Leaders are assigned to every bulletin board subject. For example, the section leader for Papermaking Technologies is an expert who can help people submitting questions or looking for answers to use the system to its best advantage. Finally, Cyberians are librarians who are especially well trained in computer technology and data and information storage. They can help anybody in searching for information to find what they need through thousands of databases and other knowledge retrieval systems.

Bob Buckman built trust among all associates by reminding everyone that the company was made up of individuals, each of whom has different capabilities and potentials, all of which were necessary to the success of the company. He also let everyone know that **this is the way we will do business**.

Many of the middle managers were confused about their new roles and resisted change. They required coaching and insistence on new behaviors. Addressing cultural issues, Buckman began with global groups of forums. It then added the Foro Latino (for South America). Later, it added forums for Europe and Asia. Excellent results began in decreasing customer response time from days and weeks, to hours.

But there remained some unresolved issues, such as alignment of reward and recognition, personal accountability and standards of participation, automated data collection and development of measures. As mentioned before, the Fourth Wave retreat gave the top 150 users recognition and reward. Later, Bob made sure that users of the system were invited to high profile meetings to look at issues confronting the company and many were promoted over time.

In 1996, Steve Buckman took over the day to day activities of running the company while Bob dedicated himself to expanding Buckman's knowledge sharing efforts and to building the Bulab Learning Center. In 1997, Bob officially opened the Bulab Learning Center. The Learning Center offered on-line learning, in five languages. Four areas of learning were offered: academic, business, industry and Buckman specific, with in-house and external development. The Learning Center grew to include classes in:

Technical Offerings

General Chemistry Primer
Introduction to Papermaking Technologies
Introduction to the Paper Machine
Introduction to Water Chemistry
Introduction to Leathermaking
BLC (British Leather Council) Basic Training
Introduction to Papermaking Technologies Chemistries
Applications Guide for Papermaking
Papermaking Boilout Techniques
Creped Products Overview
Field Lab Techniques CBTs (computer based training)
Introduction to Profitability
Profitability Primer
Statistical Process Control
U.S. Regulatory Affairs
Planning
Analysis
Financial Management
Profitability Primer
Market Profitability Analysis
Personal Productivity
Problem Solving
Effective Personal Productivity
Market Profitability
Management
Problem Definition
Seven Habits of Highly Effective People
AMA Association Seminars
Behavioral Interviewing
Coaching and Counseling
Dale Carnegie Training
Delegation
Effective Personal Productivity

Effective Writing
Feedback and Reinforcement
Financial Management
Leadership Situations
Managing Meetings
Objective Settings
Performance
Troubleshooting
Planning
Problem Solving
Project Management
Relationship Strategies
Sensitivity
Time Management

General Education – **online degrees from, among others:**
University of Phoenix
Lehigh University
ISIM University
The University of Asia
The University of Memphis

(All the above listings are partial only)

Associates dedicated solely to the development of the Learning Center are - by title:

Vice President, Learning Center
Manager, Technical Design
Manager, Systems Integration
Manager, Instructional Design
3 Instructional Materials Developers
Instructional Technologist
Senior Learning and Knowledge E-product Specialist
Business Manager
Supervisor Translations
3 Translators

The above list, though not at all comprehensive, shows the degree of progress made in a short amount of time in building the Bulab Learning Center.

THE BULAB LEARNING CENTER

Bob was much more than marginally involved in launching Buckman's variety of organizational learning – the BLC (Bulab Learning Center). He thought, planned, and examined all possible angles of the development of an onsite, online learning center through which all Buckman associates could participate. Bob was the encouragement behind the involvement of every Buckman associate who decided to take part in growing the company's knowledge through the help of the Bulab Learning Center. Most importantly, Bob championed partnerships between Buckman and other universities.

Faced with the challenges of providing continuous online learning for all associates, combined with encouraging them to share all that they learn both technical and otherwise, Buckman began experimenting with Lotus's novel educational product – Learning Space™. This experimentation led to the creation of the company's own multi-lingual, on-line learning center, the Bulab Learning Center. The mission statement for the Learning Center is as follows:

> *"The Bulab Learning Center will support the company mission by delivering and facilitating world-class training and educational opportunities, when and where it is needed. We will empower associates to manage their personal and career development, create competitive market advantage and engage customers with our products and services."*

Training and educational programs of any kind exist only to add value to sales, marketing, and business processes. In other words, they must, in a measurable way, increase customer satisfaction, sales and profitability. To realize the true value proposition of globally co-ordinated training and global knowledge standards, investments and returns on those investments should be measured, tracked, periodically benchmarked and evaluated. The only way to sustain this competitive advantage is proactive stewardship of the knowledge base residing with the company's associates.

Training expenses continue to outpace the inflation rate and are becoming an increasing burden on many a firm's overhead expenses. At Buckman, costs were measured concerning the greatest costs for training. The company found that lodging, meals, compensation for the instructor, the room, lost opportunities associated with being out of the office, equipment, and other supplies needed for the training event were by far the biggest costs associated with training. International associate expenses were even greater.

The greatest costs in the process, however, did not appear on the ledger. As the vice president of the learning center, Sheldon Ellis stated: 'Absence from the office, absence from home and hearth (which can be very stressful for some employees – single mothers, new parents, etc.) are far larger drains on the cash flow of the company. This is not to say that training is a poor investment, but rather that it must be scrutinized to provide value to the company. Our cost of training with the learning center has decreased from $1,000 per hour of learning to $25 - $40.

Bob decided to try the concept of a virtual university to provide cost-effective alternative to traditional training events, among other good reasons. Virtual learning centers can increase the value of learning events by shifting the more rudimentary
learning or knowledge to a self-paced module completed before attending class. Technology can also shift the synchronous classroom to the virtual world. Learning activities can be delivered synchronously through video-conferencing or via the computer desktop. Other content may lend itself to delivery as self-paced modules or asynchronous instructor-facilitated learning events using the various tools available today.

The challenge at Buckman proves to be the need to deliver a greater breadth and quantity of quality learning experiences to the associates and to do it cost-effectively. This challenge is becoming increasingly common as Buckman strives to unleash the potential of our collective intellectual assets and develop a sustainable, competitive, market advantage. Feedback and buy-in by senior management at this stage are crucial to the success of the program. Any effort will require significant redirection of human resources and capital. At Buckman, the Learning Center has an annual budget that equals 3% of the total budget.

> *Buckman has always had in place an extraordinary tuition plan for its associates and their dependents. Many children of parents who work in the mailroom or in house-keeping have been able to attend college through the educational program their parents were able to take advantage of for them at Buckman. Dependents are insured $135.00 per semester hour plus one-half of additional costs) In some parts of the world Buckman sponsors schools for our associates' children.*

There are two important elements of the Buckman program. One is a centralized learning effort, the majority of which is distance learning. Regardless of location, associates have completely free access to a wide range of training and educational programs. The courses range from online courses on web design to long distance Ph.D. programs. Buckman's learning system delivers training specific to the organization and the industries we support. Such training is unavailable elsewhere due to its extremely specific nature. Associates have virtually unlimited access to on-line training (currently $1,300 per associate per year) and tuition plans for distance education are prepaid.

The other important part of Buckman's program is K'Netix®, which enables associates to share knowledge through experience and expertise. Again, as our associates are dispersed all over the world and the system is electronically enabled, associates help each others to solve problems for customers, answer technical questions and share information of interest. Finally, there is an up-to-the-minute electronic library.

Buckman's knowledge sharing system has been influenced positively through the encouragement of the CEO. Anytime the CEO is deeply involved in any project, it is clear that the project will succeed. Bob had made it clear that this was going to be the way the company did business.

EVALUATION

The learning system was marked by a gradual, measured, introduction into the corporate culture. An initial program was put together in two months. BLC (Bulab Learning Center) associates, in many cases, had to write the book on distance learning because few other companies were exploring this area. Over the years, both the content and the technical aspects of the system have expanded greatly.

For the knowledge sharing system, access to the expertise of others in the company is the strongest element of the program. For the learning effort, the strongest impact is that **everyone** has an almost unlimited opportunity to learn whatever he or she chooses. Continuous learners are extremely valuable in today's world.

One reason the program is unique to our associates is that, during its design, a foremost principle was ease of use. Buckman's systems were designed to be as easy as possible for use by any associate. The cornerstone of successful learning at Buckman is based on the idea that the company sells not only chemicals, but also knowledge and creativity. Buckman is akin to a consulting company with one exception: the consulting is free. Buckman provides solutions, increases productivity and profitability for customers.

There are two aspects of the success of our knowledge sharing and distance learning. First, it benefits our customers by giving them what they need. Second, each one of the company's associates can use knowledge sharing and distance learning to help increase Buckman's success in the marketplace by working on a common goal – customer satisfaction.

Finally, many obstacles that other companies have dealt with are not issues that Buckman has encountered. There were no budgetary constraints because both the knowledge sharing program and the distance learning initiative were led by Bob Buckman. No time/management constraints occurred for the same reason. Bob was supportive of any reasonable suggestion from those who were specialists in technology, learning, culture, etc. He understands and places great value on the intellectual capital of our company.

The most important measurement of return on investment from knowledge sharing and distance learning at Buckman has been the measure of increased sales of products less than 5 years old. This is how innovation is measured in Buckman's industries and we have had extraordinary success in the past few years. The measurement of success for distance learning is: has there been a rise in intellectual capital and a sharing of new learning throughout the company? The answer at Buckman is strongly affirmative.

THE FUTURE

When the CEO of a company is a visionary in the area of knowledge sharing (management) and distance learning (organizational learning) as well as the programs most vocal and enthusiastic supporter, it is hard to do anything other than succeed. The road to that success has been vastly enjoyable and rewarding for associates at Buckman, more so than any other company initiative undertaken.

Buckman customers are now including training and e-learning initiatives in their requests for proposals. The Bulab Learning Center is becoming a profit center. Longer term and deeper customer relationships have become common.

2000 and Beyond: Implementing Virtual teams Implementing Communities of practices taking ownership of processes and areas of knowledge Implementing Extranet development for greater depth of contact and virtual relationship management

EXHIBIT ONE: COST OF LEARNING PER EMPLOYEE

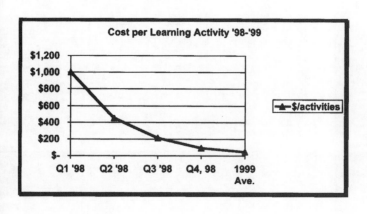

EXHIBIT TWO: NEW PRODUCT SALES

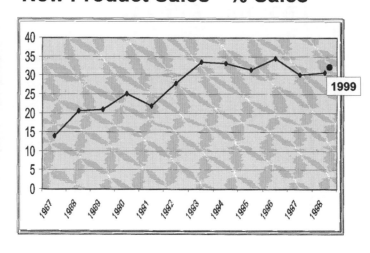

EXHIBIT THREE: RETURN ON INVESTMENT IN LEARNING

Highlights

♦ **$ per delivered hour of learning**
  – **From a high of $1,000 to $25-40/hour**

Cost to Deliver an Hour of Learning
'97 through '99

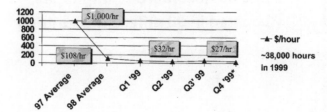

EXHIBIT FOUR: BUCKMAN EMPLOYEE PROFILE

Buckman Laboratories International, Inc.

Our Associates

- ◆ **1200+ Associates**
  - **– 400 in Memphis**
- ◆ **72 percent have College or University degrees**
- ◆ **Speak 15+ different languages**
- ◆ **Located in 90 different countries**

EXHIBIT FIVE: BUCKMAN PHILOSOPHY

Buckman Laboratories International, Inc.

Becoming a Knowledge-Sharing Organization

- ◆ We have to achieve innovation with the Customer faster than anybody else anytime/anywhere.
- ◆ We have to move the entire organization to wherever it is needed at any point in time.

EXHIBIT SIX: SAMPLE KNOWLEDGE FORUM

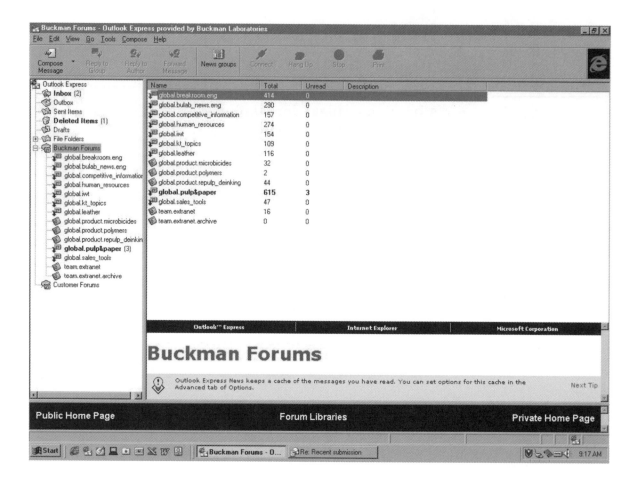

ABOUT THE CONTRIBUTOR

Sheldon Ellis is the vice president of the Bulab Learning Center and was instrumental in the early days of Bob Buckman's development of Buckman's knowledge sharing initiative. He was later charged by Bob to create a virtual learning center that could serve the training and educational needs of Buckman's 1300 associates scattered around six continents and working in over 100 countries. Today, the Buckman Learning Center has been recognized for its innovation and is a frequent 'Best Practice' site visit. A recent article he wrote for the *Journal of Knowledge Management* was awarded the "Literati Award" for quality.

Sheldon came to Buckman Laboratories in 1989 as a field sales associate in the Agrichemicals and Wood Technologies Division. Prior to coming to Buckman, he was a weed ecologist with the Colorado State Extension Service. He has held positions at Buckman in sales and was the Product Development Manager for Agriculture and Wood Technologies. Sheldon has been involved in a variety of company-wide knowledge management initiatives including co-chairing Buckman's first company-wide knowledge management initiatives including co-chairing Buckman's first company-wide openspace meeting. He has a B.S. in Soil Science from Colorado State University and a Masters in Business Administration from the University of Memphis.

Any questions regarding this chapter and its content should be directed to:
Sheldon Ellis
800 Buckman x56468
msellis@buckman.com
http://www.knowledge-nurture.com
http://www.buckman.com

7

SHELL OIL COMPANY

Shell's double-knit organization uses cross-functional teams to achieve operational excellence and learning communities to share knowledge across teams.

How Learning Communities Steward Knowledge: Shell Oil Company[1]

Knowledge-intensive organizations often swing between functional and product (or process) organizational structures. Functional structures deepen discipline expertise. Product or process structures improve efficiency. Of course, most knowledge organizations need both discipline expertise and efficiency. One of the common uses of knowledge management is to compensate for the limitations of organizational structure, providing a link between people where structure inhibits their access to each other. Shell Oil Company's Deepwater Division, located in New Orleans, has developed an organizational structure that promotes both expertise and efficiency without the drawbacks of a matrix organization. The Shell organization uses operating teams for efficiently exploring and developing deepwater oil and gas fields. Spanning these operating teams, learning communities deepen technical competence within disciplines. This approach to knowledge management is grounded in the idea that sharing tacit, fuzzy knowledge requires dialogue and collaborative thinking (McDermott, 1999a).

THE BUSINESS/TECHNICAL CHALLENGE

Deepwater Exploration

Deepwater is one of the last true exploration and production frontiers for the oil & gas industry. Major oil companies continue to find large (billion barrel plus) oil deposits across the globe. In the late 1980s, Shell Oil Co. made several large discoveries in the Gulf of Mexico. But developing these finds was a gamble. The technology for exploring and developing prospects in over 1,500 feet of water had not yet been developed and tested. Developing systems that could produce oil in water that deep would be expensive, perhaps a billion dollars or more.

Shell started deepwater (DW) exploration in the Gulf of Mexico in 1984. Its first DW Tension Leg Platform (TLP) began operation in 1994. Anchored to the ocean floor by high-tension wires, Auger, one of Shell's first large TLP floats on the surface, gently rocking with the waves, as it pumps 90 thousand barrels of oil and 300 million cubic feet of gas a day. As Auger was being developed, teams of scientists and engineers began exploring other prospects in the Gulf to see if they held enough developable reserves to justify additional deepwater platforms.

Figure 1: Tension Leg Platform (TLP) (Ram Powell)

Shifting Organizational Structures

Functional organization with project teams. Shell's Deepwater Division started as a traditional functional organization, divided into two main divisions: exploration and production. Each division was divided into departments of functional specialists. Multi-disciplinary project teams crossed functions for exploring and developing individual geographical areas. For a billion-dollar project, it was important that exploration, whose responsibility it was to appraise the size of the discovery, work closely with production, whose job it was to develop the project. This structure — functional departments crossed by multidisciplinary teams — served Shell well for its early exploration. However, it suffered from many of the common problems of functional organizations. Sharing knowledge between departments was difficult and the handoffs between departments were slow and complex. Sharing perspective between departments was even more difficult. Each discipline tended to view the project from its own perspective. This structure left a gap between the traditional exploration and production roles. Exploration focused on finding. Production on bringing the hydrocarbons to the surface. But deepwater fields are complex and mistakes costly. The organization needed to blend the perspectives of exploration and production.

Figure 2: Shell's 1980's Functional Organization Chart

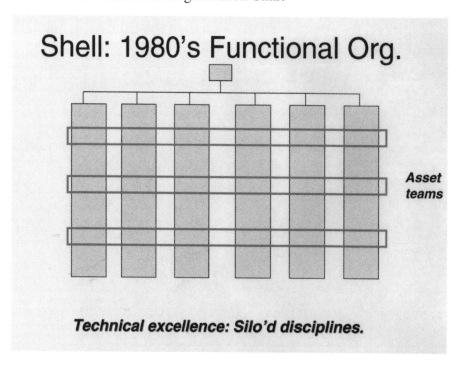

By 1994, Shell had developed two deepwater prospects, Auger and Tahoe. As the organization embarked on developing more sites, it realized that there was much inefficiency in the development process, adding to the cost and cycle time of development. For example, Exploration Department maps of a prospect were drawn to help them analyze whether a prospect was worthwhile developing. When they handed the project off to Production, the Production Department often needed to reanalyze and redraw the maps to help them figure out how to develop the prospect. Shell's managers realized that as other oil companies entered deepwater exploration, competition would increase the pressure to reduce cost. They also realized that the organization needed to be robust even with a drop in oil prices.

Rethinking the organization. Shell faced a problem that many technical companies face. How do you shift from a predominantly technical focus to a business focus without loosing your technical edge? Technical excellence was critical to develop the capacity for deepwater exploration. It continued to be critical for ongoing success in deepwater. But the inefficiencies of a functional organization led the company in 1994 to convene a design team to rethink the organizational structure. The team composed of people from different parts and levels in the organization so all perspectives could be considered. It took a "whole system" perspective, considering how the departments worked together at each stage of the process.

The Horizontal Organization

The design team recommended reorganizing the company into three main divisions, instead of two: exploration, development and production. This made it possible to make cross-functional teams the main organizational structure within each division. The new cross-disciplinary teams were designed around geographic areas, called assets. These teams contained people from all the disciplines regularly needed for the team to complete its work. Scientists and engineers from the core disciplines required to develop an asset were housed together and reported to the same general manager. They moved through each stage of the work process (find it, develop it, and produce it) as the asset developed, adding and /or subtracting staff and disciplines as the needs of project demanded. Each asset operated as a separate profit and loss center, with full responsibility for both sound scientific analysis and financial return.

Figure 3: 1994 Shell Team Organization Chart

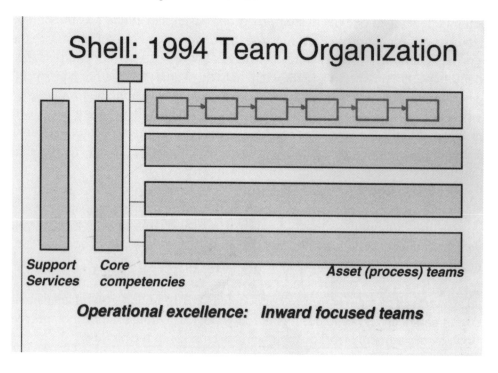

Making cross-functional teams the core of the organization changed the way people worked. With adjacent offices, the scientist and engineers could understand the full spectrum of issues in exploring and developing the site. This made much tighter integration between disciplines possible. Each discipline could more easily consider the needs of other disciplines as they conducted their work. The geologist learned more about the questions the reservoir engineer was trying to answer and was able to offer assistance. The reservoir engineer learned more about the uncertainties that were inherent in the geoscientists' maps and could incorporate that uncertainty into the development planning activity. Shared goals helped scientists and engineers better understand the financial as well as the scientific implications of the tools and approaches they used and encouraged them to choose tools that that could shorten overall cycle time and reduce costs. By working on issues together, each team member had to balance his objectives against the goals and constraints of his colleagues.

The new organization also had two staff groups to support the asset teams. Support services includes administration, finance, human resources, and information technology. Centralized support services could apply their resource where most needed. The second central group, "core competencies," served several functions. It housed people with very specialized expertise who were needed on many teams. It also served as a link between the research lab and the asset teams, providing a central clearinghouse for research and technical service projects. Finally, the new organization housed geoscience information about the Gulf of Mexico that Shell considers proprietary.

The new organization achieved its goal of integrating knowledge across disciplines. Scientists and engineers were better able to understand the technical impact of their decisions on other disciplines and the financial impact of their decisions on the project altogether. In this give-and-take environment, team members were able to change their criteria for what level of detail in analysis was good enough, what analytic tools to use, and how to integrate their findings with those of people from other disciplines.

The new organization made it more difficult to share knowledge within disciplines. For example, a petrophysicist, located at the same end of the hall with scientists and engineers from other disciplines could informally stop by and discuss the timing of key aspects of the project, the interpretation of results, or the logic behind a conclusion. However, the petrophysicists missed some parts of the old functional organization. When located with other petrophysicists, they could walk down the hall to discuss an interpretation with a colleague, find out how well a new analytic tool really worked, or hear about emerging issues in her field. In the new organization there was frequently only one petrophysicist on an asset team. To discuss an interpretation with a colleague, that petrophysicist often needed to find a colleague several floors away or make an appointment for an informal discussion. The new organization eliminated the old functional silos. But made teams into silos.

Assessing the horizontal organization. The organizational design team anticipated this difficulty and commissioned a follow-up team to address it. Using individual interviews, a survey, and focus groups this follow-up team researched the problems people had finding and using knowledge. They found five key problems.

1.   There was no standard process in place for sharing knowledge between teams. As one project engineer said, "There are a lot of things we should share between teams but we have different formats: electronic, hard copy, etc. Each project does it its own way. To retrieve information you have to go through many applications and steps. It should be a simple process."

2.   Since staff from the same discipline did not have easy daily access to each other, they spent less time talking about how they did their work. As a result, they were slower to find out about and adapt practices developed by their peers on other teams.

3.   There was no time for documenting built into work processes. Team members did not know what level of documentation would be useful to other teams so they were reluctant to take the time to document. The focus of management was on improving efficiency. Documenting was considered a luxury. Team leaders had little incentive to enforce documentation since documentation benefited other teams. As one engineer said, "Shell people are willing to share information, but since proper documentation has a perceived low value, generally it is up to the individual to take the time."

4.　　Computerization had changed the way people documented. The documentation that did exist did not contain the thought process the person used. Frequently the logic of another scientist's or engineer's thinking was more important than the output of their thinking. For example, a structural engineer could look up the design another engineer developed for part of a platform. How they calculated the stresses and why they put it together in that specific way was not in the electronic documentation. In the past, engineers' project files had been the main source of documentation and contained the notes the engineer made. Now people saw the computer as the final resting place of information and didn't put their raw notes in the file. "You could look through the project file and see what the engineer was thinking," said one engineer. "Now we don't have them." Computerization also diminished the role of the graphics department as a central repository. Now the only files were in each individual's desktop — fragmented and disorganized.

5.　　The documentation that did exist was scattered in many different file rooms, hard to catalogue or find. In the new structure there were many different file rooms. People from other teams couldn't find information they needed or the person responsible for it.

As a result of these problems, staff members spent far too much time looking for information from other teams or past projects. Some estimated that this accounted for 40% of their time. Whether the information was in someone's head or a document, there was no easy way for people to find the person or document and pull the information they needed from it.

The very thing that makes teams work well—common goals, shared focus, physical proximity, working rapport—led to the isolation of the professional staff and a myopic focus on team needs. As one team member said, "The organization of the project teams gets in the way. In the old days you would go have coffee with people in your discipline. Now it is not convenient to connect with people in your discipline."

The design team considered requiring more extensive documentation and project post-mortems. But both of these approaches push information out from one team to another. Neither addressed the complexity of information people really needed to learn from each other. An approach that would allow people to pull the right information from the right source at the right time was needed.

Push and Pull Knowledge Sharing

One way to think about the difficulties of using lessons learned, whether in a report or post-mortem meeting, is that they are usually written and distributed with a push philosophy. That is, they are usually constructed from the point of view of the team that learned the lesson, not the point of view of the potential user. At project post-mortems, for example, people are likely to hear some insights they can apply immediately, many insights they already know, and many insights they do not yet need to apply. Since their knowledge and focus are often driven by the current stage of their project, they frequently can only ask good, deep probing questions about the insights related to that stage. So the depth of understanding they can get is also often limited. As a result the timing, form and level of detail of the insights are often not quite what the users of the insights need.

A pull system for learning is very different. It is more like just-in-time manufacturing where you only make the next item when the next person in the line needs it. For sharing lessons learned, that means you share your insights when someone on another team needs it. In a pull system, questions rather than meetings drive lessons learned. The topics discussed are determined by what people need to hear. The user of the information decides the level of detail of the discussion. In this system, you know that lessons learned would never fall on deaf ears because unless someone asked for them they would never be produced. Documentation is tuned to the exact level the person who needed the insight required.

In a pull system relevance the key to producing lessons learned. It eliminates unused information and determines the exact level and focus of documentation. While it can't insure that lessons learned will be used, it dramatically increases the likelihood that they will be since the value of the lesson is already built into the request for it.

THE DOUBLE-KNIT ORGANIZATION

Communities Link Across Teams

The design team created a five-pronged approach to sharing knowledge between teams. The heart of this approach was a set of learning communities formed around topics important to both the business and community members. Each community would be responsible for managing the knowledge in its topic area. To support these communities the design team created a community support team and a set of web tools for organizing and storing documents.

Learning Communities

Spanning across the teams, communities of people who share a common discipline or interest would meet, discuss their work, and decide what to document. While the asset teams focused on generating output, the communities would focus on sharing ideas and insights. Since the communities would be formed around technical topics, their members would know what information was useful, what they should document, what help other community members really needed. While the teams' boundaries were clearly defined, the communities would be open. People could come and go as their interest dictated. While team membership was defined, community membership would be voluntary, letting the passion of participants determine their level of participation. While the teams were responsible for deliverables, the communities would be responsible for sharing learning and ideas. Since the concern that first sparked this was preserving technical excellence, the design team decided that the first learning communities should focus on technical topics, like geology, petrophysics, and reservoir engineering. This would also help implementation because the relevance of the communities was easily apparent. This new structure would knit the organization in two ways. First, asset teams would focus on outputs, and second, learning communities would focus on sharing knowledge (McDermott, 1996). As one community member said, "With so many meetings about things not related to my day to day work, it is great to go to a meeting to talk about rocks."

These communities, similar to what others have called "communities of practice (Wenger, 1998; McDermott 1999b), would:

• Conduct regular forums for community members to think together, share ideas, help each other. The design team expected that these forums would stimulate innovation and build collaboration across teams.

• Systematically find and collect best practices both inside and outside the organization, organizing that information in a meaningful way and quickly disseminating it through community forums and knowledge bases.

• Create and manage its own knowledge base within and across skill groups. Each community was expected to decide what to document and the level of detail in the docu ments. The community would also be responsible for organizing and "evergreening" the information contained in it.

•   A knowledge community infrastructure team (KNIT). This team's role was to steer the knowledge management process and support the startup and ongoing development of the communities. The team consisted of organization development specialists and technical specialists in web design and documentation. The support team helped communities get started in a two-day kick off workshop. Support team members also coached community coordinators on their role and helped the coordinators deal with the changing issues throughout the community's life.

Figure 4: Shell's 1999 Double-Knit Organization Chart

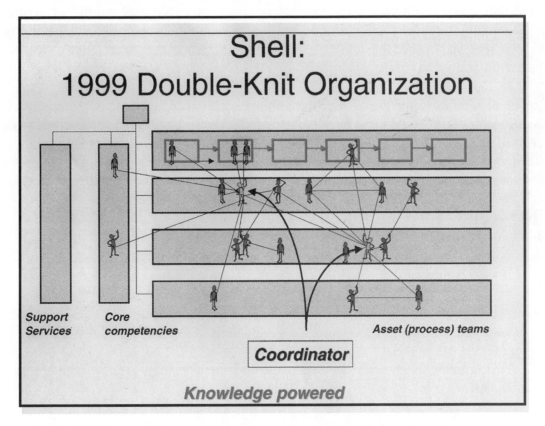

Tools

The support teams staff developed tools for the community to manage knowledge. These varied from simple web pages to more complex tools specifically designed for the community. For example, one small, well-connected group of geologists needed a way to sort through which tools they needed to use to analyze whether oil was trapped in a structure. Trap analysis is one of the most difficult and risky elements of oil exploration and Shell's research lab had developed many tools to help with it. The KNIT helped this group develop a web site that organized the tools according to the steps in the geologists' work process. The site provided criteria for deciding which tools to use and which ones worked well together. Direct links to the tool and to people who could help direct someone in its use were also listed on the site.

Community Sponsors

Each community would also have a leadership team sponsor. While generally not an active member of the community, this person legitimated the community, helped protect it during its development, and insured that it focused on issues important to the organization as well as community members.

The intent of this structure was to give the communities a wide latitude to determine what specific topics they would focus on, what knowledge they would share, what people would be involved and what they would do to enforce the use of knowledge. Rather than pushing knowledge out in documents or lessons learned meetings, this approach would pull just the right knowledge from one team to another, at just the right time, in just the right level of detail.

"Big Rules" for Community Operation

To coordinate between communities, the design team developed a set of "big rules," or principles, for the communities.

1.   Each community should own and manage its own knowledge. The design team would not dictate what knowledge the community should share.

2.   The communities should decide what to document and how to enforce and evergreen documentation.

3.   Each community should have a coordinator to facilitate contact and organize the community's knowledge.

4.   Community members should be able to get information, insights, and ideas about the community's topic either from the community coordinator or directly from other community members. The coordinator was intended to facilitate knowledge sharing, not to be an intermediary or block.

5.   The communities should use a peer review process to insure the quality of individual work. Insuring quality was one of the drivers of this double-knit organization. Since the asset team leaders did not necessarily have the discipline expertise to assess the quality of individual community members' work, the learning communities would be a resource for discipline members to get informal, technical advice and review.

How a Learning Community Really Works

Although each learning community could determine its own method for sharing knowledge, most follow an approach first developed by the petrophysics group. The petrophysics community links across teams in five different ways.

1.   First, the community holds a weekly agenda-less meetings where anyone can get input on any topic. These are very different from most agenda-driven meetings in the organization. They emphasize open dialogue for exploring issues, with no pressure to come to resolution. Members are encouraged to discuss real problems they currently face and not to use the community as a rubber stamp for analyses and decisions they have already made.   These are the public events of the community.

2.   To share knowledge that is more explicit the community hosts formal presentations by vendors on new technology.

3.   To ensure their data is consistent and widely available, the community has a data library that lets them compare data from many different sites.

4.   To ensure that informal help is available at any time, one of their members acts as a community coordinator. The community coordinator's most visible community work involves facilitating the community's meetings. The majority of this person's work is in the private space of the community, making one-on-one contact with community members. The community coordinator talks to people between meetings to ensure that the topics people bring to the meetings are interesting to other community members and that the right people for a good discussion are present. Most importantly, the coordinator maintains relationships among members, connecting people with common interests or finding people who can serve as resources for particular daily work problems.

5.   Finally, to educate people entering petrophysics from other disciplines, the community manages a mentor program. While the organization already had a mentoring program, most of the mentoring burden fell to a few senior petrophysicists. When the community took on mentorship, they were able to distribute the work of mentoring more evenly among the staff.

One of the key qualifiers of the success of the petrophysicists' community work is the tone of their meetings. They openly discuss alternate interpretations of their data, new ideas and approaches, and new technology, without incurring the obligation to act on each other's ideas.

Their meetings set a tone of thinking and reflection. While other communities vary in the details of how they work, most set a similar reflective tone.

The Public and Private Space of Community

One of the keys to community building is balancing public community events with private one-on-one relationships. In fact, the greatest error of most community organizers and coordinators is to focus too much on the public space and not enough on the private.

The Public Space of Community

Most communities have some visible, public events where community members gather - either face-to-face or electronically - to exchange tips, solve problems, or explore new ideas, tools, and techniques. These events are public in that they are open to all community members, though they are often closed to people outside the community. Public community events are good forums for seeking help with problems, finding out who is working on what, and sharing best practices. But they also serve a ritualistic purpose. People can tangibly experience being part of the community. They can see the level of sophistication the community brings to a technical discussion, how it rallies around key principles, or the influence it has in the organization. A community's public events help make it visible and present.

The Private Space of Community

Communities are formed from a network of individual relationships. While a sense of whole community identity is important, most people build relationships with other individuals more readily and more strongly in one-on-one exchanges. Coordinators call members, ask them to submit ideas or connect them directly with others. Members call each other to discuss problems and ideas. In the early stages of community development, these relationships are usually based on helping each other. In the latter life of a community, they are often based on mutual sense of responsibility for stewarding a practice. This typically involves creating standards, influencing the organization, and educating new community members. Capturing gems from these exchanges is difficult. Either the coordinator needs to follow up or the people involved need to document their gems for the community as a whole.

These dimensions are related. When people enter the public space having shared problems and ideas one-on-one, the public events are much richer. Well-orchestrated, lively public events can create more one-on-one connections. As one coordinator said, "I like to see who walks out of the room together, who hangs around and talks. The more new connections I see, the better the meeting was." Effectively coordinating a community involves working in both of these spaces simultaneously so they can mutually support each other.

"LEARN-AS-WE-GO" IMPLEMENTATION

Because learning communities were new to Shell, the design team decided to begin implementation slowly and quietly, learning about how to make communities work as they went. Of course, communities of people sharing ideas and insights is part of the underground "informal structure" of any organization. It was certainly present at Shell as well. But making communities part of the "official organization" was new. The design team was not sure how much formal responsibilities the communities could accept and still retain their informal, voluntary character. To learn about this new element of organizational structure, the design team recommended a "learn-as-we-go" implementation strategy. This involved building communities one at a time, learning what worked to make the communities vibrant and alive, monitoring costs and benefits, and revising the implementation strategy as they learned. There was a constant health check on the communities as the knowledge community infrastructure team (KNIT - the group commissioned to support learning communities) learned about community development. The design team gave the KNIT a three-year window to get the communities established before the organization would officially assessed the communities' performance and contribution. The team was confident that the data collection and reflection in the "learn-as-we-go" strategy would insure that the communities did not go off in unproductive directions during that period.

This approach fit well with the culture of the Deepwater organization. During the 1990s many corporate initiatives had passed through the organization. Some, like team management and understanding the business dimensions of deepwater exploration, were inspired by the reorganization. Others, like work process analysis, formal decision analysis, training in "Seven Habits of Highly Effective People (Covey, 1997)," and skills assessment, were corporately sponsored. Whatever their source, many staff members felt like they were suffering "initiative overload," attending far too many meetings that had little to do with their everyday work. The quiet, "learn-as-we-go" implementation approach helped keep learning communities from feeling like another initiative.

As the learning communities grew, the "learn-as-we-go" turned into a four-step process. When the KNIT formulated its "learn-as-we-go" strategy, they could not have anticipated what these steps would be. They unfolded as the KNIT responded to the demands for community building and the leadership teams' recognition of their value to the organization. The steps were:

1. establish learning pilots,

2. systematize community development,

3. institutionalize learning communities as part of the organizational structure,

4. help learning communities take responsibility for stewarding the knowledge of their

discipline.

Establish Learning Pilots

In 1997, the KNIT received seed money to start up to nine new learning communities. Their meetings set a tone of thinking and reflection. While other communities vary in the details of how they work, most set a similar reflective tone. Their meetings set a tone of thinking and reflection. While other communities vary in the details of how they work, most set a similar reflective tone. In order to concentrate their attention, they decided not to make a big fanfare about learning communities. Instead, the KNIT responded to groups that requested their help. The team focused their efforts where there was energy for community building. During 1997, fifteen groups asked the KNIT to help them form into communities. By the end of the year, seven of these were up and running and word was beginning to spread throughout the organization that communities were valuable ways to learn from peers and to get help on difficult problems. In 1998 many more groups requested their help.

The KNIT learned about community development as it implemented them. The primary vehicle of learning was to observe community meetings and coach coordinators. This not only helped the coordinators with their new role. It also helped the KNIT understand what makes a community effective day-to-day. In the course of the early implementation, the KNIT discovered many insights which later came to seem obvious. For example, one community was led by a "world's leading technical expert." The expert was terrible at facilitating the community because he couldn't resist the temptation to answer every community member's question himself. As a result, he failed to connect people with each other. Another coordinator was reluctant to go to members' offices and informally chat about their current technical issues. He waited in his office for community members to call. These early failures helped the KNIT discover the characteristics required for a good coordinator.

The KNIT also learned about managing community meetings so they are vibrant and useful to participants. For example, they discovered that discussions of real live current problems were much more engaging and useful for sharing knowledge than presentations of accomplishments. These discussions were most useful if the coordinator lightly structured them, asking participants to share their observations, then to explain the logic or assumptions of their observations. These early learnings helped the KNIT understand what it took to make a community effective.

Planned Spontaneity

Community discussions are often very informal. Typically, a member poses a question or problem he or she is having and the group makes observations and suggestions. The discussions are lightly facilitated by a coordinator who helps people explicate the logic or assumptions behind their observations. When a
speaker seems to be defensive and closed to the ideas of others, the coordinator reminds him that the purpose of the meeting is to surface many different ideas. When the group seems to be "grilling" a speaker, asking him many detailed questions without offering any alternate ideas, he reminds them that they owe the
speaker some ideas of their own. He then suggests they shift focus and discuss other ways the speaker could approach the problem. These community discussions seem very spontaneous, but this spontaneity is more planful than it appears.

Between meetings the coordinator "walks the halls." He drops in on community members, follows up on meeting items, asks people about hot issues to discuss at the next meeting, and informally lets others know about upcoming meeting topics he would particularly like them to participate in. These informal one-on-one discussions insure that the 'spontaneous" topics raised at the next meeting are truly valuable to the community and that the people attending will have something useful to add. During this early stage of community development, most communities focus almost entirely on this sort of interaction, where they help each other think through and solve problems.

During 1997, several of the most successful communities developed a rhythm. They settled into a routine of regular 7:30 AM meetings, early enough that they did not conflict with other organizational meetings. Several participants selected with meeting on different days of the week for communities in adjacent disciplines so some members could attend both. A core group of participants emerged who attended most of the meetings and contributed regularly. Several communities - Turbodudes, Petrophysics, Chemical Engineering — identified areas where they felt it would be useful to explore underlying issues more deeply and develop guidelines. The communities commissioned a taskforce of community members to develop the guidelines and report them back to the community as a whole. As they settled in, they discovered what knowledge was really useful to share, what meeting format really worked for them, and what issues in their discipline needed greater attention. Members of the research lab participated regularly in community meetings. They found the communities were good vehicles for identifying areas where they could provide technical service and short-term applications driven research. Members of the technical training department also participated in community meetings. They found that the communities were a good place to learn about emerging training needs.

Community Places

"Great civilizations, like great cities, share a common feature. Evolving within them, and critical to their growth and refinement, are distinctive informal public gathering places." - Ray Oldenberg

Neighborhood places. People who live in small towns or city neighborhoods know that community happen in places. Often, their best friends and favorite companions aren't their immediate neighbors or workmates, but they can run into friends and companions at the informal public gathering places of the community. People go to the neighborhood bar, café, park, or diner in order to see and talk with members of their local community. They meet them in the "accidental" places of the community; beauty parlors, corner grocery stores, bookstores, laundromats, drug stores, or the post office. As they go about the business of life, they are in regular, if unpredictable, contact with community members. Exchanging news, expressing opinions, and feeling connected happen in the natural course of the day.

Neighborhood places also have an emotional quality. People can talk and reflect without the pressure of work or family. Neighbors are welcome there even if they spout off their opinions, with the understanding that others have the same right. They are what Ray Oldenberg calls "third places," not home, not work, but places where the informal public life of the community happens. They are more than just a refuge from the stress of work and family. They are a kind of neutral place, where people can help and advise each other without getting entangled in each others' lives. Because they are open to all, they tend to be a leveler of status and rank. Anyone can talk, opine, or listen (Oldenberg, 1989).

Learning Community Places. Learning communities share many of these characteristics. Some communities have their own cafes. The petrophysicists built a library that also serves as their meeting and home place. Websites often serve as recognizable places communities interact. Regular weekly, monthly or annual meetings, even though they occur in different locations, also serve as places where the informal public life of the community happens. They are places where people converse and think in the presence of others. They are also neutral places where people can reflect on their experience, consider alternative approaches, express their opinion, and give advice without getting entangled in each other's projects. Like neighborhood bars or cafes, they are neutral places where people can receive advice without obligation, where they themselves are the final judges of whether the advice is worth following. They are levelers of status. But the most significant aspect of learning community places is that they are different from the workplace of operating teams. As learning community members get to know each other and gain experience thinking together, they develop their own subculture. While operating teams are dominated by a culture of action, communities develop a culture of reflection and thinking. These two cultures complement each other because the communities give people a vehicle for expressing tentative ideas, reflections and doubts that may not be appropriate in action-oriented operating teams.

Systematize

In 1998, learning communities became more widespread and the KNIT's support of them more systematic. The "learn-as-we-go" strategy led many groups to start learning communities. Some used the framework and "big rules" developed by the design team, others started on their own. This led to several different varieties of learning communities in the organization, some successful, others floundering. In early 1998, the leadership team decided to be more systematic in its approach to knowledge management and made improving the knowledge sharing between teams one of the organizations' annual goals. The leadership team announced that it considered learning communities part of the organization structure. The KNIT conducted a series of workshops for all senior managers, describing the origins, "big rules," models and experience of the organization so far with learning communities. These workshops were conducted in subunits of the organization, so the managers could discuss the learning communities in their area and what they could do to support and improve them.

Now that it had developed some experience building learning communities, the KNIT also took a more proactive role in fostering them. Rather than just responding to needs of individual communities, the KNIT reviewed the organization as a whole and determined where there were gaps in the coverage of the communities. It discovered that no learning communities existed in several areas important to the organization, discussed those gaps with the managers and offered to help build communities in those areas.

Institutionalize

In 1998, the KNIT learned that to institutionalize learning communities it needed to do more than ensure that learning communities cover the whole organization. It also needed to define the relationship of learning communities with operating teams, compensation for community participation, and leadership expectations.

In the Production Division, which had many officially sanctioned communities, the leadership team reviewed how the communities fit with the organization as a whole. Several communities were concerned about community participation, leadership team support, resources, and rewards. They were particularly concerned about whether asset teams would be required to accept community recommendations. In response to these issues, the leadership team developed a set of principles to govern community and operating team interaction. The principles asserted the leadership team's beliefs about the communities and their role in the organization.

The business strategy drives the focus of the communities

The leadership team chose which communities to fund based on business needs. For each community, it budgeted up to three full-time equivalent people. The amount of person resources available for each community varied, depending on its strategic importance to the organization. Most communities were expected to use some or all of their budgeted resources for a community coordinator. But they could also make some of that time available to people who expected to devote a substantial amount of their time to the community. The asset teams made a commitment to support the communities by encouraging asset staff to participate and release some asset team members to fill the budgeted time for community projects.

Community participation is voluntary

The leadership team expected team leaders to encourage team members to participate in communities, but the individual's interest would drive which community to join. If someone is expected to be a core community contributor for the year, they could contract with their manager to be released from their team duties for a certain percent of their time. Those who planned to participate in community meetings, but not assume core member roles, would not be explicitly released for community activity.

Communities are charged to develop products that the operating teams will adopt

The leadership team created a process to insure the alignment of assets' needs and community-developed products. Through a series of back-and-forth discussion between communities and assets, communities would identify asset needs and get preliminary buy-in to documents and products they were developing. The final decision on whether to adopt a community recommendation rested with the asset managers. If a community felt that it's recommendations were ignored, it could escalate the concern to the leadership team.

The organization values individuals' contributions to both assets and communities

The leadership team also asserted the importance of community contributions. People who played a core role in the community would receive direct input on their performance appraisal from the community so their community contribution would count.

By defining the relationship between teams and communities, clarifying the management's expectations of community members, and identifying the importance of communities to the overall business strategy, the leadership team paved the way for communities to become an institutionalized part of the organization. Most, however, still failed to do so. To be fully integrated as a key element of the organization, most communities needed to progress to one more stage of development. They needed to do more than share tips and ideas. They needed to take responsibility for stewarding a competence important to the organization.

Steward Competencies

By the beginning of 1999 there were 16 active communities in the Deepwater division. Most communities focused on helping each other, but four or five began to broaden their focus, from helping to stewarding an organizational competence. The petrophysics community, for example, began to take responsibility for defining the skills petrophysicists need and started to provide skill training.

Some communities naturally evolved to this stewardship role. Health, Safety, and Environment (HS&E) started as a loose, informal group sharing tips between TLPs on safety statistics, near misses, potential problem areas, and safety improvement ideas. As HS&E community members forged better connections between the TLPs, they took on the task of developing an aggressive company-wide safety program. They identified nine key safety areas, set company-wide goals for each, collected data on safety incidents, near misses, and first-aid calls, developed improvement plans, and disseminated safety information across TLPs. One of these areas was safety training. The safety community identified training needs, maintained a database of the safety training individuals had received, and worked with the TLPs to schedule safety training. By working with the TLP teams, the HS&E community was able to schedule training with minimal disruption to production, something the training department had been unable to do. Based on the training approach developed by HS&E, the training department changed the way it scheduled training.

Community Development: From Helping to Stewardship

Learning communities can create "virtuous cycle" of development. Turbodudes is a good example. For the first three months of its life, about fifteen members of the Turbodude community met weekly to discuss key issues in developing turbidite reservoirs, common in the Gulf of Mexico. The group consisted of leading experts in the field. Like most early learning communities at Shell, they talked about technical problems they were having in their work and thought through alternative ap proaches. During that time, word slowly spread about how the company's leading experts were talking about important geological issues. Attendance began to grow. Within a few months community meetings had evolved to reflect this growth. A small group of ten regular members contributed most to the discussion. A much larger group of about twenty "lurkers" attended regularly but contributed little. Before forcing the lurkers to contribute, the coordinator interviewed a selection of them and discovered that many were new to the organization and were using the community to learn about the field, madly taking notes during the meetings. So to keep discussions focused on cutting edge issues, he let the leading experts continue to dominate the discussion.

Stewarding Turbidite Knowledge

Like other communities, the Turbodudes are expanding their role from just helping each other solve problems to expanding, disseminating and developing turbidite knowledge. For example, in order to be more systematic about the way they analyze turbidites, they have begun distinguishing between different types of turbidite structures - sheets & channels. The distinction will help them understand how turbidite data should fit together and make it easier to predict what the structure is likely to be, even when they have limited data. Another example involves helping geologists assess the volume of oil and gas in prospects where there is little or poor data. In the past, geologists' estimates of these little-data prospects varied widely. So a taskforce from the Turbodudes researched the estimating methods community members used and developed a standard methodology. The task force reviewed their approach with the community as a whole and then rolled the approach out organization-wide. The standard helps insure that variations are really variations in the prospect, not just calibration differences among geologists. And like other communities, they have begun helping their members prepare for technical project reviews. While much of the community's discussion still focuses on helping each other, these activities are part of how the community is organizing, systematizing and creating standards of good practice for turbidite analysis.

A Virtuous Cycle of Growth

This practical problem solving led to a cycle of growth. The more the effective the community was at helping people solve real everyday problems, the more recognition it got from people and the organization. People in related fields started attending. People from other disciplines asked the KNIT to help them develop a Turbodudes -type meeting. Turbodude participation continued to grow, averaging 40-50 people per meeting, and topping off at 125. The coordinator kept the meeting focus on cutting edge issues, so they continued to be effective for core group members. The more recognition the community received, the higher the commitment of community members. The core group realized that they were onto something. Several of them started devoting more time to the community, easing some of the burden from the coordinator. As the core Turbodudes' commitment grew, they became more willing to take on more issues related to stewarding their practice. They raised their aspiration for the community. Through this cycle of effectiveness, recognition, commitment and aspiration, Turbodudes grew both in terms of attendance and the level of issue they took on. Now the community raises many topics that are worthy of forming a taskforce to develop standard guidelines and approaches.

FIGURE 5: THE VIRTUOUS CYCLE

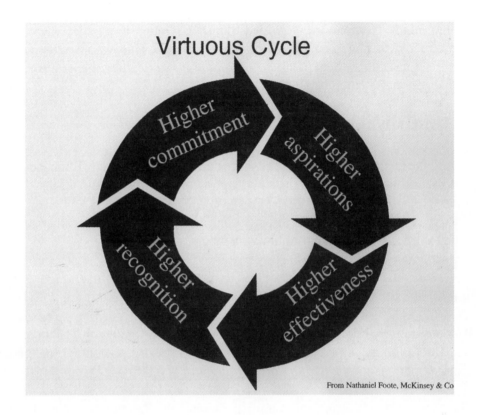

Some communities, on the other hand, were formed specifically to steward a practice. The completion community focuses on preparing a well for production. This community was formed to ensure the quality of all completions. Even though some community members originally resisted accepting that responsibility, within six months the community did, in effect, assume it. The community began with a set of project task forces that developed recommendations on technical issues. Now the community meets 3 hours a week, with 15 to 40 people attending. Its primary focus is peer assists, helping each other with daily completion problems and questions. But the community also conducts informal reviews to help members prepare for the company's official Project Approval Reviews and acts as a sounding board to help the lab define technology needs. For the organization and community members, it is the source of knowledge and responsibility for completion expertise.

In each of these cases, the community did not abandon its focus on helping each other. Rather the community expanded its focus to include broader issues.

ASSESSING THE IMPACT OF COMMUNITIES

Measuring the value of communities is very difficult. For many companies, measuring the impact of knowledge management is important, but difficult. This was also true for Shell. The KNIT identified two primary beneficiaries of community value; the organization as a whole and individual community members.

Value for the Business

By monitoring the health and development of the communities, the KNIT has identified several areas where the communities have contributed significantly to the organization.

Reduced Cost. Several communities directly contributed to reduced overall costs by using practices they learned from other community members.

• Reviewing one site with the community helped reservoir engineers figure out how to develop the site with three wells instead of four, saving $2-3 million (USD).

• By developing a training schedule that minimally interfered with TLP operations, the safety community helped improve facility uptime by one percent. A one percent improvement in uptime has an impact of about $150,000 (USD) per day.

• The chemical engineering community now manages chemical suppliers to the organization. They developed an evaluation and competitive bid process which has lowered their chemical supplies costs to one-third of that of other operators in the region.

Improved accuracy (quality)
In several cases, community members identified and avoided potentially costly errors. In reviewing a site, one community identified several errors in the way the data were posted on maps of the site. If the error had gone undetected until just before drilling begun, it would have been a $1-$2 million mistake. If it had not been caught until the well was drilled, it could have meant drilling a new well at a cost of $15-$20 million (USD). Another community, reviewing recommendations for how to prepare the well for production after drilling was complete, found and corrected a design flaw saving $5-$10 million (USD) on the well. Using the standards it developed and monitored, the safety community reduced accidents and near misses to below it targeted goal. This was accomplished at a time when two of Shell's largest TLPs were ramping up production beyond original projections, expanding the facility and nearly doubling the staff.

Reduced Uncertainty. One of the greatest gains of the Turbodude community has been to reduce uncertainty in deciding whether or not to develop a site. Much of exploration involves extrapolating from sketchy data by comparing it to known geological structures (analogues). Analogues are important because there is so little data about a site before drilling a well. They help the geoscientist decide if there are likely enough reserves to develop it. For example, one site contained layers of oil-bearing sand that were a fraction of an inch thick. Shell had to decide if sand beds that thin could extend over a large enough area without interruption for the oil in them to be pumped out. If they were large enough, the site would be worth developing. The Turbodudes made the decision by examining analogous sites. Analogues are at the heart of many "go/no go" decisions. The more certain explorationists can be about their interpretations, the greater the probability of success and the fewer exploratory wells — at a cost of $15-$20 million (USD) — they need to drill. Reviewing the site with community members helped geoscientists consider different explanations of their data, sharpen their interpretations of the characteristics of the reservoir, and reduce their uncertainty about developing it.

Improved technology transfer. Prior to the inception of the learning communities, the team structure made it difficult for the research lab to inform people of new technology. It made it even more difficult to get them to use it, since it was up to the individual scientist or engineer to decide what tools to use. Scientists and engineers tended to focus on their own team goals. They paid less attention to knowledge fairs and other events the lab sponsored to raise awareness about new tools. The lab would release new software with improved functionality, which individual scientists and engineers were "too busy" to learn. The learning communities provided a way for people to share insights on how to use the tool. When people heard about how they colleagues were using the tool, they were much more inspired to use the new functions.

Calculating the ROI of Learning Communities

Shell has not officially calculated the ROI from these communities, but a very rough calculation of the value of the Turbodudes shows an extremely valuable return. The cost of running Turbodudes, including website, support and the time the coordinator and core group members spend on it is about $300,000 (USD) to $400,000 (USD) annually. Turbodude discussions of analogues and alternate interpretations of data conservatively save drilling and testing three sites per year, at a cost of $20 million (USD) to drill and another $20 million test each well. That is a total savings of $120M annually. It is possible people would have found other ways to access these alternate interpretations. Assuming that the Turbodudes can only claim 10 percent to 20 percent of that savings, they save the corporation $12 to $24 million annually. This is an annual return of 20 to 40 times the investment.

Value for Staff

For Shell staff, the learning communities provide several other, less-tangible, but equally important, values.

Reduced time looking for information

An informal survey found that the communities greatly reduced the time people spent looking for information. In their view, this saved time increase their individual productivity 20-25%. The introduction of standardization also reduced the time people spend looking for information. Once people started sharing ideas in communities, they realized that they didn't have common tracking systems. Now several communities have introduced standard documentation processes, such as pre-and-post well review documentation forms. This makes it much easier for people to locate comparative information.

More information considered

More importantly, the learning communities have dramatically increased the amount of information people are able to review before making a decision. Sometimes, rather than spending a lot of time looking for information, people will simply proceed without it, using their best professional estimate. By connecting them with others, the learning communities provide a much greater base of information. Since looking for information is one of the least rewarding parts of their job, the learning communities have enabled them to spend more time on more rewarding work.

Greater sense of connection with peers

In the new team structure, professional staff frequently felt isolated from their peers on other operating teams. As one community coordinator said, "If we don't hang together, we will hang separately." This was particularly painful for disciplines with a small number of people in them, like petrophysics and chemical engineering. Many of the communities now have created a greater sense of connection. For example, the chemical engineering community, a small group of 17 members, peripheral to the core development and production focus of the organization. As the coordinator of that community remarked, "When we do our job well, nothing happens." That is, there are no chemically related problems on the TLP. The community has greatly improved its member's level of personal satisfaction by creating a forum to connect with peers. Three quarters of the chemical engineer staff attend their monthly all-day meetings.

Training

For many people, like the lurkers at Turbodudes, who were new to the organization or discipline, the learning communities compliment the formal technical training they receive. The learning communities expose them to timely discussions of real-time cutting edge issues. Many of those new to the Deepwater division, particularly those from overseas, have found the learning communities a very helpful training supplement. The coordinator of the Turbodudes estimates that about 40 people have used the community as a vehicle for learning about turbidites. One, in fact, has moved into the role of a Turbidite expert in another part of the organization.

Overall Benefit

Perhaps the most dramatic benefit of the communities is that they have changed the culture of Shell in New Orleans. They have transformed the organization from a single-minded focus on operating team goals to a shared focus that includes learning and sharing knowledge. By creating many welcoming, neutral forums in which people can share ideas and insights, the learning communities have made asking for help and sharing insights part of the culture of the organization. As one geologist said, "When we started, we were in a spiraling downward mentality in terms of sharing. There was no communication going on between teams. Teams were siloed. Many people working in adjacent geological areas didn't get the benefit of each other's learning. Today sharing knowledge is part of how people do their work. Not all that sharing is in the form of communities. Some of it is just in the way that teams now work."

LESSONS LEARNED

During the three years of community building in Shell, the KNIT learned numerous valuable lessons. Most of these fall into two domains: those having to do with the community development process itself; and those related to the organizational environment that supports communities.

Community Development

1.   Learning communities thrive at the intersection of business need and personal passion At Shell, most learning communities were formed around disciplines, like geology, that are central to the business. People need to think about them to do their work. Forming communities around topics important to the business gave them immediate legitimacy. As the communities were developing, sometimes with low participation, the obviousness of the business case for convening a community around that topic helped sustain them. During the production leadership team's annual community review, the communities closest to current business issues received the greatest attention and endorsement. But personal passion is equally important to community success. In the pilot communities, some members served as "representatives" of people who had greater passion for the topic, but were unable to participate because of scheduling conflicts. These representative members found it difficult to fully participate in the community or serve as effective conduits of information and insight. Because the articulation of knowledge happens in discussions of problems, knowledge and passion about the topic are essential to fully engage in the conversation.

2.   Learning communities need an active coordinator
The coordinator is the catalyst of the community. By walking the halls to connect people, they create the "planned spontaneity" seen in many communities. They keep people informed of what each other is doing and create opportunities for people to get together to share ideas. This role is also critical to the community's survival. Shell's most successful community coordinators are well-respected community members, usually senior practitioners. What is most important in a coordinator is that they are able to connect with community members on a human level. In most of the Shell communities that failed, or operated at a low-energy level, the coordinator did not have the time to devote to the community. For a large, vibrant community, this role typically was 25 percent or more of the coordinator's time.

3.   Maintain frequent enough contact among community members to build trust

Communities are primarily a network of human relationships, not a task or a web site. To build those relationships, people need contact. Only through contact can they see that they share common problems, see the value of each others' ideas, create a common etiquette or set of norms on how to interact, and learn to trust each other. The Turbodudes' coordinator tracked the number of people attending the meetings and found that the strongest predictor of high attendance is how much time he spent the previous week walking the halls. One of the great values of Shell's informal problem-solving meetings is that they gave people open time for "technical schmoozing." During those times, people shared immediate work problems or successes and helped each other, just as they would if they were informally networking down the hall. One of the most effective ways to build this relationship is through small projects. Turbodudes frequently identifies technical problems that are too big to work through to solutions by the end of a meeting. The coordinator works through some of these on his own with the input of a few community members. Small teams of community members work through others. When community members are able to work together one-on-one or in small groups, it strengthens the web of relationships and indirectly strengthens the community as a whole. People come to the meeting already connected through their projects and can focus more on exciting cutting edge issues. Even when the community's topic is very scientific or theoretical, it is the human connection that builds a base for effective knowledge sharing.

4.   Develop an active, passionate core group

Turbodudes, Chemical Engineering, HS&E and other vibrant communities in Shell have a very active core group who not only contribute but help develop the community. They share the load with the coordinator. The core group of the Turbodudes, for example, does most of the community's development projects. What makes core group members effective, like coordinators, is their heartfelt caring about the topic and the community. Coordinators can develop a core group by involving them in meeting planning, asking them to take over some meetings, host subgroups, or organize elements of the web site. The most important thing in developing potential core group members is to give them visibility in the community without requiring them to spend too much extra time.

5.   Create real dialogue about cutting edge issues in community forums

Relationship happens in true discussion, not in reports on best practices. Without real dialogue, you just get "the party line." Discussions in one of Shell's less-vibrant communities is stiff, even after several years of meeting. When the community got started some of the thought leaders in that area postured with each other in a way that said new ideas were not ok. The community has never recovered. In contrast, a good Turbodudes discussion focuses on an issue that has broad appeal where the answer is not immediately obvious. The meeting generates many different observations by different people. The coordinator insures that the tone welcomes and considers new ideas. One of the devices the KNIT uses to open a spirit of dialogue is to poll the meeting participants on whether they work in the area under discussion. Typically they find that many people do and the coordinator uses this to establish that there is expertise is in the audience as well as at the podium.

6.   Involve thought leaders

Thought leaders are "go to" people. They have the breadth and depth of experience the community needs if it is going to do something important. Thought leader's participation also legitimates the community among community members. Participation communicates a message that says that the community is worth the time, even for someone with deep expertise. One turbidite expert was reluctant to attend the Turbodudes meetings regularly because he "didn't have time." He only came to a few meetings. So the coordinator tailored his invitations, encouraging him to come when the topic was particularly important to him.

Business Environment

1.   Align rewards and recognition to support learning communities

Aligning reward and recognition is important because it legitimates community participation. In a work environment, like Shell, people are already fully committed. A reward system conveys to community members and their managers that they can put other things aside to work on community activities without getting in trouble with their operating team manger. It says that the community engages in work important to the organization. Contributing to communities is a line in Shell's performance appraisal process. However, the degree to which managers really consider it varies greatly. Except where people are specifically assigned to community activity, most managers do little to include community contribution in their performance appraisal discussions. This has limited many of Shell's communities. While they are still able to share tips and ideas, it makes it more difficult for them to steward their practice. Many more of the issues identified in the Turbodudes meetings could be worked to solution or turned into guidelines if the members felt they had more time. As the Turbodude coordinator said, "At the weekly Turbodudes meeting, I feel like I am in the middle of a rushing stream, with so many ideas and potential improvements to our work rushing by. We can work some of them on an ad hoc basis. If we had more time from community members, we could do so much more."

2.   Maintain alignment with organizational goals

One of the things that helped Shell's communities in the beginning was their alignment with the organizational goal of preserving technical excellence. Most of the communities that have remained active have maintained their alignment with organizational goals. The completion community, for example, begins ever meeting with a 20-minute informal discussion of the technology issues of the day as reflected in leadership team discussions. This helps them focus on issues with organizational as well as individual impact.

3.   Assess value while you have strong management support

When Shell's communities started, one member of the leadership team was a strong champion of the effort, and the division manager felt that "sharing knowledge is the right thing to do." As a result, the KNIT did little in the first three years of the community's development to directly measure their value. Now, the organization has a new leadership team that insists on documented value. Had the KNIT assessed the value of the communities as they developed, rather than waiting for the three-year window, justifying the current communities would be much easier. Instead, many of the communities are struggling to demonstrate their value to the organization as the new managers consider different structures for sharing knowledge and preserving technical excellence.

4.   Periodically review and renew

Learning communities naturally go through cycles of high and low activity. Sometimes they can get stuck in "vicious cycles," in which the energy dips and fewer new people participate. Core contributors have trouble "finding the time" for community activity and contribute less. As the core contributors' commitment fades, the center of the community shrinks. Since there are fewer contributions and activities, people begin to expect less from the community. As a result, the community is less exciting and less effective in sharing knowledge. In this vicious cycle less energy leads to less recognition, leads to lower commitment and more modest expectations for sharing knowledge and stewarding the practice. Several communities in New Orleans fell into this cycle. They lost sight of the excitement and principles of knowledge sharing that once drove them and fell into decline. To prevent this vicious cycle, it is important to regularly review communities, identify the vicious and virtuous cycles, and the factors that could change direction.

CONCLUSION

The Shell story shows that learning communities are effective vehicles for sharing knowledge, particularly when you don't know what knowledge will be important. By helping each other solve real, day-to-day problems, Shell's learning communities helped people build the relationships they needed to really understand each other's knowledge needs and trust each other enough to really discuss them. But Shell's most successful learning communities do more than help each other. They steward a body of knowledge. By making this shift they have become a real part of the organization. Learning communities, like other human institutions, do not mature to this stage on their own. Their development comes through people who care about the community's domain and members, people who spend the time to nurture, support and develop the community.

REFERENCES

McDermott, Richard

1999a "How Information Technology Inspired, But Cannot Deliver Knowledge Management." California Management Review. 41:4 Summer.

1999b "Learning Across Teams" Knowledge Management Review. 8:32-36 May/June

Oldenberg, Ray

1989 The Great Good Place. New York. Marlowe & Company

Wenger, Etienne

1998 Communities of Practice. Cambridge: Cambridge University Press.

ABOUT THE CONTRIBUTORS

Richard McDermott, President of McDermott Consulting, advises companies on how to improve the way they apply knowledge, learning and expertise. For nearly two decades, he has been designing knowledge-intensive organizations, working with engineering, professional service, sales, and manufacturing groups. His work typically involves developing corporate knowledge strategies, designing work processes around the flow of knowledge, designing knowledge work itself to standardize routine work and create thinking forums for innovative work, and developing mechanisms (like communities of practice) for sharing knowledge across teams and business units.

Dr. McDermott's clients include: Shell Oil Company, Hewlett-Packard, Schlumberger, Celestica, The World Bank, Ben and Jerry's, General Motors, Digital Equipment Corporation, General Electric, New England Telephone, Albany International, Work/Family Directions, Pediatric Associates of Fairfield, and Advanced Signing.

His articles on community building, knowledge management and organizational design have appeared in The California Management Review, The Knowledge Management Review, The IHRIM Journal, The Journal for Quality and Participation, Management & Innovation, Advances in Interdisciplinary Studies of Work Teams, and Info Ressources Humaines. He currently serves on the editorial board of The Knowledge Management Review.

Dr. McDermott holds a Ph.D. in social theory. He is currently conducting research on designing global organizations and completing a book on communities of practice to be published by Harvard University Press in March 2000. He can be reached at Richard@RMcDermott.com.

John Kendrick, joined Shell as a geologist in 1973. During his twelve years in Shell's Deepwater business unit, John has held several positions in both the functional and asset based organization. Since 1997, he has facilitated Turbodudes, a community that meets to work issues related to deep water reservoirs. In his "spare" time, John is working toward his MBA at the University of New Orleans.

Thanks to Mike Mahaffie for his insights implementing communities in Shell.

8

InFocus

A program of continued commitment at all levels of the company to go beyond learning initiatives and to sustain the mentality of a learning organization

INTRODUCTION

As Corporate America enters the Millennium, it is clear that topics like corporate culture, organizational learning and knowledge management will be front-runners as a management tool-set and key contributors to differentiating companies of the future.

It has not been by happen-stance that InFocus, a small high-tech company in Oregon has invested in these tools over the last decade. There has been a long-held belief at InFocus, that these types of initiatives will make an incredible positive difference in the profitability and productivity of the company. In addition, the investment in these tools has created a higher level of engagement among the InFocus workforce and has paid high dividends in terms of commitment to the company.

Over the last seven years at InFocus, the Company has held as a corporate strategic imperative to "Create and Foster an Environment where Outstanding People Achieve Extraordinary Results" and has invested a great deal in a culture of results-oriented continuous improvement, leadership at all levels and learning organization principles. InFocus is endeared to this strategy not only as an "attract and retain" opportunity, but because at the heart of the Company, it is truly believed that organizational learning is a competitive advantage that differentiates InFocus within the industry.

Over the past five years, InFocus has been consistently recognized by Oregon Business magazine as one of the top ten Best Companies to work for in Oregon. This past year, InFocus beat out competitors, such as Intel and Kaiser Permanente, with recognition as the second-best Oregon Company in the year 2000.

The Oregon Business magazine survey of the top companies in Oregon includes feedback from employees and the companies, alike, increasing the authenticity of the honor. The Oregon Best Company's are selected from thousands of company applicants and rated against these five critical corporate practices:

- Pay and Benefits

- Community Involvement

- Employee Involvement

- Advancement and Training

- Workplace Culture

ASSESSMENT PHASE

Beginning in 1996, InFocus experienced a tremendous growth rate, doubling in size by 200 percent. Key business drivers that had diluted many of the foundational elements of the culture at InFocus were identified:

- Factors of Growth

- Changing Technology

- Increased Competition

- Departure of Key Executives

- New Executive Leadership Not Grounded in the Values and Company Culture

These drivers manifested into less-than productive behaviors of short-term thinking and crisis management. Further, there was a real lack of consistency in the way leadership operated and it was evident that not everyone "was on the same page."

The Human Resources staff reached a critical decision at the end of 1998 to undertake a strategic imperative for 1999 of revitalizing the company culture.

A cross-functional team of cultural initiative members was formed with key senior members of the HR team and several other cross-functional managers representing the Quality team, Information Technology and the Service division. Members of this cross-functional team had instrumental roles to play with defining the culture initiative, assisting with culture communication strategies and demonstrating levels of influence throughout the company. The cross-functional team members were selected based on the individual's passion for the company culture and the individual's role as an influencer throughout the organization. For example, the Director of Quality participated in this team due to the cross-functional aspect of his role throughout InFocus as Director of Quality and because of his interest and passion for continuous improvement and continual learning.

The objectives of this strategic cultural imperative included:

Tangible	Intangible
Increase productivity	Create consistent behavior and practices across the company relating to values, processes and tools for effectiveness
Increase profitability	Increase level of ownership and accountability
Decrease product time to market by 50%	Better customer service
Increase quality while balancing a reduction in product returns	Stronger, productive relationships
Acquire new employee referrals	Demonstrated assertive coaching for less-than-superior performance
Achieve visibility in the industry and community as a Top Company	Create and foster an environment that encourages extraordinary results in an open, positive culture
Decrease in undesirable turnover	Re-energize the workforce
Promotional opportunities and succession planning	Enhanced capacity for effective action-taking

Step One of the Culture Assessment Phase: Gathering the Data

The cross-functional culture team was established with business objectives defined to revitalize the culture. Now it was time to move into an assessment phase of the culture data currently available to establish a clear path for a culture strategy. One outcome that seemed compelling for all team members was the desire to "fuse" the culture, by incorporating elements of the culture that had been effective since 1992, with new culture elements that would be representative of the "next generation culture" for InFocus. Thus, the effort became known as Fusion and the team took on the label of the Fusion team as an identification of the culture initiative and intent of the effort.

The Fusion team considered data from several sources to assist in the assessment phase of the culture initiative. Step one of the assessment evaluated key indicator metrics and anecdotal information gather from exiting employees:

Undesirable Turnover: Departing employees are asked to provide feedback to Human Resources about the work experience at InFocus by completing an exit questionnaire and meeting with a Human Resources representative for an informal conversation. Human Resources began to notice an increase in undesirable turnover and feedback received during exit interviews noted that InFocus was beginning to "look and feel like any other company."

While most exiting employees still listed InFocus as a great employer, there were some telling remarks by exiting employees during this timeframe that assisted in validating the Fusion team perception that the desire culture was somewhat diluted. The following sample statements from exiting employees were excerpted from exit interviews during the 1998 timeframe:

Provide any comments that you feel would be helpful in making InFocus a better place to work:

"There seemed to be a lack of involvement from some leaders. I would recommend more involved leadership that will allow employees to take some of those "informed risks.""

"PDQ needs to be a priority. A self-proven program has been forgotten."

"The company has changed a great deal in the three years I have been here. I am sure it will change a much more in the next year."

"There needs to be checks and balances from HR to see whether managers are complying with company cultures."

"Acknowledge that there is a morale problem and take steps to actively seek out and address the fundamental issues."

"As companies grow they change, not always for the better. InFocus is still the best company I have ever worked for or probably will work for. If I return to the metro area, I would talk to InFocus again about the possibility of employment."

"I truly believe InFocus went out and obtained top-notch people. If I were in a leadership position, I would do everything possible to retain and capitalize on this resource."

"So far, InFocus has done a great job balancing process development with personal empowerment. Continuing to allow individuals to perform well in their own manner will be the only way to attract and hang on to talented workers."

"InFocus has to understand that a team is not a homogenous group of people who can democratically vote on highly technical issues."

"Keep searching for the best in the people that wish to join the InFocus team. Setting high standards in applicants only makes it better for everyone. Continue with the focus and drive to the best work environment."

EXHIBIT ONE: INFOCUS EXIT INTERVIEW QUESTIONNAIRE

EXHIBIT ONE:

InFocus®

EXIT INTERVIEW

It is important to our company to conduct an exit interview with each employee upon separation. We would appreciate your honest opinion about your employment with In Focus Systems. Your objective feedback can help us improve workplace conditions and make this company a better place to work. Please complete the front and back of this questionnaire and return it to the exit interviewer. Thank you for your valued opinion.

Employee Name _____

Separation Date ____/____/____

Position Title _____

Dept. _____

Please rate each behavior for:

Agreement: The extent to which you agree with the behavior stated (please see below).

Strongly Disagree	Somewhat Agree	Strongly
Agree		

1---4---7

Department leaders model and are held accountable for the **leadership behaviors** supported by the company.	1	2	3	4	5	6	7
Department leaders support and encourage **informed risk taking**.	1	2	3	4	5	6	7
Department leaders **effectively coach and mentor** team members.	1	2	3	4	5	6	7
Department leaders **consistently recognize** work achievements	1	2	3	4	5	6	7
The **performance review** process provides for fair and consistent evaluation of performance.	1	2	3	4	5	6	7
My **workload** during my tenure with the company was about right.	1	2	3	4	5	6	7
The **nature of my job** appropriately challenged my skills and allowed me to grow professionally.	1	2	3	4	5	6	7
The **benefit programs** offered by the company provided me (and my family) with above average protection and security.	1	2	3	4	5	6	7
The **compensation** I received for my contribution to the company was appropriate.	1	2	3	4	5	6	7
The **training and development program**s offered by the company appropriately target the needs of team members.	1	2	3	4	5	6	7
The **training and development program**s offered by the company appropriately target the needs of team members.	1	2	3	4	5	6	7
Overall, In Focus is a **great place to work.**	1	2	3	4	5	6	7

<u>Productivity Metrics:</u> Productivity is the key metric InFocus had consistently tracked since the initial creation of the continuous improvement culture in 1992. The metric formula utilized was: (annual revenue divided by the number of employees, temps and contractors).

EXHIBIT TWO: FOR PRODUCTIVITY CHART EXAMPLE

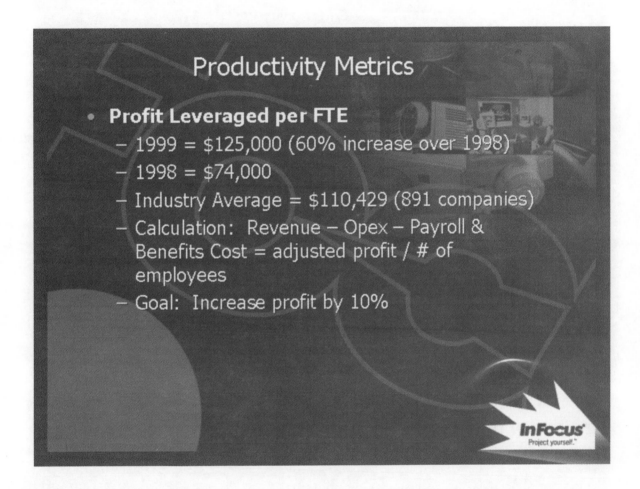

For a period of time beginning in 1996 less attention was paid to this metric as the company was driving other business factors. The Fusion team decided the company had reached a maturity level by this point that would afford the ability to track profitability metrics rather than productivity.

<u>Profitability Metrics</u>: Over recent years, profitability per employee has moved to the forefront as a key benchmark of company results. This measurement tracks: annual revenue minus op-ex (operating expense) minus payroll and benefits cost = adjusted profit/number of employees. See Exhibit Three for Profitability Chart example.

EXHIBIT THREE: PROFITABILITY CHART

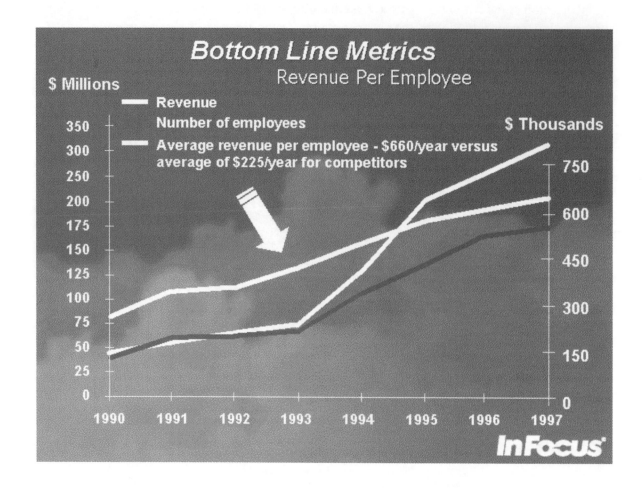

Step Two of the Culture Assessment Phase: Leveraging Past For the Future

The Fusion team had a desire to leverage past cultural success factor. An evaluation of "what's working with the InFocus culture" by the Fusion team identified several cultural strengths of InFocus that had contributed to the company business success and triggered employee engagement:

"Create and Foster an Environment where Outstanding People Achieve Extraordinary Results." This statement has been part of the corporate strategic objectives since the culture inception in the early nineties. The intention behind the statement is to illuminate that people are the driving force behind the success of InFocus. The statement remains a corporate strategic objective is to demonstrate that this philosophy of "people power" is imbedded at the heart of InFocus.

Continual Process-Improvement. The investment in continual process-improvement concepts and tools has been a long-standing focus that has reaped InFocus heavy dividends. The company has tracked metrics over the last decade that substantiate the belief that companies committed to establishing an environment of continual improvement and that enlists and supports employees involvement in this focus will have increasingly enhanced productivity in terms of cost saving.

Three key mechanisms were utilized by InFocus to drive this powerful philosophy:

1) People Driving Quality (PDQ) as a label for the InFocus culture of process improvement. When the company established the continual improvement as a core value of the company, PDQ became the acronym that represented People Driving Quality.

2) Continuous Improvement Teams (CIT). These were teams of employees who had identified a business process that could be improved resulting in a cost savings, a timesavings or increased productivity for the company or team. The results of the CIT's were tracked and highlighted at company-wide employee meetings.

3) Learning, learning, learning…tools, tools, tools. InFocus created a continual learning path that introduced everyone in the company, from new employees to tenured employees at all levels, to an effective problem-solving model and toolkit that could be used to identify and implement process improvement. The problem-solving toolkit included tools like brainstorming, cause and effect and criteria rating and ranking.

Employee Involvement. The key cultural lever for business success and for differentiating InFocus from other companies is employee involvement. Employee involvement at InFocus has been, without doubt, the most important aspect of the culture fabric of the company. In most companies, employees are hired for the knowledge and skills they bring to the equation and yet, employee input is often the most over-looked element of companies. The employee experience at InFocus is designed to increased involvement with the business direction and decisions of the company.

Step Three of the Culture Assessment: Soliciting Input from the Top

Members of the Fusion team interviewed the Executive team to solicit feedback from the top management level perspective about what culture components they ascribed value to or felt were lacking from the current culture. The Executive team had a keen interest in continuing on to engage employees, process improvement and for building in mechanisms for holistic thinking and sustainability.

Some of the interview questions utilized were:

1) What components of the company culture do you believe have contributed to InFocus business success?

2) What culture components would you like to see imbedded in the InFocus culture to enhance the opportunity for business success in the future?

3) What commitment are you willing to make in supporting the culture and aligning your management teams to support the culture?

4) In order for the culture development to be effective, from your viewpoint, what commitments would you like to see from the PDQ Culture team for rollout?

5) Which metrics do you think it is necessary to track to monitor culture effectiveness?

Culture Assessment Summary

The Fusion team reached the conclusion that it was not necessary to re-invent the Company culture. The plan was, instead, to build upon the foundational culture of continuous improvement and leadership at all levels philosophies that had been diluted by growth and lack of attention. Additionally, the team identified an opportunity to leverage the InFocus Corporate Value statements that were already an integral part of the Corporate Strategic Planning process by giving these values more visibility and connection to the desired cultural components. This provided a backdrop for linking culture topics with core values that were already existing and recognizable in the organization.

InFocus Corporate Values

Leadership at all Levels
* Effectively utilize our tools and talent
* Set challenging goals, drive results
* Identify, prioritize and execute flawlessly
* Have a positive influence and a positive attitude
* Think two levels up

Customer Intimacy
* Understand and act on our customers' compelling wants and needs
* Deliver innovative and competitive solutions that meet or exceed customers' expectations
* Create customers for life

Strategic Partnerships
* Open, effective and honest communication
* Leverage partnerships to meet shared objectives
* Treat each other fairly

Outstanding Quality
* Set and achieve best-in-class quality measures and goals
* Continuously learn, develop and improve process/products through systems thinking and other quality tools
* Meet or exceed customer quality expectations

Informed Risk Taking
* Embrace change, be innovative and take risks
* Learn from our successes and failures
* Encourage and reward innovation

Accountability
* Hold ourselves and each other accountable
* Properly plan and execute strategic goals and objectives
* Communicate intentions, set expectations and honor agreements

Honesty and Integrity
* Be honest and forthright
* Conduct business with integrity and professionalism
* Maintain confidentiality of company information
* Think, talk and act straight with each other

A Great Place to Work
* Work cross functionally, recognizing team and individual success
* Achieve balance in our professional and personal life
* Be an asset to the community
* Keep our sense of humor
* Demonstrate mutual respect
* Work hard, celebrate winning, have fun!

In consideration of the business goals identified as part of the Company's three-year strategic planning process, it was necessary to develop new skills as well. Particularly of interest to the company were the skill sets addressed in Peter Senge's <u>The Fifth Discipline.</u>[1] While InFocus had already adopted some of these ideas in its leadership development program in the mid-90s, it saw the systems thinking model as a key tool for long-term problem solving. For the Company to continue with a successful culture, it was critical to imbed a core competency of sustainability, moving from the constant fire-fighting mode into a merge of thinking and acting across the organization.

Over the course of three months, the Fusion Culture Team was able to analyze the data available and define the overall direction of the Culture Project. The culture objectives and metrics identified, core culture components were identified and a general approach plan supported by the Executive Team was established that ensured the commitment to proceed and an agreement for rollout that would honor the aggressive strategic business objectives in place.

Key Lessons Learned

Several things really help in creating consistent communication. These included creating an icon, or tag-line, such as "Create and Foster an Environment Where Outstanding People Achieve Extraordinary Results," or the "People Driving Quality" label for the initiative that the various stakeholders can relate to. These types of communication become a mechanism that people can rally around, especially if the icon/acronym is representative of aspects of the culture that are highly valued or have a history.

It is important to not belabor the culture assessment and slow down the process. As the project progresses, there is certain to be aspects that new input or considerations will cause some change of direction. In a fast-moving company, some of the culture component refinements can be identified along the way. Quickly get buy-in on the core culture components and approach and concurrently kick off the program development phase.

Absolute must have Executive support and buy-in, linked to tangible, business outcomes. Executives will more likely rally behind culture initiatives, when the key culture drivers can link outcomes to increased productivity, enhanced retention, or increased profitability.

"JUST-IN-TIME" DEVELOPMENT

With the core culture components identified through the assessment phase, the Fusion Culture task force team moved in to the program design phase. In keeping with the fast paced company environment, the team agreed the best approach for this phase would be "Just in Time" development.

"Just-in-time" development is common vernacular for the high-tech environment. In the case of culture program development, it essentially means that the design of culture workshops occurs in the timeframe immediately prior to the workshop delivery. In this particular InFocus situation, rather than take 3-6 months for the design of the six culture workshops, the workshops would be individually designed within the two-four weeks just prior to the workshop date.

Another factor that contributed to the decision to use a just in time approach was the desire by the Fusion Culture team to be able to utilize external consultants in the development and delivery process. This would enable the process to move faster since most members of the Fusion team had other corporate responsibilities and were not dedicated full-time to the project.

Two criteria factors were identified for selection of external consultants to participate in this culture design project: previous and on-going relationship with InFocus and areas of consultant expertise. Continuity with previous culture efforts was a primary driver behind the consultant selection criteria factors. There was a strong desire to use consultants that had already developed credibility with the management team throughout InFocus and that had demonstrated expertise in the core culture components identified for this culture effort. The consultants selected to participate with the Fusion team for the culture development brought with them expertise in process improvement, leadership development and aligned with the employee involvement philosophy desired.

The Fusion Culture team recognized that program development was not an inherent skill set of most cross-functional members of the team and that it would be a slow process to involve the entire cross-functional Culture team in the development phase. Therefore, it was decided to identify a smaller "core team" from the Culture team comprised of the Corporate Resources VP, the Director of Organizational Effectiveness, the Corporate HR Manager and two external consultants with process improvement and leadership development expertise.

An initial planning day was spent with the core culture team to align this development team on the vision and business objectives of the Culture effort. The outcome of this planning day was the decision to retain "People Driving Quality" as the backdrop and outline for the progression of the culture workshops to be developed. Utilizing PDQ provided an opportunity to honor and leverage the culture and leadership development work done over the years through the creation of the "People Driving Quality" environment (PDQ) and to sustain an icon that most of the InFocus workforce could relate to.

The decision to use an "arrow" as a backdrop was based upon the discussions amongst the Fusion Core Team that an arrow is representative of the concepts of an empowered workforce with shared vision around business objectives and driving for results. At InFocus, the arrow is a recognized symbol of alignment around shared vision. The PDQ arrow icon also incorporated the learning track that InFocus had invested in and sustained over recent years to develop the desire culture and obtain the workforce productivity and profitability metrics that are the hallmark of the company.

EXHIBIT FOUR: PDQ LABEL

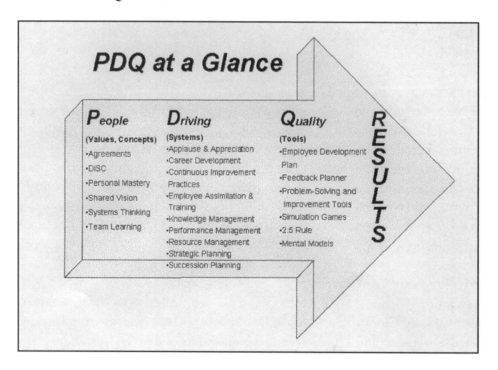

With the identified culture workshop topics and a progressive rollout path in mind, the Fusion Core Team set about creating an action plan for the development of the workshops with assignments for subject matter experts. In the interest of speed and to leverage tools already in place with the workforce, the team did not want to "reinvent the wheel." The action plan table (below) demonstrates how the Fusion Core team chose a development path that would afford the ability to enhance leadership and process improvement tools currently in place and integrate new learning tools that would increase competencies for the future; e.g. Systems Thinking.

EXHIBIT FIVE: SCHEDULE OF CULTURE PROGRAMS

Culture Topic	Subject Matter Expert	Programs/Tools Already Developed	New Programs or Tools to Develop	Due Date
Systems Thinking Introduction	Peter Senge	Upcoming Offsite Program		January 1999
PDQ Introduction & Senge Debrief	Fusion Core Team	Problem Solving Tools	Create PDQ Initiative Introduction & Senge Debrief Venue	February 1999
Accountable Leadership	External Consultant	Utilize new tools for this workshop	How We Work Together Discussion	May 1999
Communication and Feedback Vehicles	External Consultant	DiSC & Feedback Planner		June 1999
Systems Thinking	External Consultant	None available	Beer Game and Causal Loop Tool	August 1999
Strategic Planning	Fusion Core Team External Consultant	Existing Strategic Planning templates and employee involvement process		September - October 1999
Sustainable Process Improvement	Fusion Core Team External Consultant	Problem Solving Tools	Consistent Problem Solving Model	November 1999
Celebrate Success	Fusion Core Team		Leverage Mountain theme from Strategic Planning	November 1999

It should be noted, that in keeping with the just in time approach, each workshop was essentially designed in the month just prior to the identified delivery date. Over the space of six months, the Fusion Core team met several times in as needed, planning days to "fuse" the development components together and create delivery presentations that combined existing and new tools.

Key Lessons Learned

There is a price to be paid with just in time development. There was an angst felt by the Fusion Core team about not having the time to pilot a program before delivery and workshops became "learning labs" essentially using participants somewhat as guinea pigs, hoping the experiment will turn out successful.

Another factor that contributed to "lessons learned" for the Fusion team in the development phase was the realization of the complexity of logistics that occur in the final day or two, just prior to a workshop delivery. This becomes especially heightened when both internal team members and external consultants have various levels of ownership for the development of workshop segments. Basically, in the final hours before the workshop, all the pieces of are coming together (presentations and materials) and being finalized. If any of the workshop presentation depends upon external consultants with travel requirements, this adds to the time frame and must be worked through. There should be some time allotted for working through this process to ensure smooth delivery, especially in situations where workshop delivery depends upon more than one key presenter or facilitator.

That is why it is mission critical to select the best consultants and to identify an internal leader for the Culture team. This internal leader, with Organizational Development skill sets has the sole responsibility to ensure program design is created, managed to the desired timelines and developed with an understanding of the company's business objectives, dynamics of the target audience(s) and implemented according to organizational readiness.

WHILE THE INK IS DRYING: PROGRAM DELIVERY

As the culture program development progressed, new questions about program delivery emerged:

1) Who would participate in the initial program rollout?

2) What dates and times would program delivery occur?

3) What presenters would be utilized?

4) Program Logistics: how to get the participants to the program?

5) How would the culture program be rolled out to the entire company?

Program Participants

With the program development underway, it was established that the first target audience to focus on was Executive Management. The participants identified to be the "pilot audience" for the program delivery included the CEO, Vice Presidents and Director level management throughout the company. This also included Director level management of the InFocus Sales teams, even though these individuals were not all headquartered at Corporate and it would require a travel commitment for these members to participate. It was felt that it was critically important to have culture buy-in from the Company Senior leadership and many of the members of this management level were somewhat new to InFocus and had not been exposed to the culture tools currently in place. As mentioned earlier, employee feedback had identified that there was an observed lack of alignment amongst the senior leadership team, so it was essential to obtain the full involvement of this level.

For the purposes of leadership development, a few key Sr. Managers were invited to participate. Additionally, to build in sustainability and reinforcement from the onset, it was decided to include the Human Resources Strategic Partners. At InFocus each divisional VP has an HR Strategic Partner who is an adjunct member of their staff and works closely with the VP and the divisional management team. In this way, the HR team is more apprised of the business objectives and is on hand to assist each Vice President as they drive organizational effectiveness.

Program Communication

With the recognition that managers at the CEO, VP and Director level are very busy people with strategic business priorities, and given the intense desire to engage this management level, there was thoughtful consideration given to a communication strategy and logistics for the culture rollout.

The Fusion Core team felt it was important to create an identity for the culture initiative, as mentioned previously People Driving Quality ultimately took center stage in this regard. Once PDQ was chosen as the culture brand, it was imperative to use this in every communication about the culture initiative, so that participants and the company workforce and easily recognize it.

Since it was imperative for the targeted participants to understand that the culture initiative was supported from the top, initial communication and invitation for the upcoming culture programs was sent from the CEO. In addition to this, it was made clear throughout all communications, that the CEO and Vice Presidents would be participating in the culture initiative and attend all culture sessions or workshops. This emphasized the importance of the culture initiative and sent a strong message about the desired commitment level to the program. After the first PDQ introductory workshop, further communications were sent from the Vice President of Corporate Resources, who had ultimate responsibility for a sustained culture at InFocus.

Program Timing

As stated earlier, the Fusion Culture team had committed to the Executive team to ensure that culture workshops would be delivered in timeframes that would avoid impeding operations or other business issues. In this way, the Fusion team demonstrated an astute understanding that managing the culture initiative in a way that did not contribute to distracting the workforce from business objectives was key to the success of the initiative. Paying attention to industry business cycles and the impact of how those cycles play out in workload, bandwidth and sheer attention span for the targeted participants of the culture initiative was beneficial for ensuring full mind-share when it was time to deliver workshops.

One simple example of how the Culture initiative was managed around business events: InFocus participates in the largest product trade show for this industry in the United States. The trade show, Infocomm occurs around the middle of June. In addition to the representation by the InFocus Sales teams at the trade show, there is much preparation by the Engineering and Product Market teams prior to the trade show to put finishing touches on any new products that will be announced at the event. In this way, much of the workforce is involved in work activities prior to Infocomm and then out of the office for several days attending the trade show.

This is an annual occurrence and dates are set well in advance. In keeping the commitment to schedule culture workshops at optimal times for the business, the workshop delivery was scheduled for dates after the very critical Infocomm trade show.

The full schedule for the culture programs can be seen in Exhibit Five.

Taking Chances

The Fusion core team took a risk with a unique opportunity that arose. In the midst of program design phase for the first culture program, it was announced that Peter Senge would be making a rare appearance in Portland to speak on Systems Thinking. It had already been determined that it would be beneficial to introduce Systems Thinking as a core component of the desired culture, however, the plan was to focus on Systems Thinking at a much later time in the culture rollout.

Despite that the timing of the Peter Senge engagement would be a premature introduction to Systems Thinking, the Fusion team decided to seize the moment and invite the Executive management team to attend the seminar.

This turned out to be a fruitful decision. Senge spoke about Systems Thinking at an overview level and presented some very thoughtful questions that engaged attendees in compelling discussion. As a result, this created a wonderful opportunity for the InFocus participants to use the dialogue segments of the seminar to get better acquainted with each other and share thoughts about the concepts together. This offsite learning experience produced an important foundation of collegial relationship between the InFocus participant that was transported into the workshops during program delivery.

An unanticipated pay-off was the full participation of the CEO and Vice Presidents. The entire Executive team attended the Senge seminar and stayed for the duration, despite some operational issues that arose during the day back at headquarters. In essence, attendance at the Senge seminar was the first introduction to the upcoming InFocus cultural initiative that occurred for the senior management team. The CEO and VP's demonstrated an incredible commitment which modeled behavior from the inception of the culture initiative. This gave the culture initiative the best start one could imagine created a new hallmark of Executive leadership for others to follow.

Additionally, feedback from the participants during a debrief session demonstrated a new basic understanding of Systems Thinking and all agreed that there would be great benefit for InFocus to imbed Systems Thinking as a competency throughout the company.

Key Lessons Learned

Pay attention to instinct. The decision to take a risk with an opportunity when it is counter-intuitive is often the right and best choice. The Senge seminar was not ideal from a "timing" perspective for the cultural initiative, but an internal voice said that missing out on a rare opportunity to hear about Systems Thinking from the originator of the concept would be most unfortunate. Ultimately, instinct paid off.

Get the buy in and the commitment of the Executive team, especially the CEO is a paradigm that gets much publicity. Because this advice gets so much press in relation to Organizational Learning or culture initiatives in books and articles, it is sometimes easy to downplay or overlook. Time and time again throughout this culture initiative, the support and genuine commitment from the CEO and his team proved to be a critical success factor. Through the demonstrated leadership at the Executive level through consistent communication, full participation and role modeling, a very positive tone was set that created an understanding by the entire company, that this culture initiative was not just a program of the month, but rather a serious intention that required commitment by all.

Program Presenters

There was a desire to approach program delivery with a blended approach by having a few of the internal members of the Fusion core team and also utilizing external consultants in areas of expertise. This would provide opportunities for the internal members to present segments that would provide context and culture accountability and afforded the ability to use the consultants in areas where they had a particular expertise. There were several benefits to this approach:

1.   Internal presenters obtained visibility for areas of the culture that they would be responsible for reinforcing and sustaining.

2.   External consultants are often viewed as having more expertise and bring a neutral, third party perspective. In some cases, external consultants can have more freedom, particularly with Executive Management to confront tough leadership issues and emphasize culture elements that are particularly sensitive or important.

3.   When the culture team is successful in selecting the "best fit" external consultants for the type of audience within the company, many times the external consultant can provide an added appeal for participants. In this case, the Fusion core team chose to integrate an external consultant in to every aspect of the culture initiative due to the long standing relationship and credibility this consultant had already developed with senior management. This particular consultant had consistently demonstrated phenomenal classroom "presence" and most of the InFocus workforce was familiar with the consultant. Using the consultant throughout the culture initiative, both in the workshop development and delivery, paid dividends in getting and keeping participants engaged in the program.

Key Points

It is very important that any presenter used in front of participants during a culture rollout must demonstrate integrity with key culture principles being presented. In the selection of external consultants, it is critical to work with consultants that will agree to comply with unspoken cultural norms.

Unfortunately, in this culture rollout, one of the external consultants used was behind the curve in the use of electronic presentations. At InFocus, the workforce is very committed to projection devices, since that is the technology of the company. When external consultants do not use the company technology and rely on older presentation mechanisms, this can be a "quick death" for the consultant with the audience. Despite encouragement to present electronically, this particular consultant chose to use an alternative delivery mechanism and was unable to establish rapport and credibility with the participants. Additionally, the presentation style the consultant used was more of a "telling nature," which opposed essential elements of the stated desired culture of employee engagement. The factors contributed to a decision by the Fusion team to not use the consultant in subsequent culture program delivery despite the loss of expertise for one of the culture components that the consultant brought to the equation.

Program Rollout

People Driving Quality (PDQ) workshops were delivered to the Executive management team beginning in January and concluded in November. As described earlier, the workshops were delivered in timeframes that accommodated the critical business issues as outlined in exhibit #

Along the way, the culture development team chose to leverage other on-going initiatives that were already a part of the environmental fabric of InFocus. For example, over the years, the Corporate Strategic Planning process has become an increasingly collaborative process that incorporates feedback from all functions and levels of the organization.

As typical with most companies, the Executive team (CEO and Vice Presidents) spends time offsite in long-term planning for strategic objectives. Prior to this type of offsite, the InFocus Executive team spends time with the divisions collecting input and ideas from the workforce about the future of the technology and the company. Also, immediately upon return from the offsite, the Executive team shares the new strategic plan with all employees over a period of a month, collecting suggestions for refinements and ideas for accomplishing the new plan before presenting it to the Board of Directors.

A new element was added to the front-end of the strategic planning process during the PDQ culture rollout. This timeframe was chosen for delivery of the Systems Thinking workshops.

This workshop focused on the concepts of systemic thinking and introduced a new tool for the participants; causal loop diagrams. For practice, the participants were asked to create a causal loop diagram related to the success of several critical business objectives from the previous corporate strategic plan. In this way, the Executive team had practical experience applying systemic thinking to real business scenarios just prior to their Corporate Strategic Planning offsite. Once again, the timely introduction of new learning tools just prior to real-time business situations reaped an outstanding result.

Celebrating Success

At the conclusion of the PDQ Culture program rollout with the Executive team, each participant was given a crystal paperweight in the shape of a mountain. The significance of the mountain was a new element added during the Corporate Strategic Planning process. The mountain is a backdrop to all communications of the Corporate Strategic Planning process and represents the effort required to climb mountains. This is a perfect analogy for the InFocus Strategic Plan for the next three year, climbing new peaks to ascend new goals.

EVALUATING SUCCESS

Given the ongoing pursuit of excellence over the tenure of InFocus, there is significant emphasis placed on measurements of success. Of course, this holds true for the investments InFocus has placed on the culture development. Both tangible and intangible objectives with specifically defined metrics were tied to the efforts on behalf of creating a culture that sets InFocus apart as a "great place to work."

It is somewhat easier to identify tangible results for culture initiatives, as it is simple to track real data with metrics like turnover, productivity or profitability. These types of metrics can be quantified and progress can be visualized.

There can be more challenge attached to measuring the intangible goals of culture creation; for example, how do you measure whether the company is a "great place to work" or employee satisfaction with leadership?

Putting the Metrics to the Test

With real diligence, however, one can also measure the intangible culture results and the process can become part of the sustaining mechanisms. In 1996, the Human Resource team had a desire to identify any gaps that might be occurring in the People Driving Quality culture. Several members of the HR team worked closely with an existing team of cross-functional representatives (the PDQ Support team) to develop a way to measure any issues or themes that were occurring in the culture.

The extended team (HR & PDQ Support Team) worked closely with an external consultant firm to create a survey mechanism that aligned with the stated core culture and corporate values. The objective was to use the survey to measure employee perception about the culture based upon their responses to questions about areas that related to InFocus values, leadership, communication, employee involvement, quality and a great place to work.

The survey created was identified as the Climate Assessment. Every employee was invited to provide feedback about the InFocus culture by completing the survey. The survey provided an anonymous mechanism to provide employee feedback. It was set up so that the responses from the various divisional populations (e.g. Sales, Marketing, Engineering, etc.) could be tracked. Employee involvement was quite high with over 75 percent of the employees completing the survey. In addition to the empirical data provided from the 60 survey questions, many employees took the time to write comments and provide anecdotal feedback. Confidentially was guaranteed. The completed employee surveys were sent to a third-party firm to compile and summarize the data into a report that would identify any thematic cultural issues or concerns for the HR team with which to work.

This process provided the Human Resource team with some "real tangible data" about what was working in the InFocus culture and what gaps existed. With this information in-hand, the HR team set about working closely with the Executive management team to identify the targeted areas to focus on for improvement. Since the survey had tracked the responses from the functional areas, the data provided insight to any themes that were consistent throughout the entire company and helped to identify pockets of the company where certain trends/issues had more significance than other trends/issues.

Armed with the employee feedback about hot spot culture issues, the Executive management team and Human Resources spent tremendous effort in tackling the identified key themes. Throughout 1997, there was constant communication with employees about efforts in place to respond to the Climate Assessment themes.

A repeat of the Climate Assessment in the subsequent year (1997) proved that the responsive dedication and effort was exceedingly worthwhile. Employee feedback from the next year's Climate Assessment survey indicated a vast improvement in the key areas that had been identified as cultural issues in 1996.

The Climate Assessment was not repeated in 1998. Positive results gained in the preceding year led to the conclusion it was time to re-invigorate the PDQ culture in 1999. Since a major culture initiative was under-way throughout 1999, and would continue through 2000, it was felt that it was too soon to implement the Climate Assessment process as a metric in 1999.

In lieu of the Climate Assessment, however, Fortune magazine had selected InFocus to participate in the Fortune Great Places to Work Trust Index in the last part of 1999. The Fortune Trust Index process included a culture survey that would be sent to 250 InFocus employees, randomly selected. While InFocus was not identified as one of the Fortune Top 100 Companies included in the magazine article, the magazine provided Human Resources with a compilation of the results from the InFocus employee feedback.

Even though the Fortune 100 survey did not include questions specifically aligned to the InFocus culture, it did address employee feedback from five dimensions that could easily be linked to many attributes of the PDQ culture:

- Credibility
- Respect
- Fairness
- Pride
- Camaraderie

The feedback provided from InFocus employee participation in the Fortune Great Places to Work Trust Index produced at least one informal data point for whether the recent effort to strengthen the PDQ Culture is working. A bottom-line summary of the Fortune survey feedback came back with over 50 percent of InFocus respondents replying positively to all statements and in most cases (questions) the response was very positive.

The success of the current culture initiative will be measured over time with key business metrics, like productivity, profitability/employee and reduced turnover. Exhibit Six depicts the observable decline in desirable turnover from the high point in 1998 to lower levels at the end of 1999. This is just the starting point of the results; InFocus hopes to gain from renewed investments in the culture. Additionally, InFocus achieved record revenues in 1999 along with enhanced profitability/employee metrics.

EXHIBIT SEVEN: ANNUAL TURNOVER REDUCTION RATE

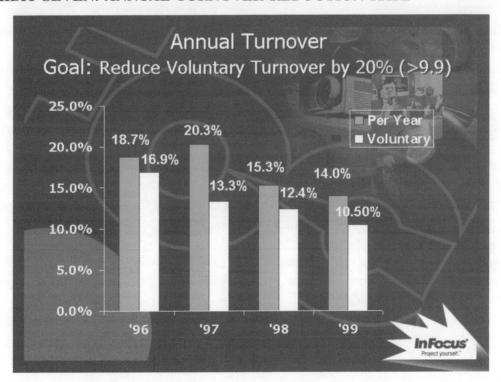

Sustaining the PDQ Culture

In order to populate the entire workforce with the PDQ culture program a rollout plan was developed for the current year.

It was decided to compress the core components of the People Driving Quality initiative into five workshop days for all InFocus managers. In keeping with recent published data that suggests that a positive experience with managers is a key retention factor for most employees, the InFocus managers and supervisors would be introduced to the same culture components and learning tools that the Executive team management team participated with. Also, there is a strong commitment at InFocus to a culture of demonstrated leadership where managers lead by example and are held accountable for results and for modeling desirable cultural behaviors. Therefore, managers were required to attend a series of workshops called PDQ Leadership, over a three-month period.

The participation requirement by all managers throughout the company was a departure from a previous culture paradigm for InFocus. In the past, all InFocus managers at all levels, have been encouraged and invited to attend culture and leadership development workshops. While there had been very strong participation, not "every" manager made the time. This is the first time workshop attendance has been made mandatory. The compelling belief is to build in mechanisms that will assist in avoiding culture dilution, particularly at the manager level.

The workshops included are the same culture components that the entire Executive Management team participated in: PDQ Leadership (Agreements), PDQ Communication (DiSC & Feedback Planner), Systems Thinking and PDQ Solutions focusing on key problem-solving tools.

As much as possible, Executive Management is invited to kick off, participate, or present on any of the core components of the PDQ Leadership series. In this way, there is consistent demonstration of the continued Executive commitment and support of the culture initiative. For most of the PDQ Leadership series, the CEO spends a bit of time at the start of the workshops stressing to participants the significance of the PDQ culture for InFocus and asking for their commitment to be involved in "making PDQ work."

In the current year, implementation plans are in place to roll out the PDQ Solutions workshop to the workforce. This workshop provides all employees with an introduction to the desired elements of the People Driving Quality culture, including the Corporate Values, Team Agreements and Problem Solving tools that support an environment of employee involvement in continuous improvement.

Additionally, the Fusion Core team developed a "sustaining mechanisms" action plan that will serve as a guidepost to continue the rollout effort and imbed the culture in the fabric of InFocus. The Fusion Core team meets quarterly for planning days to continue ensuring consistency of the PDQ workshops and identifying next steps.

EXHIBIT SEVEN: SUSTAINING MECHANISMS

Sustaining Mechanisms

Integrating PDQ Concepts/Tools Within IFS' Culture (e.g., Agreements, Lead/Manage, DiSC, Feedback Planner, Systems Thinking, IFS Values, etc.)

Stages Of Development	0 – 3 Months (Time @ IFS)	4 – 12 Months	13 + Months
Awareness *Employee is aware of concept/tool and business necessity*	Provide brief overviews and simple reference materials within PDQ Orientation Provide brief overviews and simple reference materials within New Manager Assimilation Provide a training and development resource matrix (reference catalog) that links learning objectives with development options Have senior management and/or other successful leaders (not HR) kickoff all Fusion events, and/or send e-mail announcements Develop a process for updating PDQ notebooks	Provide screen savers Publish quarterly or semi-annual schedules of PDQ efforts and training and development experiences Provide intranet marketing e-mails (e.g., a mini-newsletter) with direct quotes/testimonials from successful practitioners ("here's what I did, and here's what worked") Invite senior management and/or other successful leaders to be guest speakers sharing their experiences with PDQ, and/or co-facilitators	Publish training plans, results and trends, demonstrating how PDQ efforts are in direct response to critical business issues, and their successful impacts to date Create a "raw footage" video of desirable and undesirable PDQ behaviors Publish attendance records (to draw attention to supporters and non-supporters, and to take advantage of peer pressure) Administer charge-backs to departments with no-shows Provide bonuses or other rewards for PDQ supporters and practitioners Link training and development objectives directly to Fusion objectives and/or Strategic Plan Ensure each PDQ effort is targeted toward 2 or more measurable results
Knowledge *Employee is knowledgeable of concept/tool purpose, objectives, and potential business applications*	Provide regular marketing briefings and overviews of PDQ efforts (by HR Partners at team meetings) past successes, upcoming events, and how each team can directly apply concepts/tools OJT Designate PDQ coordinators (other than HR Partners) within each Division or Department to assist with needs assessments, program design, case development, marketing, scheduling, etc.	Administer self-assessments Administer pre-tests (e.g., on identifying product features and benefits prior to DiSC) Provide generic training experiences and participant reference materials (for new hires and make-ups)	Administer post-tests (e.g., on identifying product features and benefits after DiSC) Distribute pocket reference guides Distribute CD-ROMs Distribute a desktop accessories (mouse pad, clock, pen holder, paperweight)

Stages Of Development	0 – 3 Months (Time @ IFS)	4 – 12 Months	13 + Months
Understanding *Employee can understand how to apply concept/tool in a business case study or simulation*	Ensure all PDQ training efforts incorporate current IFS business examples and applications	Offer brown-bag refresher workshops (following generic training experience) with job-specific case applications	Provide intact team training experiences with job-specific and team-specific case applications Provide luncheon celebrations for successful practitioners (who can be presented as role models for others)
Skill *Employee applies concept/tool on the job*		Provide on-the-job coaching and reinforcement (from learning coaches, HR Partners, and/or external consultants) Design participant materials with specific action plans that tie to team objectives and/or performance appraisals Prepare 90-day post-training development plans and schedules Conduct 90-day post-training evaluations and publish highlights and trends	Provide train-the-trainer workshops to develop learning coaches Provide advanced training experience with role plays and video tape feedback Document acquired skills on performance appraisals Provide reward and recognition efforts for those who show initiative, risk, and/or succeed Organize presentations to senior management of successes experienced Assess PDQ efforts per Fusion objectives (using separate survey, culture assessment, Fortune's survey, etc.) Redesign the performance appraisal to directly assess Fusion desired behaviors/skills Link post-training measurements directly to advanced intact team business objectives

Key Lessons Learned

Keep the Executive support and commitment of the culture initiative in the forefront, continuously. Assume the Executive team will continue to demonstrate their support and task someone with keeping them involved. Find ways to have them assist in communication of the importance of the culture, invite Executives to participate in whatever way possible with current culture workshops, continue to provide Executives with updates about the on-going culture initiative updates and create visible ways to demonstrate their ongoing support. Involvement begets involvement.

Organizational Learning as part of Culture Creation

Over the past decade Organizational Learning has been touted as a competitive advantage for companies but in reality, there are few published accounts of the efforts required to create Organizational Learning. To some degree, there is still an air of mystery about the steps involved to create organizational learning, even within companies that are recognized for utilizing this "Best Practice."

There is a significant distinction between organizational learning and training. Training is the delivery of content that enhances the knowledge or skill of an individual or group of individuals. Organizational learning is the "organic" knowledge or skills that become integrated within the structure, systems and skills of the organizations throughout the company.

The company culture of InFocus is the primary lever that accelerated the ability to accomplish organizational learning. It is important that understand that organizational learning requires a solid foundation to ensure success. The effort and diligence lent toward building, maintaining and sustaining the company culture at InFocus have provided a solid foundation from which to build organizational learning.

About the Contributor

Rebecca Lynch-Wilmot (rebecca.lynch-wilmot@infocus.com)is responsible for Organizational Learning at InFocus, based in Wilsonville, Oregon. In her role of Director, Organizational Effectiveness, she provides leadership and direction for corporate culture initiatives, leadership development and systems capabilities. Rebecca has an education and leadership background and has been instrumental in the development of Learning Organization concepts throughout the company particularly the recent emphasis InFocus has embarked on to build expertise across the organizations in Systems Thinking. Throughout her tenure, InFocus has much recognition as a Learning Organization and has consistently received top honors from Oregon Magazine's Top 100 Best Companies in Oregon for the Advancement and Training with a 100% ranking in that criteria measurement.

With over 20 years experience in the fields of Education and Corporate training, Rebecca has written articles on Learning Organization implementations for several publications and has been a presenter for many conferences and university programs. Rebecca is currently involved with evolving the InFocus culture model as the company completes an integration/merger with it's largest competitor.

9

MASSACHUSETTS GENERAL HOSPITAL

An organizational learning program that led two departments into a new era of problem solving, producing quanifiable results that benefited thousands of patients

BACKGROUND

Massachusetts General Hospital (MGH), founded in 1811, is the third oldest hospital in the United States. Instrumental in the creation of MGH were two physicians, James Jackson and John Collins Warren. The founders' bold vision was two-fold: provide the most advanced, humane medical care possible and raise the standards of medical education in New England. Drs. Jackson and Warren established the New England Journal of Medicine, and ushered in an era of "firsts" – like being the first to use ether during surgery - that continue to this day. This history of achievement has resulted in MGH having the largest hospital-based research program in the United States, with a budget of more than $200 million.

In 1994, MGH joined with Brigham and Women's Hospital to form Partners HealthCare System, Inc. The objective of this collaboration is to enhance patient care, teaching, and research, as well as to provide an integrated health care delivery system to patients throughout the region. The affiliation includes primary care physicians, specialists, community hospitals, the two founding academic medical centers, McLean Hospital, Spaulding Rehabilitation Hospital, and some home health agencies. Communication within the system is of the utmost importance to prevent duplication from increasing and having the patient feel "lost in the shuffle." Indeed, the system provides care for many patients. Each year MGH admits about 35,000 inpatients, handles more than 1 million visits in its Clinical Support Services and Quality Assurance. By coordinating the health care system, there can be less duplication of effort and, more importantly, better response to patient needs.

The senior management team at MGH consists of the Chairman, Vice Chair of Quality Assurance, Administrative Director of Radiology, Managing Director of the Radiology Consulting Group, and the Senior Managers of Clinical Support Services and Quality, Management, and Education. This team has, as its overarching goal, to continuously improve patient care through the ability to leverage technology and deploy continuous process improvement efforts.

INTRODUCTION

This world-class organization, known around the globe for its superior medical care, also devotes a focus of excellence to its organizational processes. The case study will highlight the insights and performance improvement gained from careful attention and leadership commitment given to a persistent business issue. Even though the content of this issue is germane to a hospital setting, the process undertaken and the lessons learned can be applied to other organizations dealing with functional silos. First, some highlights on two specific functions.

Department of Orthopaedics

The Orthopaedics Department at MGH has as its mission to provide the highest quality musculoskeletal patient care, teaching and research, with a dedication to service and a commitment to leadership. Orthopaedics has expertise in the following specialties:

Biomotion Research and Biomechanics
Foot and Ankle Surgery
Hand and Upper Extremity
Hip and Knee
Joint Reconstruction/Arthroplasty
Pediatric Orthopaedics
Shoulder
Spine
Sports Medicine (taking care of Boston's beloved Bruins and New England's Patriots!)
Orthopaedic Trauma
Orthopaedic Oncology/Tumor

Radiology Department

The Department of Radiology provides diagnostic imaging services for MGH and its affiliates 24 hours a day, 7 days a week through its 17 specialty divisions. The department performs more than 365,000 imaging procedures annually at the radiology facility on the MGH main campus and at the Lawrence E. Martin Laboratories in the MGH Charlestown Navy Yard research complex. Routine radiologic examinations include musculoskeletal radiography, mammography, CAT scan, MRI, diagnostic breast imaging, nuclear medicine, fluoroscopy, pediatric radiography, GU studies, GI studies, thoracic (chest) radiography and ultrasound.

THE BUSINESS PROBLEM

Historically, both the Radiology Department and the Orthopedic Department have looked at the service they provide their patients independently from each other. Each organization focused their service improvement activities within their own functional area in an attempt to incrementally enhance the patient experience from that departmental perspective. No longer could each department afford to look at their processes as simply a functional/linear operation. It was simply too inefficient and costly to do so. In the words of the Special Projects Manager for Orthopaedics, functioning this way gave one the "feeling of being at the mercy of others in terms of work flow." This business problem was diagnosed by observation. Additionally, the Managing Director of the Radiology Consulting Group recognized that "[w]e had problem. We had waits that exceeded 30 minutes." The diagnosis of the problem then turned into a question. "How do we change the model so that we can provide the best possible care to our *collective* patients?"

Section Analysis

The changes necessary to reach the new objective of increased quality of patient care and throughput required interventions on two significant levels: technological and human.

Orthopaedics is a referral source to Radiology. It is the Orthpaedics patient that is sent to Radiology. A typical viewpoint of Orthopaedics was "If you want my business, I am your referral source into that type of customer. If you want my business, make sure you are delivering a good service, a good type of product."

Radiology processed patients. They strove to take images as efficiently as possible. They wanted to take quality images and get people on their way. With the old work flow, Radiology produced a hard copy which was the ONLY image. When that image was produced, the Radiology Physician would read an image and record the impressions. After doing the reading, there was a need to consult with another physician as a matter of course. The time that had elapsed was perhaps a half-hour. The patient had to then wait in a Radiology lobby for the readings to be done on those films. Then, the hard copy would be released *to the patient*, who would then carry those films back to the Orthopaedics Physician for his assessment. The patient would wait again to be seen by the physician who they saw an hour or so ago. The Orthopedic Physician would have his own interpretation of the films and they may or may not have been able to incorporate Radiology's reading into their own evaluation. It depends. The patient was then seen by the Orthopedist and, depending on how late in the day and how backed up the Orthopedist was, there would be a wait there, too. It was a very inefficient system and the patient was asked to pay in terms of time.

Inherent in this processing of patients was that Radiology knew the peak times. These spikes in the system made it difficult to predict exact staffing needs—it was either too few or too many. So, one objective would be a smoother processing of patients. One poignant example was given of how a patient was sent from Orthopaedics to Radiology to have images taken. "Mr. Brown" was sent out at 10 a.m. and he didn't return to Orthopaedics until 1 p.m. This caused significant delays. Even more interesting was the fact that Orthopedists didn't care *where* the sources of delay were. That is not to infer an indifference or apathy. They just want their patients back in a reasonable time frame. Any delay was an issue of concern for them.

Radiology stated a differing point of view at the beginning of this project. The perception there that once a patient was finished in Radiology, the commitment by the department was complete. "Hey, we're done," stated one viewpoint.. It didn't, however, work out that simply.

It was evident here that differing views have the effect of doing two things to all those involved:

(1)   They were keeping the two departments as separate entities, concerned only with what was happening in their own world, without considering the effect on the other depart ment (how many times does that happen in an organization??!).

(2)   These separate viewpoints permeated the language used. When listening to either department talk about the other, the reference made is "*They* this…" or "*They* that…" It was am "us" versus "them" dichotomy.

A Shift to "We"

This dichotomy was really evident at the beginning, when the design of the new Computed Radiography (CR) system was under consideration. Radiology and Orthopaedics had separate systems. A great deal of thought went into Radiology when they built their own general network and specified the kind of workstations and work flow desired. This raised the general question within Orthopaedics: "How could they know exactly what the Orthopedists would want? Isn't that up to the Orthopedist?" And the Orthopedist was also saying, 'We don't know anything about this…we're not so happy with this…going along with this project to save *Radiology* money.'

The new system – Computed Radiography – sounded strong. The benefits included: (1) the leveraging of technology (2) increasing service and (3) reducing cost. The implementation team went in favor of broad decentralization that can be realized from a web-based product. This allowed a physician to log onto any Partners workstation, see the image, and diagnose his patient's x-rays. The physician doesn't need a private copy. CR also reduces wait time by patients. That is its chief benefit. Because there is a decentralization, there is also dissemination. Now it was possible for the Radiologist to read the film and do their impression, while the Orthopedic Physician simultaneously looked at it and made his own assessment. Things happened in parallel instead of sequentially, so time was being saved. This was, and is, a powerful benefit.

One of the other benefits of Computed Radiography is its storage capability. With storage, you can retrieve images, filmed today, yesterday, or three months ago. This serves as added value to the patient, who is spared the inconvenience of carrying film.

In practice, this system is available on the Partners network. Image quality is very important. This was a point of contention. Another problem that emerged as a result of CR is patient throughput. Patient throughput, from Radiology's point of view, is a measured amount of time of how long a patient has to wait until the image is taken and posted to the Web.

As had been pointed out by the Special Projects Manager for Orthopaedics, "This is where Radiology had to expand their consciousness and this is where the Managing Director of the Radiology Consulting Group really started taking charge of it." He continued, "They basically had to redefine what they were doing."

As a result of this redefinition, a whole new term called Total Throughput was invented. Total throughput measures the time a patient arrives in Radiology's waiting room until the time in which an image is available to any doctor who is looking for it. It added the component of time and this had its own ramifications. Radiology was working hard to develop metrics to measure their progress and now had to add a whole new component of wait time. This change also pulled people together to view the situation from a similar perspective. They had a whole new constituency of people who were anxious to know, "Can we improve this total throughput time?"

Going Beyond the Technology

After four or five months, the improvements through technology included increased server capacity and parallel tasking type processes. They were legitimately related to the CR project. After that, the CR project became inextricably linked with the other issues of work flow and processes. As the Special Projects Manager for Orthopaedics stated, "It took awhile to realize that there were problems and they didn't have anything to do with the system." Because of the long wait times that Radiology observed, they began to ask, 'What can we do to somewhat flatten this curve so that it is acceptable from an Orthopedist's position?' Their intervention was to talk with referring physicians and patients in order to begin controlling the arrival rates.

Adding the Human Factor

Redesigned patient flow processes were implemented to improve throughput time. (The typical benchmark is 45-48 minutes.) The patient flow process includes:

Asking patients to come in a little earlier from their stated appointment time to start the paperwork, etc. (It has been observed that patients don't seem to mind if they can see the time savings out of that.);

Separating dressing rooms from exam rooms;

Adding dressing room capacity so that one can use the dressing room before and after the exam and leave the exam room just for the actual exam;

Receiving support from both the Chiefs of Radiology and Orthopaedics to form a committee to take on any issue that has anything to do with processing patients between Orthopaedics and Radiology.

The Managing Director of the Radiology Consulting Group had noted that there were not a lot of other Radiology Departments within other hospitals that have implemented this process. This was yet another first for MGH.

Focal Point for Systems Thinking and Continuous Learning

The Orthopedic/Radiology Committee (now called the Computed Radiography Committee) was formed to discuss issues and work on cooperative projects that affect both departments. As the Special Projects Manager for Orthopaedics reflected, "This is one of the factors that has boosted recognition on both sides for systems thinking. It makes sense to think of the linkage to the other department...[even though] we have different jobs that we do and it takes us in different directions, we have a big point of intersection."

This simple change of mindset – analyzing where departments intersect with other departments – can be a very powerful way of addressing common business challenges.

DESIGN OF THE PROGRAM

A Leadership Seminar Series consisting of three seminars – *Organizational Learning and Systems Thinking: Leading the Way for Managing Change; The Theory of Constraint; and Organizational Assessment and Strategic Leadership* – were provided to all Division Heads, Vice Chairs, Physicians, and Operations Managers in the Spring of 1999. These three seminars had major threads connecting each other. All three of the seminars had a pre-reading assignment for the participants. These pre-reading assignments provided the overall structure for each of the respective seminars. Key questions regarding leadership and organizational learning were then generated in the seminar for further discussion. The objectives and sequence for each of the seminars are as follows:

Seminar I: *Organizational Learning and Systems Thinking: Leading the Way for Managing Change*

The goals of this seminar were to have participants:

1. Gain an understanding of the essence of organizational learning

2. Diagnosis their organization's learning capabilities

3. View problems from the four levels of understanding: events, patterns, structure, and shared vision

4. Apply the most commonly used tool in systems thinking to recurring problems Learn how to identify key leverage points for improved thinking and effective action strategies

5. Examine how systems thinking can be applied in their organization

Sequence of Seminar:

9:00 a.m. - 10 a.m.	**Introduction to Organizational Learning and to Systems Thinking** **Application exercise**
10 a.m. - 10:30 a.m.	**Four Response Levels:** **Events, Patterns, Structure, Vision** **Learning Organization Assessment**
10:30 a.m. - 12 noon	**Systems Thinking Tools and Techniques:** **Causal Loop Diagrams** **Systems Archetype** **Systems Thinking Case Study and Debrief**
12 noon – 1 p.m.	**Lunch Break**
1 p.m. – 2 p.m.	**Hands-on, Experiential Exercise to learn Systems Thinking** **Debrief**
2 p.m. – 3:30 p.m.	**Applying Systems Thinking to your own organization** **Design and discussion using systems thinking tools**
3:30 - 4 p.m.	**Seminar Wrap-Up**

Seminar II: *The Theory of Constraint.*

This seminar was 3 hours in length, from 1-4 p.m. and focused on the main premise of *The Goal,* which is identifying the major constraint that exists in all organizations.

Discussion and application revolved around the Five Focusing Steps of the Theory of Constraints, which are:

1.   Identify the weakest link; i.e., the system's constraint

2.   Determine how to exploit the system's constraint

3.   Subordinate/synchronize all other decisions to the above

4.   Elevate the system's constraint

5.   Do not allow inertia to become the system's constraint

Seminar III: *Organizational Assessment and Strategic Leadership*

The goals of this seminar were to:

1.   Assess organizations at varying levels of management

2.   Match leadership style to the organization

3.   Achieve organizational change

4.   Discuss *The General* and organizational assessment through the ranks

This seminar was 3 hours in length, from 1-4 p.m. Its agenda for the afternoon was as follows:

Introduction
Organizational Assessment
Framework
Process
After Action Review
Discussion of *The General*
National Training Center
Conclusion

A description of the tools and instruments used in Seminar I are described in the section below. Exhibit One depicts the initial needs assessment undertaken.

EXHIBIT ONE:

Initial Needs Assessment Questions for Seminar I
1. **What do you think the doctors will want to know about organizational learning in order to improve performance?** **Response:** **The physicians will probably want to know how to employ certain behavioral practices to help adapt to the changes in healthcare.**
2. **Where do you think the major areas of concern are for them that we can address with this particular seminar?** **Response:** **Cost constraints, having to increase access and care to the patient while trying to reduce cost (simultaneously).**
3. **What do you think the "hook" will be for them to sit up and take notice? (content-wise—big picture emphasis, interpersonal issues, building a learning culture, etc.)** **Response:** **The "hook" will be in the fact that the industry is changing rapidly and environmental pressures are forcing us to change both from a business and care perspective. How do we stay ahead of the curve and meet the challenges.**

NEEDS ASSESSMENT

The input to these needs assessment questions were provided by the Vice Chairman at Massachusetts General Hospital and by the Senior Manager of Quality, Management and Education (whose title is now Managing Director of the Radiology Consulting Group). The data generated from this initial needs assessment helped to shape the objectives of Seminar I. One significant assessment tool used in this seminar was the **Learning Organization Assessment** by Peter Kline and Bernard Saunders from their book, *Ten Steps to a Learning Organization*. A copy of the **Learning Organization Assessment** is highlighted below in Exhibit Two:

EXHIBIT TWO:

Learning Organization Assessment

The thirty-six statements below could be read as at least a partial description of what constitutes a Learning Organization, and the attitudes and behaviors associated with it. This assessment asks you to think about the current reality of your own organization (or one of its subgroups/departments) and to make a judgment about how well each statement describes it.

Using the response options below, write in the blank before each statement the number which best describes your answer.

Response Options:

1=Not at all

2=To a slight extent

3=To a moderate extent

4=To a great extent

5=To a very great extent

The current reality in my organization is that:

_____ 1. People feel free to speak their minds about what they have learned. There is no fear, threat, or repercussion for disagreeing or dissenting.

_____ 2. Mistakes made by individuals or departments are turned into constructive learning experiences.

_____ 3. There is a general feeling that it's always possible to find a better way to do something.

_____ 4. Multiple viewpoints and open, productive debates are encouraged and cultivated.

_____5. Experimentation is endorsed and championed, and is a way of doing business.

_____6. Mistakes are clearly viewed as positive growth opportunities throughout the system.

_____7. There is willingness to break old patterns in order to experiment with different ways of organizing and managing daily work.

_____8. Management practices are innovative, creative, and periodically risk-taking.

_____9. The quality of work life in our organization is improving.

_____10. There are formal and informal structures designed to encourage people to share what they learn with their peers and the rest of the organization.

_____11. The organization is perceived as designed for problem solving and learning.

_____12. Learning is expected and encouraged across all levels of the organization: management, employees, supervision, "customers."

_____13. People have an overview of the organization beyond their specialty and function, and adapt their working patterns to it.

_____14. "Lessons learned" sessions are conducted so as to produce clear, specific, and permanent structural and organizational changes.

_____15. Management practices, operations, policies, and procedures that become obsolete by hindering the continued growth of people and the organization are removed and replaced with workable systems and structures.

_____16. Continuous improvement is expected and treated receptively.

_____17. There are clear and specific expectations of each employee to receive a specified number of hours of training and education annually.

_____18. Workers at all levels are specifically directed towards relevant and valuable training and learning opportunities—inside and outside the organization.

_____19. Cross-functional learning opportunities are expected and organized on a regular basis, so that people understand the functions of others whose jobs are different, but of related importance.

_____20. Middle managers are seen as having the primary role in keeping the learning process running smoothly throughout the organization.

_____21. The unexpected is viewed as an opportunity for learning.

_____22. People look forward to improving their own competencies as well as those of the whole organization.

_____23. The systems, structures, policies, and procedures of the organization are designed to be adaptive, flexible, and responsible to internal and external stimuli.

_____24. Presently, even if the environment of the organization is complicated, chaotic, and active, nevertheless, it is not on overload.

_____25. There is a healthy, manageable level of stress that assists in promoting learning.

_____26. Continuous improvement is practiced as well as preached.

_____27. The difference between training/education and learning is clearly understood. (The difference being that the learning is shared with others in the organization.)

_____28. People are encouraged and provided the resources to become self-directed learners.

_____29. There is a formal, on-going education program to prepare middle managers in their new role as teachers, coaches, and leaders.

_____30. Recognition of your own learning style and those of co-workers is used to improve communication and over-all organizational learning.

_____31. Management is sensitive to learning and development differences in their employees, realizing that people learn and improve their situations in many different ways.

_____32. There is sufficient time scheduled into people's professional calendars to step back from day-to-day operations and reflect on what is happening in the organization.

_____33. There is direction and resource allocation planned to bring about meaningful and lasting learning.

_____34. Teams are recognized and rewarded for their innovative and paradigm breaking solutions to problems.

_____35. Managers have considerable skills for gathering information and developing their abilities to cope with demanding and changing management situations.

_____36. Managers enable their staffs to become self-developers, and learn how to improve their performance.

Evaluating the Results
The results of the *Learning Organization Assessment* can be compiled, analyzed, and used in several ways. The quickest is a simple results average, dividing the sum of all the ratings by 36, the number of statements. This average indicates, on a scale of 1-5, the degree to which the respondent believes his or her organization possesses the characteristics of a Learning Organization.

During the afternoon of Seminar I, a hands-on, experiential exercise was used to engage participants more actively in the learning process. The exercise used simulated the flow and constraints in an organization. An interesting story in using the experiential exercise came up during the design phase of the seminar. The designers questioned whether actually engaging in hands-on games with physicians would go over very well. The underlying assumption was that this audience was very serious and would look upon an experiential exercise as frivolous. After asking key stakeholders at MGH, however, it was determined that this would be something that the participants would enjoy and embrace. And they were right; the participants in the seminar loved it! It was successful due to the fact that people were involved, engaged in the exercise, and they could readily identify with the flow and bottlenecks of their own system.

The participants in the *Organizational Learning and Systems Thinking* seminar were presented with the specific tools of systems thinking: causal loop diagrams and system archetypes.

Causal loop diagrams allow both individuals and teams to diagnose their issues and challenges using a "what is influencing what" type of diagram. What makes this type of diagramming different from other problem-solving methodologies is that causal loops look at the *whole* of the problem, rather than breaking a problem down to its constituent parts. Causal loops are great for team learning because members of a team are able to diagram the organizational problem or issue they are dealing with, showing the interdependencies of the variables in their story. Team members are then able to inquire into each other's thinking based on the diagram that is drawn. Diagramming a problem this way allows others to understand how the problem or issue is being viewed in its entirety. Learning to draw causal loops can take some time; however, causal loops help tremendously in understanding problems.

System archetypes take the causal loop diagrams a step further. System archetypes are generic structures that capture the underlying dynamics of the same problem so that the key leverage point for intervention can be identified. Identifying the key leverage helps to solve the problem for the long-term. A systems archetype is illustrated for the case study that was given to participants in Seminar I in Exhibit Three.

The sample case study given to the participants is as follows:

EXHIBIT THREE:

Systems Thinking Case Study: Organizational Diagnosis in Healthcare

Intermountain Health Care (IHC) is an integrated-care delivery system that includes 23 hospitals, a physician division, and a health plan (HMO) division. Healthcare services are provided to communities throughout Utah, Wyoming, and Idaho. For the past 10 years, the state of Utah has outpaced the national average in job creation. The state has also shown strong population growth over the past six years. Along with this growth, Utah has one of the lowest unemployment rates in the country.
 	
    This organization has also experienced expansion in the number of patients seen in the facilities and the number of enrollees in the health plans. After years of declining hospital occupancy, there has been a struggle to keep up with the need for hospital beds and staff. And because desirable jobs are so plentiful in our area, employees are difficult to recruit and there has been an increase in turnover rates across departments. The overall concern that all three divisions face is to sustain a competitive market advantage. In order to do this, three different strategies have been developed for three divisions in our integrated-care delivery system: (1) The hospital's strategy includes efforts to reduce labor and capital costs; (2) The Health Plans' efforts are to increase market penetration through various partnerships and increasing market share with corporate benefits plans; (3) The Physician Division focuses on efforts to align and represent MDs.
 	
    The healthcare industry is shifting towards downsizing and downskilling healthcare employees. Some healthcare organizations have sought to control the costs of health services by using entry-level employees for some tasks instead of highly trained—and more expensive—professionals. Over the last two years physician groups have started to lose substantial money on their contracts with the HMO providers. Also, prescription drug costs have been steadily increasing the last few years. This current year drug costs are resulting in double-digit increases. IHC has been affected by all of these trends.
 	
    Two projects were intended to make the hospital more efficient—one project involved outpatient surgery; the other laboratory services. While working on the projects, the conclusion was reached that, in some cases, the hospital could cut costs and better meet patients' expectations by using higher educated and higher paid staff instead of entry-level employees. In the outpatient surgery unit, for example, it was found that costs per patient could be reduced by 14 per cent by retaining an all-professional staff to carry out a reengineered patient-flow process. This counterintuitive finding led a special team to focus on the difficulty of recruiting professional staff, particularly in areas requiring specialized clinical education and experience. The one area that caused a lot of consternation revolves around the hospital's strategy of reducing labor and capital costs. This strategy is causing an increase in organizational stress. The indicators used to measure organizational stress include an increase in the turnover rate, rookie factor, workload and employee dissatisfaction. Something has to be done to address these alarming trends and consequences.

Adapted from *The Systems Thinker, November 1997, Vol. 8, No. 9. Updated May 1999.*

After reading the case study, the participants were asked to diagram the dynamics in the case using a very common system archetype entitled Shifting the Burden. A sample of this archetype is depicted in EXHIBIT FOUR.

To read this archetype: A problem is solved by applying a symptomatic solution (B1), which diverts attention away from the more fundamental solution (B2). Applying a symptomatic solution always generates side effects (R1).

EXHIBIT FOUR:

Shifting the Burden System Archetype

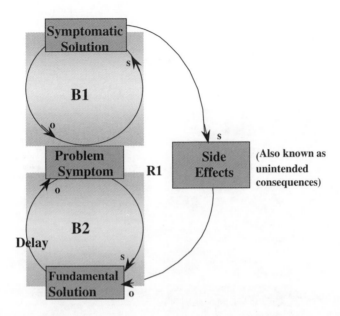

The system archetype for the systems thinking case study is illustrated in Exhibit Five, on the following page.

Case Study System Archetype.

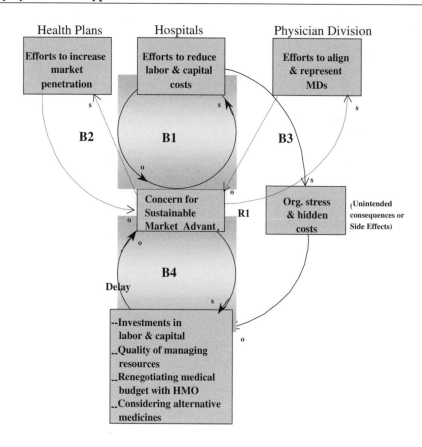

To read archetype: The problem being addressed is the "Concern for Sustainable Market Advantage." There have been three strategies developed at IHC for their three divisions as represented by Loops **B1, B2, and B3.** The hospital's strategy has caused unintended consequences to emerge in the form of organizational stress and hidden costs, which include an increase in the turnover rate, rookie factor, workload and employee dissatisfaction. These unintended consequences have the effect of both overwhelming the original problem symptom (Concern for sustainable market advantage) and over the long term, diminishes the search for the fundamental solution (**B4**).

Participants then had the opportunity to apply the systems thinking tools to their own organizational issues. Participants were broken up into teams of three and/or four. They were asked to identify a business issue, problem, or challenge and then to diagram that issue based on an appropriate systems archetype that represented the fundamental structure of their business issue. From there, participants discussed the key leverage point for helping to solve the problem. Discussion of possible consequences of this intervention point was also undertaken. All the small teams then reconvened into one large group to discuss their business issue, the archetype chosen, the key intervention point and the consequences of that leverage point. Feedback to the team was provided by the facilitator and by other seminar participants.

Two other significant tools were implemented from Seminars II and III. The first was applying the Theory of Constraints— identifying where the "weak links" are in any given organizational issue and utilizing Another was the After Action Review, which is a debriefing tool to focus on what worked, what did not, and what should have been done differently. Both of these tools highly complement systems thinking.

REINFORCEMENT OF CHANGE

Continuous improvement is the hallmark for Radiology and Orthopaedics in their efforts to reach their goal of providing the best in patient care and throughput. One program has already been discussed: the creation of the Computed Radiography Committee to meet regularly to discuss issues that affect both Radiology and Orthopaedics. Another continuous improvement and learning effort is the continuation of the Leadership Development programs which are developed around their strategic direction and objectives. There is an emphasis to develop programs which strike a balance between their clinical and business objectives.

The interviews that were conducted asked for feedback on the seminars. They produced numerous responses. Open-ended questions were asked that revolved around these questions:

Tell me about the changes that have occurred in your respective area

Describe the process before and after these changes

Talk about the metrics used to measure improvements

How is systems thinking and organizational learning being used…what are the challenges?

What do you see as the "next steps" for further improvement and growth?

The interviews and discussions conducted revealed best practices. These best practices were a result of the strategy, objectives and programs put in place at MGH to continually reinforce and strengthen its leadership position. The best practices are highlighted in
EXHIBIT SIX:

Best Practices at MGH
• **Reputation for Quality Care**
• **Recognized Industry Leadership**
• **Reputation for Excellence in Patient Satisfaction**
• **Process Improvement with Patient Throughput**
• **Forum for Cross-Functional Issues**
• **Open Communication Channels**
• **Turning Business Problems into Higher-Level Questions**
• **Adaptation for Measurable Process Improvement**
• **Committed Leadership and Staff**

EVALUATION

The evaluation will be presented in three sections:

Quantitative measures. Improvements in patient throughput and tracking of this measure (which links directly to the original objective) is done monthly and is posted on the wall in Radiology for all to view. By leveraging technology and systems thinking, patient throughput time was reduced by 34%. An example of the latest figures on patient throughput from Radiology is presented in Exhibit Seven:

EXHIBIT SEVEN:

Radiology's Statistics on Patient Throughput for the Month of February 2000

Data ACC5 Radiology: Daily Patient Wait Times and Exam Volume

Day/Date	Daily Patient Wait Time	Exam Volume	Mean Wait Time by Week	Mean Wait Time by Month
T 6/29	12.1	200	11.2	10.95
W 6/30	9.8	81	11.2	10.95
Th 7/1	12.6	121	11.2	17.62
F 7/2	10.3	123	11.2	17.62
M 7/5	0	0	16.05	17.62
T 7/6	24.7	198	16.05	17.62
W 7/7	11.9	121	16.05	17.62
Th 7/8	17.4	184	16.05	17.62
F 7/9	10.2	68	16.05	17.62
M 7/12	38.4	129	17.62	17.62
T 7/13	15.1	171	17.62	17.62
W 7/14	7.3	80	17.62	17.62
Th 7/15	14.5	158	17.62	17.62
F 7/16	12.8	106	17.62	17.62
M 7/19	53.6	171	24.6	17.62
T 7/20	18	171	24.6	17.62
W 7/21	18.5	131	24.6	17.62
Th 7/22	20.2	186	24.6	17.62
F 7/23	12.7	117	24.6	17.62
M 7/26	14.7	144	17.9	17.62
T 7/27	24.1	212	17.9	17.62
W 7/28	15.1	150	17.9	17.62
Th 7/29	14.3	166	17.9	17.62
F 7/30	21.2	144	17.9	17.62
M 8/2	10.6	107	14.8	16.64
T 8/3	23.2	208	14.8	16.64
W 8/4	10.3	116	14.8	16.64
Th 8/5	14.4	180	14.8	16.64
F 8/6	15.5	118	14.8	16.64
M 8/9	9.8	119	14.7	16.64
T 8/10	25.9	192	14.7	16.64
W 8/11	10.1	128	14.7	16.64
Th 8/12	17.6	132	14.7	16.64
F 8/13	10.2	100	14.7	16.64
M 8/16	13.8	118	16.56	16.64

T 8/17	20.9	164	16.56	16.64
W 8/18	16.5	160	16.56	16.64
Th 8/19	19.5	182	16.56	16.64
F 8/20	12.1	84	16.56	16.64
M 8/23	14.3	110	19.8	16.64
T 8/24	28	150	19.8	16.64
W 8/25	21.3	148	19.8	16.64
Th 8/26	22.2	151	19.8	16.64
F 8/27	13	93	19.8	16.64
M 8/30	13.2	136	15.1	16.64
T 8/31	23.7	188	15.1	16.64
W 9/1	9.6	96	15.1	23.66
Th 9/2	17.2	131	15.1	23.66
F 9/3	12	109	15.1	23.66
M 9/6	0	0	34	23.66
T 9/7	43	167	34	23.66
W 9/8	30.4	148	34	23.66
Th 9/9	28.3	166	34	23.66
F 9/10	34.2	157	34	23.66
M 9/13	24	154	26.2	23.66
T 9/14	52.1	202	26.2	23.66
W 9/15	17.1	130	26.2	23.66
Th 9/16	20	132	26.2	23.66
F 9/17	17.9	133	26.2	23.66
M 9/20	40.5	167	33.3	23.66
T 9/21	41.7	199	33.3	23.66
W 9/22	39.5	142	33.3	23.66
Th 9/23	21.9	154	33.3	23.66
F 9/24	22.9	130	33.3	23.66
M 9/27	9	124	17.3	23.66
T 9/28	13.2	214	17.3	23.66
W 9/29	10.8	140	17.3	23.66
Th 9/30	15.2	142	17.3	23.66
F 10/1	38.2	140	17.3	20.81
M 10/4	14.4	139	14.52	20.81
T 10/5	15.9	186	14.52	20.81
W 10/6	14.9	128	14.52	20.81

Th 10/7	16	158	14.52	20.81
F 10/8	11.4	115	14.52	20.81
M 10/11	0	0	16.05	20.81
T 10/12	27.8	210	16.05	20.81
W 10/13	11.5	118	16.05	20.81
Th 10/14	12.8	149	16.05	20.81
F 10/15	12.1	115	16.05	20.81
M 10/18	27.4	168	24.6	20.81
T 10/19	38.3	228	24.6	20.81
W 10/20	13.8	137	24.6	20.81
Th 10/21	19.1	179	24.6	20.81
F 10/22	24.4	130	24.6	20.81
M 10/25	28.6	176	27.8	20.81
T 10/26	32.9	209	27.8	20.81
W 10/27	19.8	134	27.8	20.81
Th 10/28	21.8	168	27.8	20.81
F 10/29	36	132	27.8	20.81
M 11/1	11.1	133	11.4	17.48
T 11/2	14.7	199	11.4	17.48
W 11/3	16.9	130	11.4	17.48
Th 11/4	6.3	101	11.4	17.48
F 11/5	8.2	113	11.4	17.48
M 11/08	11.2	154	13.04	17.48
T 11/09	14.9	174	13.04	17.48
W 11/10	11.9	154	13.04	17.48
Th 11/11	15.5	141	13.04	17.48
F 11/12	11.7	92	13.04	17.48
M 11/15	18.6	167	26.2	17.48
T 11/16	44.4	206	26.2	17.48
W 11/17	15.6	141	26.2	17.48
Th 11/18	32.2	190	26.2	17.48
F 11/19	20.2	140	26.2	17.48
M 11/22	32.2	165	28.9	17.48
T 11/23	40.5	188	28.9	17.48
W 11/24	13.9	98	28.9	17.48
Th 11/25	0	0	28.9	17.48
F 11/26	0	0	28.9	17.48

M 11/29	15.0	150	22.7	17.48
T 11/30	29.6	183	22.7	17.48
W 12/01	12.4	119	22.7	21.33
Th 12/02	38.3	161	22.7	21.33
F 12/03	18.1	108	22.7	21.33
M 12/06	39.2	156	27.3	21.33
T 12/07	43.5	186	27.3	21.33
W 12/08	17.1	129	27.3	21.33
Th 12/09	25.5	142	27.3	21.33
F 12/10	11.2	74	27.3	21.33
M 12/13	44.6	163	30.4	21.33
T 12/14	30.2	151	30.4	21.33
W 12/15	21.8	162	30.4	21.33
Th 12/16	22.4	140	30.4	21.33
F 12/17	33.0	104	30.4	21.33
M 12/20	36.7	163	24.25	21.33
T 12/21	36.9	164	24.25	21.33
W 12/22	14.4	134	24.25	21.33
Th 12 23	9.0	106	24.25	21.33
F 12/24	0.0	0	24.25	21.33
M 12/27	7.4	82	9.10	21.33
T 12/28	9.5	80	9.10	21.33
W 12/29	10.4	85	9.10	21.33
Th 12/30	9.1	83	9.10	21.33
F 12/31	0	0	9.10	21.33
M 1/03	16.2	148	18.86	18.90
T 1/04	31.4	206	18.86	18.90
W 1/05	12.1	109	18.86	18.90
Th 1/06	21.0	142	18.86	18.90
F 1/07	13.6	119	18.86	18.90
M 1/10	20.3	132	18.66	18.90
T 1/11	34.5	174	18.66	18.90
W 1/12	17.2	116	18.66	18.90
Th 1/13	10.6	116	18.66	18.90
F 1/14	10.7	107	18.66	18.90
M 1/17	0.0	0	19.63	18.90
T 1/18	32.0	191	19.63	18.90

W 1/19	12.2	126	19.63	18.90
Th 1/20	14.3	161	19.63	18.90
F 1/21	20.0	128	19.63	18.90
M 1/24	14.5	149	19.36	18.90
T 1/25	12.6	130	19.36	18.90
W 1/26	13.9	123	19.36	18.90
Th 1/27	22.9	195	19.36	18.90
F 1/28	32.9	157	19.36	18.90
M 1/31	15.1	146	16.26	18.90
T 2/1	25.2	201	16.26	16.60
W 2/2	14.8	137	16.26	16.60
Th 2/3	9.7	148	16.26	16.60
F 2/4	16.5	134	16.26	16.60
M 2/07	15.8	131	19.44	16.60
T 2/08	36.4	206	19.44	16.60
W 2/09	13.1	142	19.44	16.60
Th 2/10	11.1	153	19.44	16.60
F 2/11	20.8	126	19.44	16.60
M 2/14	13.9	177	13.42	16.60
T 2/15	16.2	194	13.42	16.60
W 2/16	10.4	149	13.42	16.60
Th 2/17	15.0	192	13.42	16.60
F 2/18	11.6	122	13.42	16.60
M 2/21	0	0	16.93	16.60
T 2/22	25.7	193	16.93	16.60
W 2/23	12.4	152	16.93	16.60
Th 2/24	17.1	155	16.93	16.60
F 2/25	12.5	127	16.93	16.60
M 2/28	9.9	158	17.22	16.60
T 2/29	23.8	178	17.22	16.60
W 3/01	10.3	156	17.22	17.47
Th 3/02	20.6	171	17.22	17.47
F 3/03	21.5	130	17.22	17.47

Post-Leadership Series Survey. Radiology sent out a Participant Survey to gauge the effectiveness of the Leadership Seminar Series. The participants' feedback is used to adjust the content and format of future lecture series. Notice how Questions 4 and 7 link the seminar back to the department's/organization's strategy. The questions are given below.

EXHIBIT EIGHT:

Post-Leadership Series Participant Survey

Rating Scale Used: 1-5, with "1" being excellent

1. As applied to my operational area, the subject matter of Course #X was:
2. How effective was the lecturer in communicating the seminar material?
3. In order to facilitate interaction among the course participants, the pre-course "homework" was:
4. Rate the level of understanding you gained by participating in Course #X regarding strategic implications to your operational area:
5. Did you think the pre-course "homework" was a good idea? ___Yes ___ No Why?
6. Have you previously been exposed to material on Organizational Learning and Systems Thinking? ___Yes ___No Where?
7. Do you feel that this course has provided you skills that supplement your ability to manage strategically on a daily basis? ___Yes ___No Why?
8. Was this course valuable for interacting on a social level with your fellow leaders?
9. Would you recommend courses similar to X in the future?
10. Comments:

An evaluation received from Seminar I, *Organizational Learning and Systems Thinking*, indicated that "Many were impressed by how relevant [your] strategic technique was to their operational area and have subsequently been utilizing techniques taught during [your] seminar."

Qualitative Impacts – "That Human Thing"

Qualitative impacts of the changes occurring within Radiology and Orthopaedics have been, and continue to be, significant. The subtle, yet profound shifts, revolve around changes in the culture from being one of an intense, frenetic, reactive environment to one of cooperation and collaboration (not that it's not still crazy there!). According to the Unit Operations Manager in Radiology, the environment within Radiology three to five years ago "got to the point where it was just so heated." People were working very hard. "They were just complaining bitterly…so much so, that it went all the way up to Administration." However, at the same time, changes were happening in Administration; management was restructured. With these changes came an Administrative Director who started to look at things differently. He started working with the Unit Operations Manager and was highly instrumental in implementing positive changes. As the Unit Operations Manager stated, "we started to put information together…we look at operations, run reports, get data to be able to say, quantitatively, 'this is what's going on in the operation and this is what you can do if you add a resource or take a resource away.'" This intervention by the Administrative Director at this point in time was very significant. As the Unit Operations Manager confided, "At that point I was getting pretty burnt because I felt like I was fighting this problem, which was so frustrating, all alone…it was such a relief to have [the Administrative Director] giving me some direction."

There were also a lot of changes happening in Orthopaedics, too, including a new Chief of Orthopaedics and the transition to CR. Based on observations from the Unit Operations Manager, "People weren't thrilled with that transition to CR. They were rockin' and rollin' in Orthopaedics - let me tell you!" The new Chief of Orthopaedics brought with him a very forward-looking vision and philosophy that laid the foundation to helping these changes take hold.

The Computed Radiography Committee that was formed with representatives from Radiology and Orthopaedics has a spokesperson from Orthopaedics, an Orthopedic Oncologist, who is able to take things back to his group and say, in effect, "Look, let's be reasonable. This is what they have to work with and if we can make a small contribution here, then it can possibly make a big difference." This Orthopedic Oncologist has been highly credited with being open to new possibilities.

Even though measurable gains have been made with this new process, there has been some unintended consequences. The attention to patient flow has brought a lot of regimentation and a lot of loss of control over one's job. As the Unit Operations Manager commented, "that human thing can sometimes get a little bit lost." Yet, the leaders from Radiology and Orthopaedics strive to be proactive, work at finding that middle ground, and keep morale up. According to the Unit Operations Manager, "I have a great group of techs on staff." As a hospital that is known for its many outstanding accomplishments, MGH's Radiology and Orthopaedics also have leaders and staff who are willing to make great things happen behind the scenes to achieve excellence in patient care.

BIBLIOGRAPHY

Interviews with John Couris, Managing Director of Radiology Consulting Group; Patty Marotta, Unit Operations Manager; Clint Sours, Special Projects Manager for Orthopaedics, Massachusetts General Hospital, February-March 2000.

Kelly, D. "Systems Thinking: A Tool for Organizational Diagnosis in Healthcare. *The Systems Thinker*, November 1997, pp. 9-11.

Kline, P. & Saunders, B. *Ten Steps to a Learning Organization.* Virginia: Great Ocean Publishers, 1993.

On-line source for background info, Orthopaedics and Radiology at MGH: www.partners.org

Zulauf, C. "Systems Thinking." No. 9703 (March 1997). Alexandria, VA: American Society for Training and Development. Revised edition: Spring, 2000.

ABOUT THE CONTRIBUTORS

Dr. Carol Ann Zulauf, Associate Professor in Adult and Organizational Learning at Suffolk University in Boston, co-designed the Master's Program in Adult and Organizational Learning which focuses on applying systems thinking and organizational learning tools to practical applications. Carol is also President of Zulauf & Associates, a consulting company which provides training in the areas of leadership and team development, systems thinking, and emotional intelligence. Carol is the 1995-1996 recipient of Suffolk University's "Outstanding Faculty" award; was nominated for the "Outstanding Faculty" award in 1999; and is the recipient of "Women Leaders" at Suffolk award, 1999.

John Couris, Managing Director of the Radiology Consulting Group at MGH, is responsible for the leadership and implementation of all operational improvement activities at both a strategic and tactical level.

Cliff Kennedy, a Babson MBA, has spent ten years doing government research on a wide variety of topics. In addition, he has done leadership consulting in the private sector. His objectivity and insight have proven invaluable in case analysis.

NORSKE SKOG FLOORING

An experiential learning model designed to help launch a new product by quickly communicating features and benefits to sales professionals and consumers—because people won't sell, or buy, what they don't understand.

BACKGROUND

COMPANY SNAPSHOTS

Norske Skog Flooring is the world's leading manufacturer of laminate flooring equipped with mechanical locking systems. It is a division of Norske Skogindustrier AS of Norway, one of Europe's largest paper and pulp companies, with $3.5 billion in annual sales and 11,000 employees

Celemi is a global company that creates learning processes to support large-scale change and improve business performance. Celemi's Launches & Branding division specializes in creating learning methods and tools that support or enhance marketing efforts, including shortening product launch time, communicating complex messages, raising product/corporate awareness and more.

BUSINESS OVERVIEW

When Norske Skog Flooring developed a unique mechanical interlock flooring system, the company realized it had not only created a revolutionary new product, but had created a whole new flooring category.

Already one of Scandinavia's largest flooring manufacturers, Norske Skog Flooring was contemplating a move to expand into some of the world's most competitive markets, including North America and Europe.

The critical issue was clear: How would the company get everyone in the flooring business around the world to understand the features and benefits of this product, and make room for a new flooring brand on store shelves?

For this product launch, Norske Skog Flooring was reluctant to invest the time and money required to roll out traditional training methods, which had a history of lackluster results.

In addition, the product was constructed in a unique way—which would be unfamiliar to professionals in the flooring industry. For this reason, the company needed something more than the usual marketing and sales collateral.

But Norske Skog Flooring also understood that a sales force, and in turn, a distributor network, with insufficient knowledge would mean lost sales and lost market share.

To solve this product launch and marketing challenge, Norske Skog Flooring teamed up with Celemi's Launches & Branding division, which specializes in creating learning tools and processes to support or enhance marketing efforts, and developed a creative alternative—a learning program that served as a key element in the marketing mix.

The program, which could be implemented in a matter of hours, proved effective. Retail store owners who took advantage of the manufacturer's learning program reported an unprecedented 50% increase in sales of the new flooring product within six months.

The methodology embraced by Norske Skog Flooring, and outlined in this case study, can serve as a model for any company looking to launch a new product and strengthen brand recognition, in a short time frame.

PHASE ONE: NEEDS ASSESSMENT

Under the brand name, Alloc™, Norske Skog Flooring's newest innovation made it possible for anyone to lay a new floor quickly and easily with precision results—simply by snapping laminate boards into place.

The magnitude of the educational challenge was immense. Norske Skog Flooring had already made a strategic decision to become, within ten years, one of the major players in hard-surface flooring, and the Alloc family of products was an integral part of reaching this goal.

At the same time, the American flooring marketplace presented a unique cultural difference for the Scandinavian company. In the United States, distributors, retailers, installers and sales staff have varying degrees of flooring knowledge, unlike the Scandinavian countries where the people who work in the flooring industry are regarded as craftsmen, often from a lineage of skilled carpenters.

Another barrier: the network of retail outlets across America ranges from tightly run chain stores with formal training systems to more casually managed "Mom-and-Pop" shops, with little or no resources for training and development programs. Early in the planning process, top executives from Norske Skog, including the president, the vice president of marketing and sales, and key sales representatives made a careful assessment of the marketplace.

After a series of retail store visits and reviewing the results of research reports conducted by the company, Norske Skog Flooring realized there was only one way to break through to the floor-buying consumer without spending millions of dollars in consumer advertising: they would have to get retail sales personnel interested in promoting the Alloc product. This approach required extra consideration because Norske Skog Flooring had seen good products fail due to lack of knowledge and high turnover among retail sales professionals.

Working together, Celemi's Launches & Branding Division and Norske Skog Flooring created a unique learning program designed to set the company apart from the competition. The program would achieve two specific goals:

1.   Enable the company's sales force to demonstrate the features and benefits of their new snap-in flooring product to busy distributors, retailers, installers and others; and

2.   Demonstrate their long-term commitment to the US marketplace by offering storeowners the opportunity to educate their own sales force, which would ultimately improve sales in all flooring categories.

EXHIBIT ONE: LEARNING IN THE MARKETING MIX

People won't sell or buy what they don't understand. The more complex a product or its application, the more important it becomes to communicate clear, concise messages not just to your customers, but to the people who are selling your product. For this reason, many marketing professionals have come to rely on training
initiatives. However, these often prove ineffective or may only have a short-term impact.

At Norske Skog Flooring, it was imperative that a range of flooring sales professionals, who did not work directly for the company, be able to communicate quickly and knowledgeably about the features and benefits of Norske Skog Flooring's new product.

The most effective approach, it turned out, was an emerging new marketing specialty, one that Celemi calls Learning Marketing™. Learning Marketing draws on some basic principles of behavioral science—how we think, behave and learn. In any situation where you rely on the knowledge and capabilities of a third party (or sales partner), you need each partner to represent and position your product, or range of products, in the right way, at the right time, to the right customer. How then, can you ensure that every time a sales person or distributor stands before a potential customer he or she automatically recalls the key messages, and translates them into appropriate (or desired) actions?

Think also of the "brand experience" your company may have promised through advertising or other
communication channels. How do you ensure a consistent brand experience when you have little control over, or contact with, your selling partner? Many companies are finding the answer in Learning Marketing. Learning Marketing does not challenge the concept of marketing; it targets and alleviates some common difficulties in certain marketing situations, such as these:

- Distribution of the product or service depends on non-payroll distributors or sales agents.
- Distributors or sales agents represent competing products (i.e., cellular phones sold through a consumer electronics store).
- The consumer formulates opinions and makes judgements about a product or brand based on an in-store or third-party experience.
- Ensuring a consistent brand experience is important.

Expressed as a behavioral challenge, Learning Marketing ensures, for example, that the sales agent's behavior, while representing your brand, consistently reflects the brand experience you want your customers to have—or have promised that they will have.

Today, we see marketing leaders address such challenges using an array of brochures, product manuals, videotapes, CD-ROM and a host of traditional training techniques. But these have proven ineffective for their passive (one-way) communication, lack of feedback, lack of control over the information as it is being received, and lack of consistency in communication or misinterpretation. Traditional training techniques, in particular, frequently fall short of expectations. When speed to market counts (such as in the case of almost any
electronic or technology based product), significant losses can occur in the time it takes to hire and train teachers. In many cases, the "teachers" are less knowledgeable than the selling partners, who are out with the customers on a daily basis. And, in a lecture-based approach, the teacher owns and controls the learning process.

On the other hand, an effective Learning Marketing program is characterized by the following:

- A professional design of the learning process and materials, which is tailored to the audience and complexity of the information to be shared.
- The individual participants own the learning process. They interact, discuss and exchange ideas in an engaging, dynamic environment.
- The learning process is led by colleagues, who guide discovery and provide on-going support back on the job.

As the learning program developed for Norske Skog Flooring demonstrates, knowledge gained through a

PHASE TWO: PROGRAM DESIGN

A NEW APPROACH TO LEARNING

Norske Skog Flooring, which had some 15 years of experience launching and selling new flooring products at the time, turned to Celemi on this occasion to ensure the program would help reach a strategic objective: distinguish Norske Skog Flooring from the competition and capture market share.

Norske Skog Flooring's learning program would reflect some critical common-sense rules, which were important to the company.

1. Norske Skog Flooring did not want to force information onto the retail sales professionals. The company would look to the retailers to discover what they needed to learn, and then provide them with the opportunity to learn it.

2. The program would offer opportunities for repeat sessions, to address turnover issues.

3. Knowledge presented would be applicable to all levels; simple facts would leave room for logical interpretations based on background and experience, not right and wrong.

4. The learning process would be fun, engaging and provide for interaction among all participants so everyone could contribute to business improvements. On the other hand, the learning process would provide opportunities for in-depth learning for participants seeking to enhance their own knowledge.

5. The learning experience should be as realistic as possible, closely matching the actual work environment.

6. The process would be easy to understand, execute and facilitate. Norske Skog Flooring did not want elaborate instruction manuals or professional "trainers."

To accomplish all of this, Norske Skog Flooring involved retailers, distributors, installers and their own employees in numerous interactive sessions led, in part, by Celemi. In addition, the company provided Celemi's project managers with industry data and current research findings on all their current and prospective markets.

The result was a simulation-based learning program that not only helped Norske Skog Flooring sell the product to distributors, but in turn, helped the distributors reach their retail customers with a tool to help them improve the general flooring knowledge and customer service skills of their own sales staff.

At the heart of the program are four WorkMats™ (highly visual, poster-size sheets) customized to reflect the daily issues and concerns of those in the flooring industry—distributors, retailers and installers. (See Exhibit Three)

Named the Alloc Learning Program, the goal of the plan was to communicate the added value of the product and how Alloc's features translate into benefits for the retail shop as well as the flooring customer.

Since it is a "hands-on" experience, participants discover for themselves how Alloc can help them improve the performance of their own businesses.

EXHIBIT TWO: THE VALUE OF THE EXPERIENTIAL MODEL: REAL LIFE LEARNING

Celemi uses a variety of media in its learning solutions, including simulation models, special WorkMats™ that provide a unique bird's- eye view of the information, CD-ROM, video, learning guides and Web applications.

Each of these venues brings participants together in groups to foster a spirit of teamwork, share experiences and generate enthusiasm. Messages from strategic planning programs and customer surveys are routinely incorporated into the model. This approach offers a number of advantages over traditional "teaching" methods:

- Experiential learning is fast and cost effective. Client companies have been able to reach over 100,000 employees in just five months.

- Participants are engaged in real-life, meaningful experiences that give them the opportunity to develop their own knowledge. They draw their own conclusions, and can apply what they've learned directly to their jobs.

- Managers and staff work together in discussion groups to solve problems. This builds teamwork and creates an atmosphere that encourages individual initiatives.

- Large-scale learning processes are cost effective, since they reach large groups of people simultaneously and effectively.

Aha! Learning by Doing

The very nature of the simulations—lots of teamwork and interaction— is a significant departure from literature-based and lecture-style learning methods so prevalent in the industry. The Alloc Learning Program actually guides participants through all aspects of the new product— the economic life cycle, installation, utilization and reuse. This way, Norske Skog Flooring reasoned, the distributors, retailers, and sales force would understand the total value of the product, and be able to communicate these value-added benefits to the customer, not just the purchase price.

At the heart of this methodology is the concept that certain conditions, or critical success factors, must be present in any learning program if you wish to change a mind-set or provide information that is valued, and used, by the learner. (See Exhibit Four)

EXHIBIT THREE: CRITICAL SUCCESS FACTORS FOR AN EFFECTIVE BUSINESS SIMULATION

The Context: Sets the stage for new knowledge to be created and establishes a clear, practical relationship to its application in the workplace. **Key points:**

> **Validate the conceptual framework**
>
> **Link to supportive initiatives and messages**
>
> **Define expected result**

The Nature of Learning: Guides the development and organization of the learning experience. Ensures participants get just the right amount of information at the right time during the experience. Key points:

> **Go for the cognitive base—create the "big picture"**
>
> **Recreate the learning process**
>
> **Leverage the basic conditions for learning**

The Implementation: Role of the facilitator is critical. He/she has direct bearing on the motivation of the participants. Key points:

> **Use the medium as the message (the method gives participants responsibility
> for their own learning; echoes management's desire to support new
> attitudes when people return to daily tasks.)**
>
> **Link to actions and desired behavior**
>
> **Establish conditions for continuous learning and growth**

By nature, effective learning is spontaneous and exciting. Think of a child who receives a new toy. Children explore new toys thoroughly by touching and manipulating them. Their curiosity drives them to push a button or turn a knob. Aha!, and instantly they understand.

The Nature of Learning

As adults, we are so experienced in learning that we do not usually think about how it works. Yet, if we want other people to share knowledge that we already have, we must have some idea about the conditions necessary for learning.

Each element of the Alloc Learning Program engages participants by using a six-step process called the Learning Spiral, which creates and builds on the Aha! experience.

EXHIBIT FOUR: THE LEARNING SPIRAL

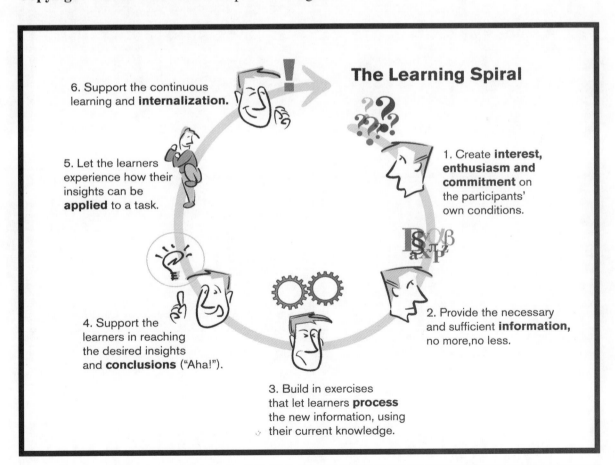

As a flooring manufacturer, Norske Skog Flooring rarely sold products directly to retail customers. The company would normally work through a network of distributors, who in turn, would sell to the retailers. And installers could work for anyone—a distributor, a retailer, independently with customers, or in any combination of these.

This multi-step sales process presented a bit of a challenge. The learning program had to be highly flexible and readily adaptable. Norske Skog Flooring's sales force may have the luxury of several hours to engage distributors in the simulation, but distributors might have only an hour to spend with retailers in the smaller shops.

Another challenge was the small size of some retail shops. Smaller retailers might find it difficult to set aside time to develop their people and might also have difficulty organizing a group of participants diverse enough to reap all the learning benefits of the program.

To come up with the right solution—the set of four interchangeable WorkMats—Norske Skog Flooring had to work very closely with Celemi. Together, they followed a basic project model that served as a guide to quality control.

EXHIBIT 5: THE LEARNING DEVELOPMENT PROJECT MODEL
Copyright © 2000 Celemiab Group AB. All rights reserved.

1. **The Draft Outline Phase**

   Feasibility study is conducted and verified. Objectives of the learning program are clearly defined. A time-line for program rollout is created.

2. **The Conceptual Development Phase**

   Draft material prepared and presented. A conceptual test is performed to verify the flow and presentation of information and concepts. A test group is engaged. Content is evaluated and approved.

3. **The Design Phase**

   Feedback from Phase II is incorporated into a more detailed design, for both content and visuals.

4. **The Verifcation Phase**

   A pilot test is conducted with a test group representing the target audience. If fundamental changes are indicated a second pilot test is required. This phase ends when there are no more fundamental changes.

5. **The Finalization Phase**

   Adjustments indicated by pilot test results are incorporated. Full scale WorkMats and other program elements (video, CD-ROM, and other collateral) are sent out for final approval.

6. **The Production Phase**

   All program material is produced and delivered. A "Facilitator Manual" is finalized and delivered.

7. **The Follow-Up Phase**

   Internal and external facilitators are prepared. Multiple language versions are created as needed. Participant evaluations are conducted to ensure the program reaches the objectives defined in Phase I.

PHASE THREE: IMPLEMENTATION

EXHIBIT FIVE: THE LEARNING DEVELOPMENT PROJECT MODEL

Norske Skog Flooring had to implement the learning program with four distinct audiences, each with a different objective:

Flooring Distributors: Distributors decide whether or not to inventory a product or brand, and sell product to the flooring retailers. All four WorkMats in the Alloc Learning Program are used with this group, which has a stake in understanding the features and benefits of product lines carried.

Retailers: Primarily it is the distributors who sell product to the retailers. Distributors use the Alloc Learning Program to introduce the new product to shop owners and chain store managers. The content of the program ensures that they present all key messages. The program is readily adaptable, allowing the distributors to facilitate any or all of the WorkMats as time allows.

Retail Sales Professionals: Retailers can opt to have their sales staff participate in the simulation as it is facilitated by the distributor, or they can easily facilitate the program themselves, taking people off the sales floor at their convenience.

Installers & Contract Estimators: Installers and estimators may work for a retailer or they may act independently. Distributors and retailers may invite installers and estimators to participate in a full session, or use only the installation WorkMat.

The Program: A Closer Look

In the first simulation, sales professionals work in small teams to analyze the nature of their own store environment and the customers they serve. Using a WorkMat, they discuss trends and characteristics of different flooring options like carpet, sheet vinyl, ceramic tile, hardwood and laminates. They compare product samples, and consider the buying habits and reasoning process of customers.

In this phase, participants "open the doors" to their own simulated retail store and "meet" customers who have general flooring concerns.

"Price is not an issue as long as I get the quality I want," reads one customer profile card, which also indicates that this customer values "prestige." Such general statements help participants practice their response strategies.

In the second simulation, participants take a closer look at the features and benefits of Alloc. The snap-in flooring product is pictured on a new WorkMat, along with benefit statements and photos of the product life cycle. Participants analyze the product's design features and match them to corresponding benefits—an engaging process that reinforces their new knowledge.

The third simulation brings everything together. Sales professionals test their understanding of Alloc's features and benefits and their customer service skills in an environment where mistakes won't cost them a sale.

On the third WorkMat, new customers with specific questions about Alloc are introduced. Participants confront a range of statements. Some comments came from consumers who were confused about the price differences between types of laminate floors. Others came from installers and do-it-yourselfers wondering which type of saw to use or how to cut a metal scarf joint.

Using role-playing techniques, participants prepare responses, sharpening their customer service skills and their product knowledge.

In a fourth component, customized to reach floor covering installers and estimators, participants plan project installations and develop price quotes for both Alloc and regular glued laminate flooring. They also work hands-on with the product to practice installation. In an hour, they have experienced the ease of an Alloc installation and discovered its distinct competitive advantages: it's simple to install, easy to remove and reuse, durable, good-looking and cost effective.

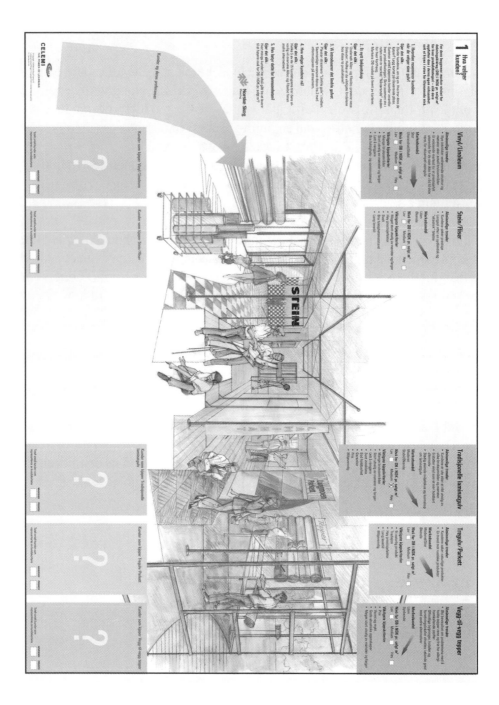

EXHIBIT SIX: WORKMAT NUMBER ONE
Copyright © 2000 Celemiab Group AB. All rights reserved.

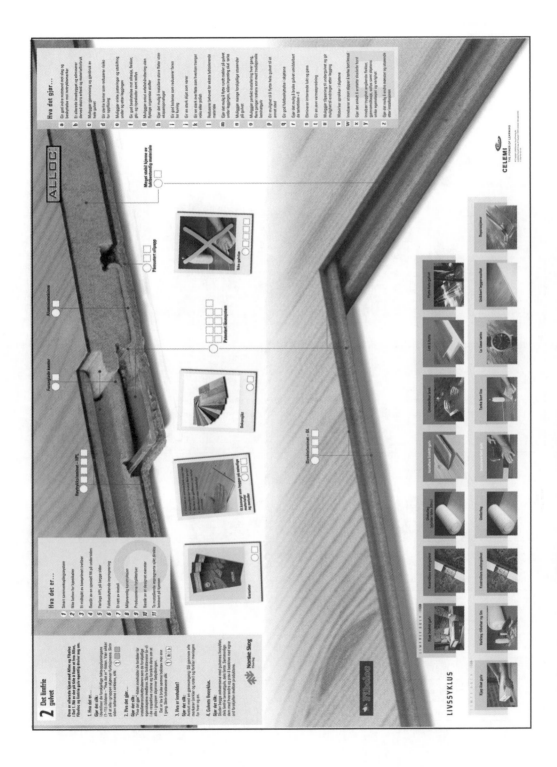

EXHIBIT SEVEN: WORKMAT NUMBER TWO

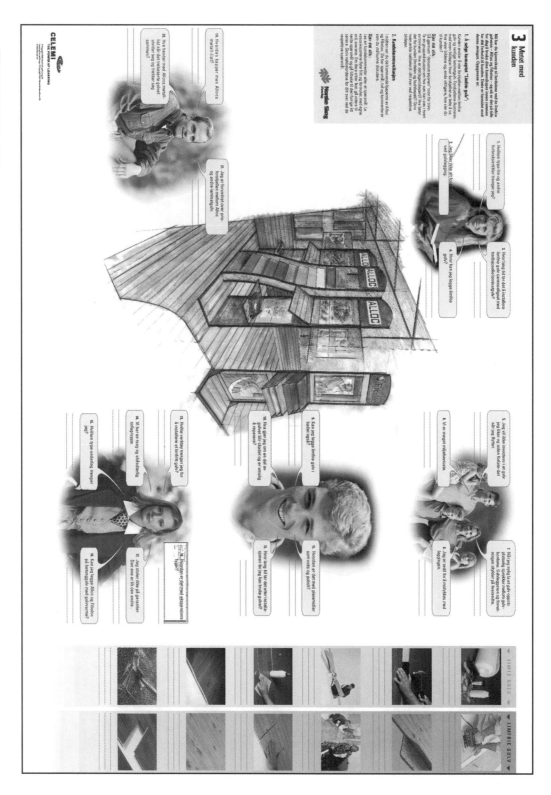

EXHIBIT EIGHT: WORKMAT NUMBER THREE

Participants noted three basic features of the Alloc Learning Program as having the most impact:

1. The learning process itself was considered different than anything they had seen before;

2. It was simple— visual and "hands-on"; and

3. Engaging, fostering teamwork and knowledge-sharing opportunities.

In fact, retailers and participants were so enthusiastic about the opportunity that Norske Skog Flooring did not have to offer traditional incentives for participation. They did, however, recommend that sessions be run at times when participation would be most convenient and encouraged some social connection, a lunchtime session, for example.

In summarizing the cornerstone of learning at Norske Skog Flooring, President Claes Wennerth notes, "Most people cherish the opportunity to learn. We try to provide the opportunities."

Phase Four: Enabling Knowledge to Grow

At its core, each part of the Alloc Learning Program is a simulation of reality. Careful research, industry statistics and real life examples were combined to create the set of four WorkMats, leaving little chance that the new insights and knowledge gained would not apply once the participants—distributors, retailers, sales professionals or installers—returned to their jobs.

To foster the implementation process, sales representatives from Norske Skog Flooring went through the simulation first, then demonstrated the process for the distributors. The distributors' representatives, at times together with Norske Skog Flooring, then demonstrated the program to the retailers. Norske Skog Flooring also offered central "open" sessions to participants who wanted to increase their facilitation skills.

Because the learning program is aimed at external audiences, Norske Skog Flooring includes it in all of their presentations. It has become an integral part of the product concept and package; and, therefore, is reinforced all the time.

In addition, Norske Skog Flooring provides every participant with a certificate upon completion of the program. Participating retailers are tracked and supplied with product updates, and store performance is measured. The results are passed on to distributors to encourage their continued interest and support.

The Alloc Learning Program is not static. Norske Skog Flooring continues to develop new components for the learning program, and is responsive to participants' feedback.

As a "living" process, the program ensures new knowledge, and the WorkMat concept contains specific elements that inspire long-term learning benefits.

"The opportunity to work with Norske Skog Flooring provided Celemi with an opportunity to grow as well," explains Lasse Hansen, director of Celemi's Launches & Branding division. "This was the first time we worked with a flooring company to address its unique marketing challenges in a very competitive marketplace. Although we were able to draw on our vast experience with other product launches, the Alloc Learning Program broadend the experience of everyone involved in its development."

EXHIBIT NINE: WAYS TO ENGAGE THE LEARNER
Copyright © 2000 Celemiab Group AB. All rights reserved.

MORE WAYS TO ENGAGE THE LEARNER

1.   Go for the root causes

The signs and symptoms are one thing; the root causes are quite another. Find out what is meaningful to the audience members; know which buttons to push.

2.   Ensure consistency

A consistent message is an obvious prerequisite. Alignment with other messages from the organization is just as important in order to avoid contradictions, confusion, and disappointment.

3.   Represent reality

Use a working model that mimics reality and allows people to use, challenge and expand their prior knowledge and views.

4.   Demand results

When rolling out the program, tie it closely to what you want to achieve; the desired behavior and performance.

5.   Keep up the momentum

Create the conditions necessary for the learning to make its mark and hit the bottom line.

PHASE FIVE: EVALUATION

The results speak for themselves.

In a random survey conducted by Norske Skog Flooring, some six months after introducing Alloc, retailers who used the learning program reported sales of the product 50 percent above those who did not.

After learning of these results, some retailers who initially declined the program decided to give it a try. A few months later, this "late start" group reported Alloc sales that were 32 percent ahead of those who never opted to use the program.

Norske Skog Flooring openly credits the Alloc Learning Program with the successful introduction of the new product into the competitive American marketplace.

"People are very enthusiastic," said Steve Bunch, Vice President of Marketing for Norske Skog Flooring. "First, you have a revolutionary product to show them. Then, you take them through a learning process that is very different, and effective. Within minutes they realize the potential impact that this product can have on their own business."

Some participants have called the Alloc learning process a good team-building tool—a comment that Mr. Bunch was delighted to hear. "Each sales person must see the potential for this new product category, even if he or she is selling carpeting or tile. It is important for people to realize that Alloc means more business for their shop, which also means more business for everyone."

An important component of the Alloc learning process is its ability to give participants the opportunity to practice using their newfound knowledge. "We help them see how this new product category fits into their current business and creates a win-win situation—their customers are satisfied and they earn more money," he added.

Feedback from the Field

"The beauty of the program is its flexibility," commented Shane Calloway, a Regional Manager with Norske Skog Flooring. "We use it with distributors, retailers or installers, and adapt the program according to their specific needs and the time they have available."

The program also helps set Alloc apart.

"I haven't seen anything else like it," said Bill Baker, Flooring Manager with Acoustical Specialties in Louisiana, a Norske Skog Flooring client and Alloc distributor. "It helps us sell the product to our retail customers because it covers all the details, so we don't forget key points. It's a professional way to educate people, and that's a benefit for us and the retailers."

"Retailers are reluctant to carry a product that can't 'sell itself'," noted Claes Wennerth, President of Norske Skog Flooring USA, "until they see the impact a knowledgeable sales force can have on their entire business."

Stepping Quickly into the World Market

Within two years of launching the product and the learning process, over 1,500 flooring professionals throughout North America have experienced the program.

In the next phase, Norske Skog Flooring plans to roll out the Alloc Learning Program in the European marketplace and anticipates that thousands of people will eventually take part in the process.

"Using this methodology has made it possible for us to have many people learn more in a shorter amount of time than otherwise would have been possible," concluded Mr. Bunch. "And the learning process is fun. It is the perfect way to launch a revolutionary new product into the worldwide marketplace."

ABOUT THE CONTRIBUTORS

Claes Wennerth is president of Norske Skog Flooring USA. He is a business consultant specializing in start-ups, strategic development, marketing and sales planning. In his role as President of Norske Skog Flooring USA, he is charged with introducing the Alloc Flooring brand in North America and establishing a firm position in this competitive marketplace. Claes attributes the new product's success to a good product concept, innovative marketing and sales initiatives, as well as the Alloc people who embody the Alloc spirit and share the strategic vision —a combination that enables them to consistently overcome marketplace challenges.

Claes brings to his position a strong background in international business experience. Previously, he served as President & CEO of Arjo, Inc., the North American subsidiary of Arjo International (Sweden & Holland), a world leader in patient care equipment used in health care facilities. He was also President & CEO of Swedish Match Consumer Products in North America; and earlier, Director of Corporate Development for Swedish Match Corporation, a $1 billion international operation with business in building products and consumer disposables. Claes earned his M.B.A. from the North European Management Institute in Oslo, Norway, and holds a B.A. in Economics from the University of Lund, Sweden.

Lasse Kjaer Hansen, Senior Vice President, Launches & Branding at Celemi, is a specialist in marketing and strategic planning. Lasse leads Celemi's global Launches & Branding division, which is dedicated to helping client companies quickly and consistently communicate brand values, and product features and benefits to sales partners and consumers worldwide. As Senior Vice President, Lasse is charged with growing the division's visibility in some of the world's largest markets, including the United States. He is also spearheading Celemi's efforts to create a global understanding of the integral role learning plays in the marketing mix.

Lasse brings to Celemi a strong background in international marketing and management. Previously, he served as Vice President, Strategy and Branding, for OAG, the international airline flight guide and travel information specialists based in Chicago, Illinois. Prior to that, he worked for Budget Rent A Car, where he held several positions, including Director of Marketing in Europe and Director of International Marketing in the United States. He also worked for Avis in Denmark as Manager of Marketing Programs. Lasse holds a bachelor degree and M.B.A. in Economics from Copenhagen Business School, and a M.B.A. in Marketing from Northwestern University's Kellogg Graduate School of Business (Chicago, Il).

Part Three:
Conclusion

RESEARCH: KM/OL TRENDS & FINDINGS

To provide additional context for the case studies presented in this book, we asked our contributors to reflect upon elements critical to their knowledge management and organizational learning initiatives. These areas included:

1) Time and Resources Devoted to the Initiative
2) Tools and Methods of Assessment
3) Competitive and Strategic Business Challenge
4) Key Instruments of Implementation
5) Factors for Successful Reinforcement of the Program
6) Measurements of Success
7) Critical Factors for Overall Success

Although the questions covered a broad range of topics, the overriding success factor in nearly every initiative was the development and cultivation of communities of practice. It was important to acquire knowledge. The overriding goal was for employees to learn from each other through sharing of ideas, common experiences, best practices and lessons learned. Some companies did this via technological tools such as the worldwide web or their own internal intranet. Others conducted focus groups and constructed pilot groups that went on to meet informally to share these experiences. Whatever the case, continuous learning required continuous efforts on the part of everyone involved in the initiative.

Within this section, you will see that we have researched the most pressing questions essential to developing, implementing and maintaining a successful knowledge management and organizational learning initiative.

COMPANY BACKGROUND

The organizations in this book represent a range of employee sizes, revenues and industries. The average revenue for the companies represented in this book is $19.8 billion. The breakdown of industry is as follows:

Table One: Participating Companies, by industry

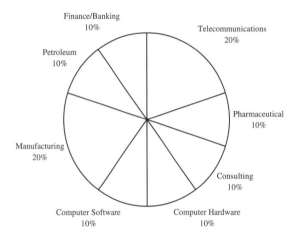

TIME & RESOURCES

The average amount of U.S. dollars spent on a KMOL initiative was over $1 million, annually. The highest of these was $55 million and the lowest was less than $10,000. These averaged out to approximately $9.5 million per program. Though most initiatives (8 out of 11) had initial pilot groups, all but one of the KMOL initiatives were eventually dispersed organization-wide. All companies affirmed a positive, quantifiable result that they directly attributed to their KMOL initiative.

MOTIVATION FOR KMOL

Assessment feedback and results can provide a clear-cut path for planning the KMOL strategy. The driving force of that strategy varied throughout the groups. The top two overriding factors, however, were far and above the remaining top three. Reasons behind the KMOL strategy were often 1) a need to increase productivity; and 2) a need to increase the customer base. The top five reasons for the change are illustrated in Table Two.

Table Two: Top Reasons Organizations Engaged in KMOL

Top Reason for Change, ranked in order of importance

1	Looking to Increase Productivity and Profitability
2	Looking to Improve Customer Base
3	Globalization
4	Data Mining & Information Storage Issues
5	Changing Needs of Training

ASSESSING THE STATUS QUO

The need for a KMOL initiative is often the end result of an analysis based upon a perceived problem within the business. To determine the intricate layers of the issues related to that problem requires an assessment of the facets and details involved in the crisis. The top five methods used by contributors are illustrated in Table Three. Interestingly, in an area incorrectly perceived as "technology based," methods of assessment relied heavily on human contact, including customer surveys and employee surveys.

Table Three: Top Methods to Evaluate the Need for KMOL

Top Methods, ranked in order of importance

1	Customer Surveys
2	Employee Surveys
3	Behavioral Indicators
3	Focus Groups
4	Benchmarking
5	Performance Reviews

PLANNING AND DESIGN

Participants were accomplished practitioners in the field of KMOL. When planning the programs, specific business challenges were addressed. The focus of each initiative often centered around these challenges. Participants were asked to "indicate how each of the following competitive and strategic business challenges impacted the FOCUS of your Knowledge Management and Organizational Learning Plan by rating them using a scale of 1 (most important) and 10 (least important)." FIrst, the most important challenges that the KMOL successes targeted are ranked in Table Four. Improving customer focus was ranked the highest. Ten out of 11 contributors ranked it as the most important factor in their strategy.

Table Four: Top Ten Competitive and Strategic Business Challenges Impacting KMOL, in order of Impact, (1 being higest impact, and 10 being least impact)

Challenge	Average Rank
Improving Customer Focus	1.4
Need to Increase in Sales and Profits	2.14
Other	2.42
Shift in Corporate Vision	3.2
Technology Changes	3.7
Competitive Pressures	4.42
Rapid Growth in Data Accumulation	5
Resistance to Change	5
Decrease in Productivity	5.14
Increase in Costs	5.14
Retention and Recruitment	5.71
Entrance into New Market	5.8
Strategic Partnerships	6
Post-Merger Integration	8.8

EXECUTING THE PLAN

In implementing their KMOL plan, each contributor used key instruments and tools that led them down the path of success. The perception of KMOL may be that managing data and information requires technology. Technological tools played a role in connecting humans together as well. Nearly all contributors agreed that technology solutions were one of the most important tools in their programs. Table Five shows the most important instruments, tools and models that aided the implementation of a KMOL directive.

Table Five: Top Tools Used to Execute the KMOL Plans, ranked in order of importance (1 being most important, and 5 being least important)

Tool	Average Rank
Tech Solutions	1.74
Benchmarking	2.4
Training	2.4
Performance Management	2.8
Internal Marketing	3.5
Shared Vision	3.71
Mental Models	4
Intranet Development	4
Web-Based Tech	4
Action learning	4
Systems Thinking	4.28
Personal Mastery	4.42
Competency Modeling	4.42
360 Feedback	4.42
Team Leading	5.28

CHANGING CORPORATE CULTURE

Contributors were asked what steps were taken to reinforce success of their KMOL initiative once the initial KMOL program was in place. Many of them agreed that the culture and behaviors of employees cannot continually change without nurturing and growth. Practitioners who contributed to the book stated the importance of generating feedback through focus groups and other sources to continually improve upon the KMOL system. It was also important to gauge the use and involvement of employees through metrics, or measurements of use. This was done in several ways, including measured hits on an intranet, tracking of submissions to virtual communities and forums.

Table Six: Ongoing Reinforcement and Support -- Factors for Success, ranked in order of importance to success of on-going reinforcement and support stage

Top Success Factors for On-going Reinforcement and Support, in order of importance

1. Feedback Sessions/Focus Groups
2. Metrics in Measuring Employee Use and Involvement
3. Empowerment of workforce in access to knowledge sharing
4. Rewarding Employees for Providing and Increasing Enterprise Intellectual Capital
5. Recognizing Employees for Adding value to Intellectual Capital
6. Developing Communities of Practice
7. Development of Different Applications in Managing tacit and explicit knowledge
8. Coaching and Mentoring

EVALUATION

Contributors in this book presented the best in world-class offerings for true knowledge management and organizational learning. How they were able to demonstrate this is clear: these initiatives showed quantitative results directly correlated to aspects of the program. Numbers, beyond anything else, speak for themselves. Increases in productivity, profitability, customer sales and acquisition of new customers are just some of the results that practitioners in the book achieved through their KMOL programs. Of the organizations that reported that metrics were the method of evaluation, several quantifiable results were indicated including:

1. productivity improvements of up to $26M,
2. reduction of operating costs by 25%,
3. increased revenue per person,
4. increased employee retention,
5. improved employee satisfaction rates,
6. improvement in quality of services by 25%.

When asked what the top evaluation methods for measuring the return on investment for their initiatives, our best practice practitioners indicated that evaluation of metrics was the most impactful method. We also tested for the use of other evaluation methods such as Donald Kirkpatrick's four methods of evaluation as Kirkpatrick identified in *Evaluating Training Programs* (Barrett-Koehler Publishers, 1998).

1.) Reaction Evaluations measure the participants initial response or feeling from the training

2) *Learning Evaluations* are administered in the form of tests or questionnaires and measure how well participants have learned facts, ideas, concepts, or theories.

3) *Behavior Evaluations* measure the effect of training on job performance.

4) *Results Evaluations* measure the effect of training on the achievement of organizational goals.

Table Seven: Top Evaluation Methods

Top Evaluation Methods, in order of usage
1. Metrics (measured "hits" on the intranet, monitored use of access to database, measurements taken from performance reviews, customer satisfaction, employee satisfaction, and sales revenues, etc.)
2. Reaction Evaluation
3. Results Evaluation
4. Learning Evaluation
5. Behavior Evaluation

Additionally, qualitative results, less number-oriented but still crucial in achieving long-term benefits, were established through KMOL programs. Contributors indicated several qualitative results from participants including, "We now view problems from a common perspective; not an 'us versus them' mentality. It's been a true shift of paradigm," and " The KM program transformed our company into knowledge communities. It enabled peer support and best practice sharing. It became part of the user's daily routine."

CONCLUSION

Contributors were asked to rank the four most important critical factors of their KMOL program in order of importance. The factor with the highest ranking was developing communities of practice. In fact, in all but one case study, contributors in this book rated communities of practice as one of the top four success factors of their initiatives. Table Seven highlights these factors critical to success.

Table Nine: Top Critical Success Factors, ranked in order of importance, (1 being highly important and 5 being of least importance)

Success Factor	Median Rank
Communities of Practice	2.5
Senior Buy-In	3.14
Creating a Convincing Business Case	3.28
Overcoming Resistance to Change	4.28
Enabling Leadership Development	4.42
Technology Implementation	4.85

Each initiative in this book viewed the term knowledge management and organizational learning differently. They shared common characteristics, though, of any program that seeks to change the organization at its core. Buckman Labs, who began its knowledge management and organization learning over twenty years ago, maximized broad, sweeping changes that transformed the company into a learning organization. Other companies in this book have also sought to change the organization at every level. Hewlett Packard, Ernst & Young and AT&T have successfully intergrated KM/OL into their employee's daily life. With the lightening speed of developing technologies, it seems only fitting that other organizations will develop a need to tap human resources in addition to the deep well of tangible information.

KNOWLEDGE MANAGEMENT RESOURCES

To Order Any of These Best-Selling Titles, Please Call 781-862-3157
or Visit Us on the Web at www.linkageinc.com/library!

Harvard Business Review on Knowledge Management
Knowledge management-the way companies generate, communicate, and leverage their intellectual assets-has only recently emerged as the information economy's essential source of competitive advantage. The Harvard Business Review was among the first to identify the importance of knowledge management, and now the cutting-edge thinking and practical applications that are defining the field are conveniently close at hand in this timely and authoritative collection.   OKM / $19.95

The Infinite Resource: Creating and Leading the Knowledge Enterprise,
Edited by William Halal, Raymond Smith, and Cedric Crocker
In all of history, there has been no resource resembling knowledge. Unlike commodities or industrial capital, knowledge is inexhaustible and only increases when shared. And now that the Knowledge Revolution has taken hold, organizations are scrambling to find ways to capture and leverage this most important of competitive advantages. In this unprecedented volume, nineteen of the best minds on business and government cut through the myriad myths and theories surrounding the knowledge phenomenon. Each offers today's shell-shocked managers and civic leaders a clear vision of how organizations must reinvent themselves to remain viable in the not-too-distant future – to thrive in a world remarkably different from the one we have come to know.
IR / $32.95

Knowledge in Organizations, by Laurence Prusak
There is a growing realization among executives that an organization's knowledge is its only sustainable advantage. Knowledge in Organizations offers sound insights into how companies can harness and cultivate this elusive but all important subject of knowledge. This anthology of key articles represents a variety of perspectives, including sociology, economics, and management science. This book provides robust solutions to anyone seeking to develop and enhance their organization's knowledge base. KIO / $21.95

If Only We Knew What We Know: The Transfer of Internal Knowledge and Best Practice, by Carla O'Dell, C. Jackson Grayson Jr., with Nilly Essaides
Carla O'Dell and Jack Grayson explain for the first time how applying the ideas of Knowledge Management can help employers identify their own internal best practices and share this intellectual capital throughout their organizations. Knowledge Management (KM) is a conscious strategy of getting the right information to the right people at the right time so they can take action and create value. Basing KM on three major studies of best practices at one hundred companies, the authors demonstrate how managers can utilize a visual process model to actually transfer best practices from one business unit of the organization to another.   IOWK / $30.00

KNOWLEDGE MANAGEMENT RESOURCES

To Order Any of These Best-Selling Titles, Please Call 781-862-3157 or Visit Us on the Web at www.linkageinc.com/library!

Knowledge Management Fieldbook, by Wendi Bukowitz and Ruth Williams
Using an elegantly simple framework for thinking about the knowledge management process, the authors advocate a strong link between tactics and strategy that will appeal both to in-the-trenches managers and senior executives at the helm who are grappling with how the knowledge economy impacts upon their business. Filled with case examples based on the authors' original interviews with more than 50 organizations, *The Knowledge Management Fieldbook* provides a structured process for thinking about knowledge management that helps managers build a detailed action agenda.   KMF / $29.95

Web Warehousing and Knowledge Management, by Rob Mattison and Brigitte Kilger-Mattison
Web Warehousing and Knowledge Management helps you understand the new world of web commerce, and come up with the right answers to today's competitive business challenges. This balanced, objective resource gives you the background information, technology know-how, business insight, and case studies necessary to evaluate your own systems and discover your own unique solutions. If you are involved with designing, implementing, or evaluating Web warehousing solutions or if you are wrestling with the challenges of building corporate computer systems for the 21st century, Web Warehousing and Knowledge Management is the complete solution you've been waiting for.
WWKM / $49.00

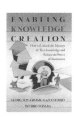

Enabling Knowledge Creation, by Georg Von Krogh, Kazou Ichijo, and Ikujiro Nonaka
Weaving together lessons from such international leaders as Siemens, Unilever, Skandia, and Sony, along with their own consulting experiences, the authors introduce knowledge enabling – the overall set of organizational activities that promote knowledge creation – and demonstrate its power to transform an organization's knowledge into value-creating actions. They describe the five key "knowledge enablers" and outline what it takes to instill a knowledge vision, manage conversations, mobilize knowledge activists, create the right context for knowledge creation, and globalize local knowledge. EKC / $27.50

Intellectual Capital: Realizing Your Company's True Value by Finding Its Hidden Brainpower, by Leif Edvinsson and Michael Malone
One of the greatest challenges facing any business today is the gap between its balance sheet and its market valuation. This gap, representing the bulk of a company's true value, consists of indirect assets – organizational knowledge, customer satisfaction, product innovation, employee moral, patents, and trademarks – that never appear in its financial reports. Intellectual Capital will transform the nature of doing business by establishing the real value of enterprises for those who manage them, work in them, and invest in them. The result will be a revolutionary transformation of the modern economy. IC / $25.00

Page 324

KNOWLEDGE MANAGEMENT RESOURCES

*To Order Any of These Best-Selling Titles, Please Call 781-862-3157
or Visit Us on the Web at www.linkageinc.com/library!*

Managing Knowledge Workers: New Skills and Attitudes to Unlock the Intellectual Capital in Your Organization, by Frances Horibe

This hands-on guide gives managers practical, doable strategies for motivating and keeping knowledge workers without breaking the bank or sacrificing productivity and quality. It goes beyond the quick-fix of throwing money at the problem and offers realistic solutions for effectively managing the human side of intellectual capital. It features case studies, anecdotes, and examples of companies using the new managing techniques, including IBM, Deloitte & Touche, and Transport Canada. MKW / $29.95

Working Knowledge: How Organizations Manage What They Know, by Thomas Davenport

The definitive primer on knowledge management, this book serves as the hands-on resource of choice for fast companies that recognize knowledge as the only sustainable source of competitive advantage. Drawing from their work with more than 30 firms, the authors examine how all types of companies can effectively understand, analyze, measure, and manage their intellectual assets, turning corporate knowledge into market value.   WK / $29.95

The New Organizational Wealth: Managing & Measuring Knowledge-Based Assets, by Karl Erik Sveiby

This book outlines the conceptual framework for changing business strategies to focus on intangible assests. Using its guidelines, managers can learn how to identify the indicators for their companies intangible assets – their emplyees talents and strengths, their customers' support and interest, and their supplier's reliability and ingenuity. Case studies of companies such as WM-data-s, Skandia AFS, and Celemi, that have developed systems for measuring intangible assets and publicly reporting the results, provide models can use in leading their companies to increased profitability and long-term organizational success.
NOW / $29.95

Linkage Inc's Best Practice Library

*To Order Any of These Best-Selling Handbooks, Please Call 781-862-3157
or Visit Us on the Web at www.linkageinc.com/library!*

Linkage Press publishes best practice handbooks that detail what the world's leading practitioners are doing by way of Leadership Development, Organization Development, and Human Resources Development. They help senior executives, practitioners, students, and managers to immediately analyze, design, develop, support, and evaluate their organization's initiatives. These handbooks have received critical acclaim by leading experts, senior executives, and thought leaders around the world as being highly informative and providing an exceptional amount of detailed and clearly written research and in-depth information at an unusually low price. They include all of the tools, instruments, models, forms, and benchmarking information necessary to successfully implement a best practice initiative.

The very popular **Linkage, Inc.'s Best Practices in Leadership Development Handbook** has been endorsed by such leadership gurus as Warren Bennis, Bev Kaye, Jay Conger, Deepak (Dick) Sethi, and a host of leadership development executives and practitioners from major corporations worldwide. The handbook includes **15** leadership development systems from the world's foremost organizations including BP Amoco, SmithKline Beecham, Motorola, Bose Corporation, Barclays Global Investors, Colgate Palmolive, Allied Signal, and Abbott Labs. Leadership development case studies include instruments, training, competency models, research and a full breakdown of the process of building the leadership development system. Leadership development systems presented in the book include assessment-based programs that leverage such tools as 360 assessment, action learning programs, team building, and strategic change programs.

The handbook covers five of the hottest management topics today: organization development & change, leadership development, recruitment & retention, performance management, and coaching & mentoring. OD/HRD case studies include models, tools, assessments, training, and a full breakdown of the change process. Learn how 17 world-class organizations achieved their change objectives including how Westinghouse created a safety culture that has become the world-wide standard for safety practices and how Dow Corning implemented an award winning coaching and mentoring system. Benchmark against Sun Microsystem's 22 behavioral competencies, SmithKline Beecham's use of the Burke-Litwin Model of Organizational Performance and Change, Case Corporation's 15 leadership competencies, Dow Corning's Three-Circle Profile, Media One's 360 degree feedback tool, Boeing's 19 executive competencies and more!

ORGANIZATIONAL LEARNING RESOURCES

To Order Any of These Best-Selling Titles, Please Call 781-862-3157
or Visit Us on the Web at www.linkageinc.com/library!

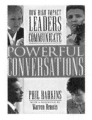

Powerful Conversations: How High Impact Leaders Communicate, by Phil Harkins
Powerful Conversations, Harkins illustrates, are neither mystical nor unattainable. This book outlines the processes to follow to eliminate communication barriers to foster learning and growth. He explains why and how powerful conversations are effective tools – and how to use and measure them to know when you've had a productive powerful conversation. Packed with real-life examples from great leaders and communicators such as Jack Welch, Oprah Winfrey, and Howard Schultz, Harkins provides a step-by-step blueprint for mastering the craft of powerful, productive conversations. PC / $24.95

Dance of Change: The Challenges to Sustaining Momentum in Learning Organizations, Peter Senge
The Dance of Change, written for managers and executives at every level of an organization, reveals how business leaders can work together to anticipate the challengs that profound change will ultimately force the organization to face. Then in a down-to-earth and compellingly clear format, readers will learn how to build the personal and organizational capabilities needed to meet those challenges. This book provides an insider's perspective on implementing learning and change initiatives at such corporations as British Petroleum, Harley-Davidson, Hewlett-Packard, Mitsubishi Electric, Royal Dutch/Shell, Shell Oil Company, Toyota, the US Army, and Xerox. DOC / $35.00

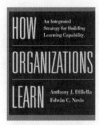

How Organizations Learn: An Integrated Strategy for Building Learning Capability, by Tony DiBella, and Edwin Nevis
DiBella and Nevis maintain that all organizations have learning capabilities and styles that vary with individual corporate cultures, and they show why distinctive styles should be regarded as sources of competitive advantage. From theory and research to practical applications, How Organizations Learn presents a productive framework for any organization that that wants to learn more fully and adapt more quickly to the fast changing marketplace. HOL / $32.95

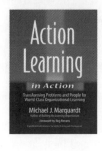

Action Learning in Action: Transforming Problems and People for World Class Organizational Learning, by Michael Marquardt and Reginald Revins
Michael Marquardt brings together step-by-step guidance and the personal accounts of frontline managers to show how to create and implement an action learning program in any organization. This book uses solid research results and extensive real-world examples to make the critical connection between action learning and organizational learning. It includes lessons from such global leaders as McKinsey & Company, General Electric, Bristol-Myers Squibb, and Arthur Andersen to demonstrate how to leverage the benefits of action learning. Marquardt addresses all aspects of design, implementation, and assessment, including the important facilitator role and the special needs of organizations with multicultural workforces. ALIA / $38.95

ORGANIZATIONAL LEARNING RESOURCES

*To Order Any of These Best-Selling Titles, Please Call 781-862-3157
or Visit Us on the Web at www.linkageinc.com/library!*

Effective Training Strategies: A Comprehensive Guide to Maximizing Learning in Organizations, by James Davis and Adelaide Davis
For managers, supervisors, trainers, engineers, and consultants alike, Effective Training Strategies demonstrates how to facilitate the many types of learning required to ensure that individuals, groups, and teams do their jobs more effectively, efficiently and, sometimes, even more creatively. This compendium of solid theory and current practice challenges the quality expectations that organizations have for learning, takes the guesswork out of training and development, and offers a rich set of real-world examples drawn from various types of organizations from around the world. ETS / $49.95

Organizational Learning From World Class Theories to Global Best Practices, by David Schwandt, Michael Marquardt
Organizational Learning: From World Class Theories to Global Best Practices starts with a review of significant learning theory and research accomplished over the past 20 years. This research is integrated into an action-centered theory of organizational learning. The authors present best-practice application of the Organizational Learning System Model by companies from around the world, including Arthur Anderson, Price Waterhouse, Beloit Corporation, Motorola, and Meralco. These are companies that have taken the leadership in developing learning systems on a organization-wide basis. This book provides practical steps and strategies for developing and applying organizational learning in the workplace. OLF / $34.95

Organizational Learning Capability: Generating and Generalizing Ideas With Impact, Arthur Yeung, Dave Ulrich, Stephen Nason and Mary Von Glinow
Through this book the authors assist practicing managers by providing several examples of successful and unsuccessful organizations and by describing ways in which they have helped organizations improve learning capability in their consulting practices. Based on detailed case studies, a review of past literature, and data gleaned from a worldwide survey of companies, *Organizational Learning Capability*, is an accessible and useful guide for managers competing in the information economy. It turns abstract ideas into practice, offers tools that managers can use, and presents a simple yet profound road map for making learning a reality.
OLC / $29.95

Results: How to Assess Performance, Learning, and Perceptions in Organizations, by Richard Swanson, and Elwood Holton
Why measure results in HRD? If HRD is to be a core organizational process, it must act like one and hold itself accountable. Assessing results, particularly bottom-line performance results, is key to gaining support from top management. And those who measure results ultimately find it a source of program improvement and innovation as well as pride and satisfaction. Results is both theoretically sound and firmly rooted in practice. The practical five-step assessment process the authors present gives readers a simple and direct journey from analysis inputs to decision outputs. This book provides the tools required for effective and efficient assessment of the outcomes resulting from development efforts in organizations. **RHAP / $34.95**

ORGANIZATIONAL LEARNING RESOURCES

To Order Any of These Best-Selling Titles, Please Call 781-862-3157
or Visit Us on the Web at www.linkageinc.com/library!

Developing and Managing Organizational Learning, by Karen Overfield
Developing and Managing Organizational Learning is a practical guide for
trainers who aim to lead learning in their organizations. This easy-to-
understand book contains tools that will help trainers to manage training
programs efficiently and effectively. In addition, the book shows the training
program manager how to link these program-planning skills to skills in project
management and critical thinking to produce training programs on time and
within budget. DMOL / $26.00

Cross-Functional Teams Toolkit, by Glenn M. Parker
Implement cross-functional teams in your organization. This useful toolkit is
packed with examples and ideas for effective team building. The toolkit gives
you six invigorating ice breakers, five experiential team-building activities,
five insightful assessment tools, five useful abstracts and reports, six detailed
case studies and much more. The loosleaf binder format facilitates quick
preparation: photocopy what you need, and you're ready!

**Organizational Learning at Work: Embracing the Challenges of the New
Workplace,** Pegasus Communications
Compiled from articles appearing in recent volumes of The Systems Thinker
Newsletter, this book presents the insights of the field's most respected
thinkers. Each chapter in Part One tackles a common obstacle to
organizational learning, including "superstitious learning," misconceptions of
the "causes" of success, and damaging organizational addictions. Part Two
takes a further step to support continuos learning by introducing innovations
in key processes such as decision making, strategic conversation, and transfer
of best practices.
OLAW / $24.95

**Turning Training Into Learning: How to Design and Deliver Programs That
Get Results**, by Sheila W. Furjanic and Laurie A. Trotman
In *Turning Training into Learning*, the authors share their original, time-tested
method for how to help trainees internalize a skill so that it sticks. In detail,
the authors show you how to take the traditional training cycle (assess, design,
delivery, evaluate) and align it with their step-by-step system, which they call
"LEARN." This revolutionary approach examines the adult mind, and shows
you how it deals with new information and skills – how it perceives, evaluates,
tests and finally accepts what it has learned. This book is packed full of
practical advice, guidelines, models, checklists, forms, templates and much
more.
TTIL / $39.95

About Linkage, Inc.

Linkage, Inc. (www.linkageinc.com) is a global leader in creating organizational development, leadership, coaching and mentoring, and corporate education programs, research, and resources that achieve measurable business impact. Combining the world's most renown thought leaders, "best-in-class" educational resources, and a highly experienced team of consultants, Linkage has delivered programs to more than 9,000 individuals, including employees of 80 of the Fortune 100 companies. Clients include Lucent Technologies, Merck, Harvard University, Skudder Kemper Investments, McDonald's, Toyota, Xerox, and a host of other organizations in the major vertical industries.

Linkage's Suite of Leadership and Organizational Development Products & Services

Linkage, Inc. prides itself in providing practical, cost-effective, and results-oriented leadership and organization development programs and systems. Linkage provides one-stop-shopping for its clients leadership and organizational development needs.

World class consulting, training, research, distance learning programming, videos, tapes, and books.

Leadership/Organizational Development Consulting and System Development— Through a multimode systemic model for building an organizational or human resource development program, Linkage provides "best-in-class" OD/HRD consulting. Linkage leverage's its multimode model for designing, implementing, and providing ongoing support for OD/HRD systems such as performance management, leadership development coaching and mentoring and change management. Clients include Brown University, Case Corporation, Toyota, American Home Products, Ralston Purina, and ITOCHU International.

Global Institute for Leadership Development (GILD)—Co-chaired by Warren Bennis (leadership author and expert) and Phil Harkins (Linkage's president and CEO), GILD provides high-level programs and services targeted at the long-term leadership development of individuals and teams from the world's foremost organizations.

The Executive Leadership Development Program—This program, Linkage's core leadership workshop, is an experiential, interactive session that provides proven models, tools, and processes to help participants become more impactful leaders. The program is designed to provide an intensive 3-day session that helps leaders to continuously improve skills, increase knowledge, and develop their leadership competencies.

The Best of Organizational Development Conference (ODC)—The event brings together Organizational Development, Organizational Effectiveness, HR professionals, academics, and practitioners to address the compelling issues and challenges facing Organizational Development professionals today. ODC is designed to provide the most comprehensive learning forum and a compilation of the best thinking and applications of OD tools, skills, and methodologies.

The Essential Coach—Enables managers and leaders to shape and direct their behavior to increase their personal effectiveness by measuring the critical capabilities required for powerful coaching. The Essential Coach is available as both a self-managed assessment and a 360-degree assessment.

Leadership Assessment Instrument (LAI)—Developed by Linkage, in partnership with Warren Bennis, the LAI measures the critical capabilities required for high-performance leadership across all industries and functions. The LAI is available as both a self-managed assessment and as a 360-degree assessment.

Complete Consultant—Categorizes the broad range of roles that HR/OD consultants perform by measuring the competencies within each role that drive superior results and work outputs. The Compleat Consultant is available as both a self-managed assessment and a 360-degree assessment.

Action Research—Linkage's Research Group provides benchmarking and best practice research to help guide decision making on key leadership and organizational development issues, bringing the industries' key leaders and best practitioners to work directly with the client.

ABOUT THE EDITORS

Phil Harkins
President and Founder, Linkage, Inc.

For over 30 years, Phil Harkins has helped leadership teams develop their missions, vision, and values, and drive their business strategies by impacting the way people work to achieve bottom-line results. An authority on the subject of leadership and communications, he is an expert coach and management consultant who works with CEOs and senior executives to strengthen their individual leadership skills and build agendas for change. Author of Powerful Conversations: How High-Impact Leaders Communicate (McGraw-Hill, 1999), Phil has consulted to senior teams at such organizations as Kraft Foods, Ralston Purina, Prudential Real Estate, and Xerox, enabling them to identify and implement critically needed changes for maximum savings and productivity. He has also led major Human Resource projects at such organizations as Morgan Stanley, Chiron, Brigham and Women's Hospital, The Franciscan Hospital System, Lifespan, and American Express Bank, and sits on the board of Keane, Inc. An expert in leadership assessment, Phil collaborated with Warren Bennis in creating the Leadership Assessment Instrument (LAI™), a validated multi-rater assessment instrument based on state-of-the-art research on leaders worldwide. He and Warren Bennis also co-chair the Global Institute for Leadership Development, a common forum for the hundreds of emerging leaders who have attended its Leadership Conferences around the world. In 1988, Phil founded Linkage, Inc. on the principles he espouses: practical tools, clear road maps, and connecting competence and work to the reality of budgets and industry guidelines. As president of the company, he has led Linkage to become one of the 500 fastest-growing companies in the United States in 1997 and 1998. Phil received his doctorate from Harvard University, taught at Boston University, and held the Senior HR position in such organizations as Raytheon and Keane, Inc.

Lou Carter
Publisher/Consultant, Linkage, Inc.

Lou Carter is publisher and consultant at Linkage, Inc. Working with Linkage's senior consultants, product development specialists, and associate editors, Lou is responsible for the creation of best practice educational resources, as well as training and development programs. Prior to joining Linkage, he served as vice president for business development and change for an insurance and financial services organization where he designed and delivered change management initiatives and customized training. Lou was also an analyst for two Wall Street investment banking firms, and a Cambridge, Massachusetts-based strategic analysis think-tank dedicated to Fortune 500 Internet and Online Services Organizations. His handbooks, Linkage, Inc.'s Best Practices in Leadership Development Handbook and Linkage Inc.'s Best Practices in Organization and Human Resources Development Handbook (Jossey Bass and Linkage Press 2000) received critical acclaim from leaders in the industry. Lou was also a radio personality in college where he ran his own news and pop rock music show, has worked for Don Imus on his morning radio show, and was a business news writer for New England Cable News. He is also a certified partnership coach and change agent and has designed and delivered best practice workshops and forums for ASTD's regional and international conferences. Lou received his BA cum laude in Government and Economics from Connecticut College and has studied organization development and management at Brown University, Harvard University Extension School, and American University/National Training Labs Master's of Science in Organizational Development program.

Amy J. Timmins
Editor

After concluding that the business of lawyering was not for her, Amy Timmins resigned her post as designated attorney to pursue her imaginative nature and compile organizational development handbooks. Prior to her work at Linkage, Amy was an online reporter, legal analyst, journalist and independent desktop publisher. She graduated *magna cum laude* from Point Park College in Pittsburgh, Pennsylvania with a B.A. in Journalism & Communications. She conferred her Juris Doctor Degree from Duquesne University of Law in Pittsburgh where she was named to the Justice Louis Manderino Honor Society and placed in the Moot Court Hall of Fame for Outstanding Achievement in Advocacy. She spent two years clerking for the Honorable Kim R. Gibson before moving to Waltham, Massachusetts to be with her husband, Will.

Brainbench, formerly tekmetrics.com, is the leading service for online skills assessment and testing. Launched in 1998, Brainbench provides secure, web-based computer adaptive testing (CAT) and related services to help businesses target their recruiting and training. Our suite of tests include technical, financial, sales, administrative, management, customer service, languages, job fit – an expected 400 different tests available by year-end 2000. Likewise, professionals rely on our online certification and testing to verify their skill level and to enhance their job search.

Brainbench
Mike Russiello, CEO
111M Carpenter Drive, Sterling, VA 20164
T 703-437-4800, F 703-437-8003
mike.Russiello@brainbench.com
www.brainbench.com

Calian is a professional and technical services company helping its clients become more successful through three strategic offerings: e-Business solutions, human asset management solutions, and systems engineering solutions. Calian's e-Business solutions focus on helping its clients take advantage of new e-business technologies to leverage their knowledge capital, and make their workforces more productive and better informed. Human asset management solutions give our clients the ability to exercise critical workforce control. Systems engineering provides leading-edge communications infrastructures to the telecommunications and government sectors.

CALIAN
Christine McPherson, Account Executive
2 Beaverbrook Rd.
Kanata Ontario, Canada K2K 1L1
T 613.599.8600, F 613.599.8650
c.mcpherson@calian.com   www.calian.com

Correlate provides innovative solutions for business-to-business and enterprise information exchange. The company has developed a powerful suite of information exchange applications that provides a comprehensive, cost-effective platform through which enterprises can assemble, manage and share strategic knowledge and project related information - including word documents, presentations, spreadsheets, email and web content.

Correlate Technologies, Inc.
David Dexter, VP Business Development
601 Gateway Blvd., Suite 600, South San Francisco, CA 94080
T 650.827.8888, F: 650.827.8889
ddexter@correlate.com
www.correlate.com.   Page 335

Penn State Executive Programs offers experience, value and impact. Our strategic intent: to work in partnership to enhance organizational effectiveness and leadership development. Work with us. We take the time to understand your organization and your developmental needs, then offer solutions to meet your needs.

Penn State Executive Programs
Mr. Peter J. Steinberg, Manager of Client Development
310 Business Administation Building
University Park, PA, 16802-3003
T 1-800-311-6364 T(Int'l) 814-865-3372
F 814-865-3372
psep@psu.edu
www.smeal.psu.edu/psep

PENSARE

Pensare develops Knowledge Community(TM) online learning solutions that drive business results, teamwork and creativity through the innovative use of validated content from industry experts and top-tier business schools, leading internet community technology, applied learning tools, human interaction and the latest cultural adaptation methodology.

Pensare, Inc.
Margaret Hughes, VP of Corporate Communications
5150 El Camino Real, Suite C-32, Los Altos, CA 94022
T 650.967.5000, F 650.967.5100
margaret@pensare.com
www.pensare.com

Personnel Decisions International is a global consulting firm based in organizational psychology. We use our expertise to define, measure, and develop the capabilities needed to make organizations successful by growing the talents of their people, improving customer relationships, and increasing organizational performance. By unleashing the power of their people, we help our clients accelerate success and increase their competitive advantage.

Personnel Decisions International
Kelly Wold
700 Peavey Building, 730 Second Avenue S
Minneapolis, MN, 55402
T 612-904-7103, F 612-904-7120
kwold@pdi-corp.com
www.pdi-corp.com

Knowledge Management & Organizational Learning Providers

SARATOGA INSTITUTE℠

Saratoga Institute, a division of Interim Services, Inc. is the global leader in providing a unique, comprehensive approach to the study of "human capital management" – that is, *maximizing the talent of a company's people.* Using this approach, companies can track the cost of recruiting, hiring and turnover of employees, and most importantly, the ROI of human capital management. Saratoga Institute is the prime reference for human capital performance benchmarks and measurement methods for the American Management Association, American Productivity and Quality Center, Conference Board, Society for Human Resource Management and many trade associations.

Saratoga Institute:
Vicki Vigo
3600 Pruneridge Ave, Ste 380, Santa Clara, CA, 95051-5958 - USA
T 408-556-1150, F 408-556-1155
vickivigo@saratoga-institute.com
www.saratoga-institute.com

LEARNING INNOVATIONS UW

University of Wisconsin Learning Innovations (UWLI) provides e-learning consultation and courseware design services that help organizations develop customized online training using various multimedia tools and interactive technology for measurable learner outcomes, UWLI transforms on-site training into an online format that is accessible anywhere, anytime.

UW Learning Innovations
Mike Offerman, Executive Director
505 S. Rosa Road, Madison, WI 53719
T 608-265-9378 F 608-262-3878
offerman@learn.uwsa.edu
http://learn.wisconsin.edu